DA 591 · B55 B00

WITHDRAWN
FROM STOCK
QMUL LIBRARY

D0261674

MAIN LIBRARY
QUEEN MARY, UNIVERSITY OF LONDON
Mile End Road, London E1 4NS
**DATE DUE FOR RETURN**

NEW ACCESSIONS

CANCELLED

1 4 JUN 2004

WITHDRAWN
FROM STOCK
QMUL LIBRARY

# BOOTHBY

*By the same author*

The New Economy
I Fight to Live
My Yesterday, Your Tomorrow

# BOOTHBY

## Recollections of a Rebel

HUTCHINSON OF LONDON

The extracts from *The World Crisis* and *Great Contemporaries* by Winston Churchill are reproduced by permission of Hamlyn Publishing Group (Odhams Books) and the lines from A. E. Housman's *A Shropshire Lad* are reproduced by permission of Jonathan Cape and Company Limited.

QM LIBRARY
(MILE END)

Hutchinson & Co. (Publishers) Ltd
3 Fitzroy Square, London W I P 6JD

London Melbourne Sydney Auckland
Wellington Johannesburg and agencies
throughout the world

First published 1978
© The Lord Boothby 1978

Set in Monotype Baskerville

Printed in Great Britain by The Anchor Press Ltd
and bound by Wm Brendon & Son Ltd
both of Tiptree, Essex

British Library Cataloguing in Publication Data

Boothby, Robert John Graham, *1st Baron Boothby*
Boothby, a rebel remembers.
1. Boothby, Robert John Graham, *1st Baron Boothby*
2. Politicians – Great Britain – Biography
941.082'092'4          DA566.9.B57

ISBN 0 09 134830 7

*For Wanda,*
*with love and gratitude*

*

**MOTTO OF THE BOOK**

*'L'extrême félicité à peine séparée par une feuille*
*tremblante de l'extrême désespoir, n'est-ce pas la vie?'*

ST BEUVE

(with acknowledgements to William Somerset Maugham)

# Contents

# Illustrations

Buchan in daylight

'In the News' (reproduced by permission of the BBC)

'Face to Face' with John Freeman (reproduced by permission of the BBC)

Caxton Hall at last! Two wedding photographs (reproduced by permission of the Keystone Press Agency Limited)

Buchan at twilight (reproduced by permission of the Radio Times Hulton Picture Library)

*Letters reproduced in the text*

# Prologue

Soon after the Second World War, Robin Day asked me, on television, how I accounted for my total failure in politics. I said that I did not think it was total; but I agreed with him that, on all the major political issues in which I had taken an active part in Parliament, I had been hopelessly beaten. I have lived my life in opposition to what has now become known as 'The Establishment': in the 1920s to our return to the Gold Standard at the pre-war parity of exchange which led, inevitably, to a General Strike and massive unemployment for many years, and to our disarmament; in the economic crisis of 1930–31 to Snowden's policy of continued deflation; in the 1930s to appeasement, to our failure to rearm, to our betrayal of Czechoslovakia at Munich, and to our unilateral guarantee to Poland without Russian support; during the war to our betrayal of central and eastern Europe at Yalta; and after it in favour of a united Europe, and against the Bretton Woods agreement, the American loan, and Suez. I told him that I could never have been a minister for more than a very brief period, because on all these issues I should have resigned. He was good enough to say that perhaps my political failure had not been as total as he had imagined.

Some time afterwards I received a letter (later quoted) from Lord Salter, one of our greatest civil servants, in which he wrote that no one had been so uniformly right on each of the great issues on which he has fought as I had.

I thought about this for two years, and finally reached the

rather immodest conclusion that, on the whole, it was true. Apart from the persistence and encouragement of my wife, it is the reason, and the sole reason, which has prompted me to write this book.

In *Great Contemporaries* Churchill wrote of the first Earl of Birkenhead: 'He had reached settled and somewhat sombre conclusions upon a large number of questions, about which many people are content to remain in placid suspense.' So, at a far lower intellectual level, have I. I have recorded them in a chapter of a book called *What I Believe*, published by Allen and Unwin in 1966. Other contributors included A. J. Ayer, Margaret Cole, Daphne du Maurier, Edward Glover, Jacquetta Hawkes, Malcolm Muggeridge, J. B. Priestley, and Barbara Wootton. Together with Professor Macneile Dixon's Gifford lectures, subsequently gathered together in a volume called *The Human Situation*, it remains my bedside book. But I have not repeated a word of it. I do not want this book to be sombre. I have enjoyed life too much; but I realize that it is because, with a handful of others, I have been sitting at the top table. The vast majority of mankind live in poverty, misery and fear; and never more so than in this century.

For many years I thought that emotion and beauty, however derived, gave significance to life. Now I am not so sure. I am inclined to agree with Maugham that, like everything else, they too are ephemeral and of no lasting importance. Churchill may have been right when he said that the journey had been well worth making – once. For my part I would certainly not like to repeat it. As Balfour once said: 'This is a singularly ill-contrived world.'

This is not an autobiography. Still less is it a diary. I have never kept a diary. It is a book of memories which might otherwise be forgotten. I am well aware that I shall be accused of name-dropping. It is a charge to which I plead utterly guilty. Indeed it is the main point of the book. Fate or chance has enabled me to meet, and sometimes to know well, a number of the great figures of our time, in various fields. The impression they made on me, and the things they said to me, are still vivid in my mind. And my chief concern has been to write them down before memory fades, in the hope that they may throw an occasional beam of light on the tumultuous events of the century in which all of us have had to live, and on those who shaped them.

In the earlier chapters I have drawn on a book I wrote called *I Fight to Live*, published in 1947 by Victor Gollancz – Livia Gollancz has very kindly given me back all the rights; and the account of an afternoon with Churchill in the south of France, abbreviated here, appeared in another book I wrote, *My Yesterday, Your Tomorrow*, published in 1962 by Hutchinson. Both these books have been out of print for many years; and I have thought it better not to fiddle about with the things which I believe are worth keeping on record. That would be holding the door on memory. I have also quoted from two articles I wrote about Lloyd George and Churchill for *Books and Bookmen*. What I have succeeded in doing is to avoid quotation at any length from my own articles and speeches, which are on the record. And there is, in this book, far more new stuff than old.

I am deeply grateful to Lord Montgomery of Alamein for allowing me to publish two letters from his father, which seem to me to reveal, more than anything that has yet been recorded, how far his vision extended beyond the battlefield; to the literary executors of Somerset Maugham for permission to publish one letter he wrote to me; and to the late Sir Dingle Foot for letting me publish a verse of a poem he once wrote about me.

I would like also to give thanks to my wife, to whom I owe my life. Twice she has nursed me back to health. For thirty years I suffered from a psychological fixation. I thought that the answer to my own life was marriage. It wasn't. I was married to my constituency. I tried often, but never with success. One evening at my villa on the Lake of Como there was, to my acute discomfort, a discussion about my private life. Next morning Maurice Bowra said to me, at breakfast: 'Well, old boy, how are you? Still suffering from a jilt complex?' On another occasion, when he was staying in my flat, the telephone rang. When I put down the receiver he looked at me suspiciously, and said: 'What was that?' I said: 'Only a girl who said she was going to sue me for breach of promise. She won't.' He became very agitated, and said: 'You must take this seriously. Get on to your solicitor at once.' Then he gave a deep sigh, and added: 'With you one never knows what is going to happen next.' In 1921, when I was standing alone with my mother at sunset by Lake Como, she said to me: 'I hope that one day you will marry an Italian girl.' Nearly half a century later, I did. My wife is an almost perfect linguist, in Italian, English, French and Spanish. But to begin with she was not word-perfect. Soon after we got married I became quite seriously ill, and had to go to hospital. A friend of hers rang her up to ask how I was, and she said: 'He is better today, but still under heavy seduction.'

I would like, finally, to express my deep gratitude to Mr Anthony Whittome for the invaluable assistance which he has given to me at every stage.

During my life I have watched the Decline and Fall of the British Empire from a front row in the stalls; and tried in vain to prevent it. All I have tried to do in this book is to paint a picture of the drama as it unfolded, and of some of the principal actors as I saw them.

I have nothing much to boast about, and few constructive achievements to record. The two things I am proudest of are that my father and I are the only father and son who have been respectively Captain of the Royal and Ancient Golf Club and Rector of the University of St Andrews; and that I have sat in Parliament for fifty-four unbroken years.

ROBERT BOOTHBY 1978

# I

# The First World War

The summer of 1914 was glorious. Churchill has well described
it in the first volume of *The World Crisis*. 'Nations and Empires
crowned with princes and potentates rose majestically on every
side, lapped in the accumulated treasures of the long peace. . . .
The old world in its sunset was fair to see.' But 'there was a
strange temper in the air. Almost one might think the world
wished to suffer.' Distant thunder muttered; and suddenly,
at Sarajevo, there was a flash of forked lightning, unnoticed
at the time. As a boy of fourteen at Eton I attended my first
and last cricket match against Harrow at Lord's in time of
peace. It was a glittering scene. The ladies in the latest
fashions. The men (including the boys) in top hats, and
wearing carnations. The coaches of the aristocracy. Straw-
berries and cream. In my House we had a member of the
eleven, of whom we were very proud. His name was C. S.
Vane-Tempest. He went in first, and made 37. Like almost
every other boy of his age he was soon to be killed.

Also in my House was a slim volume of poetry recently
published, called *A Shropshire Lad*, which I kept beside my bed.
I had turned down the page at one poem:

> On the idle hill of summer,
>   Sleepy with the flow of streams,
> Far I hear the steady drummer
>   Drumming like a noise in dreams.

Far and near and low and louder
  On the roads of earth go by.
Dear to friends and food for powder,
  Soldiers marching, all to die.

East and West on fields forgotten
  Bleach the bones of comrades slain,
Lovely lads and dead and rotten:
  None that go return again.

On the second day of Lord's my father introduced me to a small man, with alert and kindly eyes. 'Take a good look at him,' he said, 'because you will hear of him again.' It was Jellicoe. And a fortnight later he was Commander-in-Chief of the British Grand Fleet in war.

During the First World War I lived, at school, a life of my own. I did enough work to keep my place, but I thought of nothing but the war. To the surprise of my house-master the only photographs on the wall of my room were those of Jellicoe and Beatty, on whom our survival depended. It is difficult to exaggerate the traumatic effect of the casualties in France upon the lives of boys who grew to maturity during the years between 1914 and 1918. Every Sunday the names of the fallen were read out in College chapel. As we saw all the heroes of our youth being killed, one by one, and not far away, our whole attitude towards life changed. 'Eat and drink and try to be merry, for tomorrow you will surely die' became our motto. Neuve Chapelle, Loos, the Somme and Passchendaele bit deep into our small souls. If early and bloody death was apparently an inevitable consequence of life, what was the point of it?

My home outside Edinburgh was near Rosyth. From 1914 to 1916 the Battle-Cruiser Fleet, under Beatty, was based there. Then, in 1917, after he had become Commander-in-Chief, Beatty brought the Battle Fleet down from Scapa, so that the whole of the Grand Fleet was based at Rosyth. In 1918 I counted fifty dreadnoughts at anchor above and below the Forth Bridge. At week-ends our house and garden were always filled with naval officers who came to eat, drink, play tennis and talk; and as a boy I got to know many of them well. One Admiral who was particularly good to me was

Arthur (later Sir Arthur) Leveson. At the beginning of the war he was Director of Naval Operations at the Admiralty, but he didn't get on with Churchill (he once told me that, if he had had his way, he would have taken him out to the back garden and shot him), and went to command a division of the Battle Fleet (*Orion*), in which he took part in the Battle of Jutland. From there he went on to command the Second Battle-Cruiser Squadron in *Australia*, and finally the Fifth Battle Squadron (*Barham*), the fastest and most powerful of them all. His Flag-Captain in *Australia* was Oliver Backhouse, a great ornithologist, a fascinating man, and a brother of Sir Edmund Backhouse, who has now been immortalized by Professor Trevor-Roper in his book *A Hidden Life*. Leveson had a very strong personality, and a formidable brain; and people were rather afraid of him. I had no need to be. Like many similar characters, he would talk more freely and easily to a somewhat precocious boy, who was not under his command, than to his officers; and enjoyed it. A cousin of mine, Philip Warre, was his Flag-Lieutenant; and he used sometimes to take me out for sub-calibre gunnery practice in the Firth of Forth. But he would not take me out to sea with the Fleet.

The Battle of Jutland fascinated me at the time, and has fascinated me ever since. It was one of the decisive battles of history just because it was indecisive. Victory for either side would have brought the war to an end quite soon. If Jellicoe had won we could have put an end to the U-boat campaign, which nearly destroyed us in 1917, by a close blockade of all German ports; and reached Russia through the Baltic. If Scheer had won, Britain would have been wide open to invasion, with her armies cut off on the continent. And this takes no account of the psychological consequences, which would have been tremendous. Victory for neither side, which happened, condemned Europe to a long war of attrition, and wiped out a whole generation. The consequences remain with us. I have written, as Appendix 1 (pages 257–61), a footnote on this crucial battle, based on conversations I have had with many of the senior officers who took part in it.

There was never another fleet action in the North Sea. The Germans turned to the U-boats. And Beatty, as Commander-in-Chief, Grand Fleet, was so shocked by the report of the

Projectile Committee after Jutland that he informed the Admiralty that he had decided not to try to force a fleet action until he had new shells. The end came with the surrender of the German High Seas Fleet in the Firth of Forth in November 1918.

It was then sent to Scapa Flow. Leveson took me up in the *Barham* when his Battle Squadron was sent on guard duty. We cruised round it in his barge; and I suppose that, apart from the Orcadians, I am one of the very few civilians who ever saw the High Seas Fleet riding at anchor in that vast harbour. When we got back (it is always a moment when an Admiral is piped on board his flagship), he went straight to his cabin aft, and said: 'Now I am going to make a signal to the Admiralty asking for permission to take the German crews off those ships.' I asked him why, and he replied: 'Because, if we don't, they will be scuttled.' A day or two later he was relieved by another Battle Squadron under Admiral Sydney Fremantle, who took it out for gunnery practice; and, while he was at sea, the High Seas Fleet was scuttled. Perhaps it was better so. It should never have been built. In the 1920s Leveson, as Commander-in-Chief, China Station, reported to the Government that Singapore could never be defended from the sea alone. He said that in the event of war, the Japanese would invade and take it from the land. He was interviewed by a Cabinet Committee; and, as usual, his advice was disregarded. He told me afterwards that, despite their old animosity, the only minister who listened to him was Churchill.

Apart from training for the Guards, and death, I have no other personal experiences of the First World War. But afterwards I learnt a lot from Lloyd George and Churchill. Lloyd George told me, often, that he never wanted to replace Asquith as Prime Minister; and Lord Beaverbrook, who was deeply involved in what became known as the political 'plot' of 1916, confirmed this. What Lloyd George wanted was the direction of the war, as Chairman of the War Committee of the Cabinet. Both Lloyd George and Churchill told me that, as Chairman of the War Committee, Asquith spent much of the time writing letters, in his own beautiful hand, to Venetia Stanley. Women played a great part in his life, not always to his advantage. When Venetia Stanley fled to the arms of Edwin Montagu, he turned to Mrs Pamela McKenna who, together with her husband, and also Margot Asquith, hated Lloyd George.

In fact the agreement Lloyd George reached with Asquith would have put himself in an invidious position, because he would have had to bear all the odium for the misfortunes which were bound to come. It was Asquith who broke it. The influence of Mrs McKenna doubtless played a part. But the decisive factor was a leading article in *The Times* which Asquith thought was inspired by Lloyd George, but which had actually been written alone at Cliveden by Geoffrey Dawson, the Editor. It would have been best if Asquith had accepted the Lord Chancellorship and an Earldom in a Lloyd George Government. As it was, Lloyd George became Prime Minister, with a small War Cabinet of his own choice; and, in Churchill's words, 'set out upon his march as High Constable of the British Empire'.

The real argument at the end of 1916 was not between Lloyd George and Asquith, but between Lloyd George and Lord Lansdowne. Lloyd George wanted victory, Lansdowne wanted a negotiated peace before Europe completed her own destruction. In retrospect, Lansdowne was unquestionably right. But was it possible? I think not. After the war I made great friends with von Kühlmann, who as Foreign Secretary of Imperial Germany negotiated the Treaty of Brest-Litovsk with Trotsky – one of the harshest peace treaties ever signed. When he returned to Berlin he advised the Kaiser to make a reasonable peace, immediately, with the Western Allies. He was bitterly opposed by Hindenburg and Ludendorff, who thought they could achieve a quick and total victory in France by means of a knock-out blow. Not for the first time the Kaiser made the wrong decision. Kühlmann was sacked, and Hindenburg and Ludendorff took complete control. As a result Germany lost the war, and the Kaiser lost his throne.

In the 1920s Kühlmann lived in great elegance in a flat in Berlin, with French Impressionist pictures on his walls. He took no further part in politics, but talked freely; and I used to lunch or dine with him whenever I was there. One day, when I was Parliamentary Private Secretary to Churchill, he came to London. I mentioned this to Churchill and, rather to my surprise, he told me to invite him to lunch at 11 Downing

Street. There were just the three of us. Kühlmann was very nervous and, to Churchill's evident concern, had a nose-bleed. After that, the conversation between these two men was fascinating. Both of them had known the Kaiser well, and all the ground was covered. But I was not quite sure of how it had gone until, a few days later, I got a red-ink minute from Churchill saying: 'Tell Kühlmann that, if he is going to write his autobiography, I should not be ill-disposed to write a preface.'

At this time he had just completed the sixth volume of *The World Crisis – The Eastern Front*. Although the least read it is, in some respects, the best; because it is written through the eyes of a historian, not a participant. The research had been prodigious. He talked to me about it often, and at great length. He made me read the diaries of General Hoffmann, which I still possess. His conclusions are there for all to read, and I shall not repeat them all. But two remain vivid in my memory.

The first was that, when all had been written and read, final responsibility for the First World War must rest on the shoulders of three men: Princip, the assassin, who killed the Archduke Franz Ferdinand and his wife; Count Berchtold, the Austrian Foreign Minister, who started it; and the Kaiser, who could have stopped it. Since then A. J. P. Taylor has rightly added another: the chauffeur who, by mistake, drove down the wrong street in Sarajevo. It is on these things that the lives of millions, and the fate of the world, depend: and that is why it is inadvisable to take life too seriously. Only one man of political eminence in the Central Powers fought hard and persistently to prevent war. That was Count Tisza, the Minister-President of Hungary. It is typical of life that he was the only one to be killed by an assassin who believed he was avenging the people for the miseries that had befallen them. So the green light was given to the General Staffs, when mobilization was authorized in Vienna, Berlin and – reluctantly – St Petersburg. Then the vast military machines, prepared for so long and in such meticulous detail, clanked into action. And after that there could be no turning back.

The second conclusion was that by far the ablest general on either side in the First World War was Max Hoffmann. 'No clearer brain', he wrote, 'or more discerning eye could be found in the élite of the General Staff. His was the mind behind most of the German plans on the Eastern Front. We shall often recur to his sagacious wisdom.' When Prittwitz the German Commander-in-Chief in the East, lost his nerve and decided (without telling his staff) to retire to the Vistula, he was recalled by Moltke, the Chief of Staff, and replaced by Hindenburg (from retirement) and Ludendorff. When this formidable pair reached their Headquarters they found, to their surprise, that all the plans for what became known as the Battle of Tannenberg had been made by Colonel Hoffmann, on the staff of Prittwitz's Eighth Army. All they had to do was to execute them. Unlike Jutland, Tannenberg was one of the decisive battles of history. By disobeying, at a critical moment, an order from Ludendorff, General von François, commanding the First German Corps, pulled off a brilliant stroke. But chief credit for the victory must go to Hoffmann. Thence he went on to defeat the Russian armies in the field. At Brest-Litovsk he was at Kühlmann's side. He said afterwards that, if he had known what was going on inside Russia, he would have marched to Moscow, thrown out Lenin and Trotsky with a couple of divisions, and installed a government which met with his approval, to which he would have given much better terms. Thus the whole course of history might have been changed.

Anyone who has studied Hoffmann's diaries carefully, as I have done under the direction of Churchill, can only reach the conclusion that he was seldom wrong. He wanted to win the war in the East, and then make peace with the West. He was bitterly opposed to Falkenhayn's attack on Verdun. He sharply criticized Ludendorff's tactics in the March offensive of 1918; and the only conclusion that can be drawn from his subsequent writings is that he was against it. Today he is an unknown and unremembered figure. The historians have not done him justice.

Like all the generals in 1914, Hoffmann found himself in possession of a new and deadly weapon, the machine-gun. He knew how to use it. He also knew that battles are won by manoeuvre – occasional retreats, followed by out-flanking advances. In a word, movement. As against this, the strategy

of the generals on both sides in the Western Front was static.
All they could think of to put up against the machine-gun was
human bodies. And the bullets won. Instead of fighting a war
of movements by means, on occasion, of tactical withdrawals
followed by surprise attacks elsewhere, they fought for weeks
and months for a few fields of mud, at colossal loss of life.

My last memory of the First World War is a dinner with my
uncle, Lord Cunliffe, during the winter of 1918–19, just after
it was over, at his home, Headley Court. He was Governor of
the Bank of England from 1913 until 1918, when Beaverbrook
persuaded Bonar Law, as Chancellor of the Exchequer, to
sack him. But he remained a Director, and was still powerful,
because Lloyd George had appointed him, with Lord Sumner,
to advise the Government on reparations at the Peace Conference; and Keynes had already christened them the Heavenly
Twins. Hot water remained in short supply, and what there
was of it I used; so, after a cold bath, he came down not in the
best of tempers.

Beaverbrook once said to me: 'Your uncle Walter Cunliffe
was the hell of a bully.' I replied, 'Not to me.' They lived next
each other in Surrey, and, if they ever met walking in the
woods, cut each other dead.

My own relationship with him was very similar to my relationship with Admiral Leveson. Like Leveson, people were
frightened of him; but he rather enjoyed letting himself go to
a cheeky boy. He, in turn, stood in awe of Lloyd George. He
made no claim to be an economist – I think he rather despised
them. But he was shrewd; and when the inevitable financial
crisis arose on the declaration of war in August 1914, he
handled it with cool determination and marked success.

After dinner, when my aunt left us alone together, he
remained silent for a while. This neither surprised nor disconcerted me, for he was a taciturn man. Then, suddenly,
he began to talk. He told me about Lloyd George as Chancellor
of the Exchequer in 1914; how good he was as an administrator, and how well they got on together – 'we never had a
disagreement'; and about the Balfour Mission to the United
States, of which he was a member. He then said that two problems weighed on his mind, and I think they should be recorded.
When I asked him what they were, he said: 'I had, as one of

the directors on my Court, a very remarkable man. His name is Montagu Norman. He has a strong personality, and great charm. During the war he had what he thought was a nervous breakdown, and went to Switzerland to consult a psychiatrist – I think the name was Jung. I knew this wasn't the answer. The answer was work. So I recalled him, and made him Assistant to the Deputy-Governor, Brien Cokayne. This means that, when Cokayne goes, he will become Governor. And when he does, he will never give it up. This is wrong in time of peace. There should always be two or three members of the Court who have "passed the chair". It means that, in course of time, the Court will consist of his own nominees. It also means that, sooner or later, the Bank will be nationalized. As you are a Communist, you won't mind. But I shall.' I then said: 'And the second problem?' His reply was not only shrewd, but prophetic. 'Keynes will write a brilliant book about the Peace Conference, which will do unfathomable damage to the world.'

*The Economic Consequences of the Peace* established the legend of the Versailles '*Diktat*', and became the bible of the Nazi movement. In the event, none of Keynes's dire forebodings came true, and the reparations clauses of the Treaty were not carried out. Lloyd George once told me that, in the fevered and emotional atmosphere of the time, they were inevitable; but that he always regarded them as provisional, pending a general settlement – he wanted cancellation – of inter-Allied debts, for which he strove in vain at the Genoa Conference of 1922. One blunder followed another in the economic field, accompanied by acrimonious personal quarrels behind closed doors. The French were obdurate, the Americans difficult. Bonar Law himself nearly resigned as Prime Minister over the American debt settlement negotiated, as Chancellor, by Baldwin. Cunliffe made a fatal mistake when a committee, of which he was chairman and Bradbury and Pigou were members, recommended that we should return to the gold standard at the pre-war parity of exchange. No attempt was made to achieve effective co-operation between central banks. Thus the way was prepared for the gradual and, as it seemed, helpless drift into an economic morass.

# 2

# Into the World

I have described elsewhere* my three years at Oxford, 1919–22. I came down with my mind in a turmoil. Oxford immediately after the First World War was, basically, a homosexual society. By this I do not mean that all the undergraduates slept with each other. I simply mean that, with the exception of one week in the summer when the Colleges gave balls, girls never impinged upon our lives at all. I remember how shocked we all were when John Strachey brought two of them, Elizabeth Ponsonby and Yvette Fouque, to Magdalen. For this the emotional back-lash of the war was partly responsible. So was our extraordinary educational system, unique in the world, under which, in the so-called upper and middle classes, the sexes were completely segregated from the age of ten to twenty-two. In the universities this has now broken down, but in many of our schools it still prevails. But the primary factor was, I think, the pervading influence of ancient Greece, which provided intellectual and aesthetic enjoyment at the highest level, but had no relevance to the world that lay ahead of us. It was not Mr Joseph of New College, but Poincaré, Stalin and Hitler who should have given undergraduates sleepless nights. As a result the generation which grew to maturity during the years between the two great wars was ill-prepared to face their challenge, and failed to meet it. For my part, I detected the danger, and sheered away from it. Namier, then perhaps our greatest historian, took hold of me,

* *My Oxford*, Ed. Ann Thwaite, Robson Books, 1977.

gave me much of his time and trouble, and taught me what the modern world was all about. As for the homosexual phase, most of the undergraduates got through it; but about ten per cent didn't. Homosexuality is not indigenous in Britain, as it is in Germany, Scandinavia and the Arab countries; but it is more prevalent than most people wish to believe. Before I left Oxford I made up my mind that, if ever I went into public life, I would stop talking about it, and instead do something practical to remove the fear and misery in which many of our most gifted citizens were then compelled to live. In this, eventually, I succeeded.

Quintin Hailsham is a great advocate of an 'élitist' society. It all depends on who the 'élite' are, and whether they are fit to cope with the problems and difficulties that confront them. Manifestly, the élite of the inter-war years was not. 'Pop' at Eton, 'Greats' at Oxford, and a Fellowship of All Souls proved to be a sorry preparation for life in the modern world. Quintin himself, for whom I have the greatest admiration and regard, when he was rightly regarded as the star product of Oxford, fought and won what was for me a shocking by-election in defence of Neville Chamberlain's policies. True, he made amends afterwards by voting to bring Chamberlain down in 1940. But by then it was too late. As for All Souls, with a few notable and courageous exceptions – Amery, Salter, Rowse – it became the intellectual power-house of the policy of appeasement. In an uncontradicted letter to the *Spectator*, I wrote: 'No one can estimate the damage done to this country at that disastrous dinner table.'

I was launched into the great world by three men, Archie Clark-Kerr, Compton Mackenzie and Walter Monckton. In 1922 Archie, who had been with me at Bushey training for the Guards, and who was then Consul-General in Tangier, asked me to stay with him for a farewell tour of Morocco before he left for Cairo, where he had been appointed First Secretary to our High Commissioner, Allenby. When I got there he told me that we were to spend the first week pig-sticking, and the second shooting snipe; and that he would give me his best Arab pony. I had to make a split-second decision whether to tell him that I had not been on a horse since the age of ten, or not. But when he told me that Arab ponies were not trained to trot, and that there was nothing between an all-out gallop and a walk, I decided to bluff it out.

On the first day all went well until a horn sounded, denoting the presence of a pig. I was walking quietly down a ravine, when my pony pricked its ears, and then started off. A French Colonel, in full uniform, was in front of me, and held out his arm in warning. I tried to stop my pony. As well try to stop a whirlwind. We stormed past him, knocking him off the path. I carried my spear at right angles, and it removed his cap. Afterwards he complained, bitterly and justifiably, to the Master of Hounds. But the culprit was never found. The next thing that happened was that I found, to my horror, that the boar was immediately in front of me. This time I managed to rein in my pony just enough to enable another French officer to stick it. After that, there was a cross-country race. There were a lot of cactus bushes. I never knew whether my pony was going to swerve to the right or left, or to jump them. My only concern was to stay on. I won the race with both my feet out of the stirrups, my arse out of the saddle, and my arms clasped round its neck. Afterwards a young French officer, who had confidently expected to win, referred to me as '*ce jeune jockée Boozby*'. Alas, I was no Lester Piggott.

The snipe-shooting was better. I think I must have the mind of a snipe. In flight they jink. In order to kill them you have to guess which way they are going to jink next. More often than not I guessed right.

Then we set out on our tour of Morocco. Malcolm Robertson, Archie's successor; Ivone Kirkpatrick, from the Foreign Office; Ian Campbell, later to become Duke of Argyll; Walter Harris, the famous – and mischievous – correspondent of *The Times*; Archie and myself. We rode on mules through the dark streets of Fez, Rabat and Marrakesh, lit by oil lamps, where the craftsmen were still plying their wares, to dine with some local potentate – El Glaoui, the Pasha of Marrakesh, was the most powerful. One day we were taken to visit a large gathering of tribesmen. Harris introduced us in the local dialect. Robertson made a speech in which he said that he was happy that the relationship between Britain and Morocco had been so good for so long, and that his chief ambition was to strengthen still more the bonds of friendship between us. After about three minutes of this the tribesman began to shout. Then they all got up and left, with gestures of contempt and even disgust. It later transpired that Harris had introduced us as a troup of famous English acrobats, who would give them a performance they would never forget.

Towards the end of our tour Archie was invited to lunch by a chieftain in the foothills of the Atlas mountains. At this distance of time I cannot remember the exact name. It was something like the Sherif of Tamshlat. Robertson had another engagement, and Archie fell ill in Marrakesh with influenza, so he asked me to represent him – my first official appointment. At lunch there were twelve courses of chicken, each cooked in different herbs. The form was to tear off the breast of a chicken with your fingers, suck it, and then dip your hand in a bowl of rose-water. We all sat on the ground. After brief speeches by the Sherif and myself, translated by an interpreter, I was presented with a magnificent white Arab pony. I was embarrassed until Harris, who was standing behind me, whispered in my ear: 'Take it. And give it to me.' I did.

The Governor-General, Lyautey, Marshal of France, was absent on leave. But wherever we went we felt his presence. His power, exercised discreetly and almost invisibly, and his influence, pervaded the whole country. He will go down in history as one of the greatest proconsuls ever sent to Africa by Europe.

The subsequent career of Archie Clark-Kerr deserves a brief description. In Egypt he made a serious error of judgement when, in the course of some minor dispute, he advised Allenby to threaten to cut off water supplies. For this he was sent, in disgrace, to Guatemala. But he was far too good to be left there. He came back to the top of the Diplomatic Service via Stockholm. Meanwhile he married a very pretty Chilean girl called Tita because, as he told me, he fell in love with the back of her neck on a beach at Santiago. Subsequently he divorced her, and then re-married her. I always liked her; but I was against all three of what I regarded as reckless actions on his part.

In 1934 I went to visit them in Stockholm when he was Minister. There I met Madame Kollontay, the Soviet minister, who believed in free love. She was a remarkable woman, and still a force to be reckoned with, but did not survive the full rigours of the Stalin régime. When I asked Tita whether she was enjoying herself, she said: 'The three things I hate most in life are darkness, smoked fish and bridge. That's what you get here.'

When war broke out in 1939, Archie found himself Ambassador in Chungking. There he was a tremendous success. He got on well with the Chinese, and established a firm personal friendship with Chiang Kai-Shek. So it was not altogether surprising when he was chosen to succeed Sir Stafford Cripps as Ambassador in Moscow. This was a key position in the war; and again he was a tremendous success. Not surprisingly, everyone was frightened of Stalin. Not he. They spent most of one night together in an air-raid shelter, and he told me that they never stopped talking. 'From time to time I teased him,' he said, 'and he seemed to like it.' I don't suppose that anyone else ever attempted that. Archie added that, whatever else might be said about him, Stalin was a great Commander-in-Chief. The tremendous Battle of Kursk, the biggest tank battle ever fought, which decided the Second World War, was directed by him. His marshals obeyed him. Churchill once said to me: 'Your friend Clark-Kerr is an extraordinary fellow. At the Teheran Conference he suddenly said to Stalin, "It's sissy to smoke cigarettes".' I said, 'What happened?' Churchill replied: 'To my amazement, he stubbed out his cigarette, and lit a pipe.'

After the war Archie was chairman of the Allied Commission which gave independence to Indonesia; and then returned to London in triumph. There it should have ended. But Ernest Bevin, as Foreign Secretary, pressed him very hard to go to Washington as Ambassador. He came to talk to me about it at my home in Scotland. I begged him not to go. 'I know you so well,' I said. 'I know why you are so good with orientals, and why you will be so bad with the West. You have an oriental mind. They understand your jokes, and you understand theirs. You are subtle, and so are they. The Americans are quite different. You will never understand them, or they you. I could do it because, when I am in Washington, I not only look like a Senator – I feel like a Senator. But they will bore you stiff. For God's sake rest on your laurels.'

For a few days he hesitated. Then Bevin put on further pressure, and he succumbed. He became Lord Inverchapel, and went to Washington. It turned out just as I expected. He was a great failure. And he was miserable. At his first press conference he said that cricket was the most boring game on earth. Coming from a British Ambassador, this would have amused the orientals. But the Americans didn't like it. On the top of that, he was no good with the press. This doesn't matter in the East, where the press doesn't count. It matters like hell in the United States, where it does. Finally, he made no claim to be an economist. But this is a subject which any British Ambassador in Washington must know something about. Sir Berkeley Ormerod, *our man in New York* for many years, gave me his verdict. When I asked him which, of all the Ambassadors he had served, was the best, and which the worst, he said: 'Lothian the best, Inverchapel the worst.' For this Bevin's lack of judgement was primarily responsible. I am sad that such a glittering career ended in anti-climax. But that often happens. I have an enormous file of Archie's letters, written to me over many years with a quill pen. They make fascinating reading, and some of them may one day be published. I cherish his memory, because he was one of the best friends I ever had.

Next, Compton Mackenzie, known to a host of friends as 'Monty'. I first met him at Magdalen, his old college, in 1920; and at once fell under his spell. Charm, vitality, wit, great good looks, a brilliant mimic (almost a lost art), marvellous company – he had everything. He was still basking in the fame of his early novels. Now, at his *Casa Solitaria*, he was the uncrowned King of Capri; and there he introduced me to the literary world. Every evening he held court on the piazza, in a panama hat; and Norman Douglas, Munthe, and the mad genius D. H. Lawrence, sat at his feet. I shall come back to him in my chapter on authors.

Then, by a piece of amazing good luck, I went into Walter Monckton's Chambers at the Bar. He had the biggest of all the junior practices. In 1923 I received an invitation from Baldwin, after he had become Leader of the Opposition, to join his Secretariat. His sons had been with me at my private school at Rottingdean; he was a friend of my father, who had beaten him in the fathers' race by accidentally winding him with his elbow, which he took with perfect equanimity, and a benign smile. At this distance of time. I can't remember exactly how it all happened; but I know that J. C. C. Davidson then head of his Secretariat, Storr and Geoffrey Fry played a part. I went to consult Walter who was, as usual, immersed in briefs. Characteristically, he put them all aside, and listened to what I had to say. When I had finished, he sat silent for a few minutes. Then he said, 'I think you have the makings of a good criminal advocate but, unlike mine, your heart is not in the law. It is in politics. Throw your cap over the windmill, and go into politics.' Thus he decided my life.

# 3

# Into Politics

The resignation of Bonar Law in 1923 had thrown British politics into turmoil. Curzon confidently expected the succession; when he received a telegram from Lord Stamfordham, private secretary to King George V, asking him to come to London, he began to form his government. Meanwhile the King had summoned one or two senior statesmen, including Balfour, to give him advice. Balfour was ill in bed in Norfolk, but got up immediately and travelled to London. When he returned, one of the members of his very select house-party said: 'And will dear George be Prime Minister?' 'No,' replied Balfour placidly, 'dear George will not.' So when Stamfordham called on Curzon the next morning, it was only to tell him that Baldwin was already at the Palace.

Indolent by nature, Baldwin in those days was rather impetuous. To the consternation of most of his Cabinet colleagues he plunged the country almost immediately into a General Election by remarking, casually but with truth, that if we went 'pottering along' without protecting our industries, we should have grave unemployment for the rest of time.

I went to see Colonel (later Sir) Patrick Blair at the Unionist Headquarters in Edinburgh to ask him what I could do to help. To my astonishment he said: 'I have just received instructions from headquarters in London to fight every seat. This means I must find candidates for the Western Isles and Orkney and Shetland, neither of which we have contested for many years; and I must find them today. I have already asked W. S.

Morrison to take on the Western Isles because he speaks Gaelic, and he has accepted. Would you like to take on Orkney and Shetland yourself? We will pay your expenses if you don't lose your deposit.' I went immediately to consult my father, who was deeply alarmed. He thought that, at the age of twenty-three, I was far too young. Then, after further thought, he said: 'If you want to do it, I will not stand in your way.' So next day I found myself in a train bound for Thurso, and the following day in a small boat crossing the Pentland Firth from Scrabster to Kirkwall. As usual, it was a rough voyage. On board was my Liberal opponent, and the sitting member, Sir Robert Hamilton. He advised me to wear warm clothing (it was mid winter); and, when we got to Kirkwall, introduced me to my own Agent, who was awaiting us on the pier. That night I looked out over the vast expanse of Scapa Flow. Last time I had seen it, the German High Seas Fleet was there. Now it was empty. I was pretty thoughtful when I went to bed.

It did not take me long to discover, to my delight, that I was among Scandinavians. I am myself Scandinavian. The original name of my family is Bothe. It was not until they came to East Anglia from Denmark that the 'by' was added. The Western Isles and Orkney and Shetland are the only two constituencies in Britain where most of the electioneering has to be done by sea, some of it in a sailing-boat. Twice, when a storm blew up, we had to make for the shore. This involved a two-mile walk along the beach, and an hour's wait for the audience. They were accustomed to it, and did not mind.

It was not only Scandinavians that I found in Orkney and Shetland. I found also something that I have loved all my life – light. In what was perhaps the most brilliant of all his television programmes, Kenneth Clark talked about light when he reached the Dutch painters; and made me see, for the first time, why it had meant so much to me. I have been lucky. I found it again in Buchan, my constituency for thirty-four years; in the Baltic; in the wolds of Lincolnshire, from which I come; in Holland; on the Romney Marsh, where I lived in the 1930s; and, on occasion, in the Hebrides. Different in quality and translucence from the Mediterranean.

In Orkney I got a majority. But the incredulous crofters of Shetland could not bring themselves to believe that a beneficent Tory government would really give them a pound an acre, whether they grew anything or not. As a result I was beaten by 800 votes; but I did not lose my deposit. If I had won, I am pretty sure that I would have foreshadowed the experience of Jo Grimond. I would have remained in the House of Commons as long as they kept me there. I would have plunged into the whirlpool of national politics, and then extricated myself as soon as possible. Above all, I would have lived there. I dare say I would have had a happier life.

Meanwhile a number of Aberdeenshire farmers, headed by Bailie Booth of Peterhead, had been buying cattle in Orkney. They came to one of my meetings. When he got back, Booth said to the East Aberdeenshire Unionist Association: 'We are looking for a young candidate. I have just seen one. His name is Bob Boothby. He knows nothing about agriculture or fishing, but we can teach him; and, when he gets up to speak, he goes off like an alarm clock.' As a result I was invited to meet the Association, and adopted as candidate. Then I went to Baldwin, who had lost the election, and was now Leader of the Opposition.

It was a great treat, and a great experience, to work for him; because, apart from anything else, he and my father were the nicest men I have ever known. He never stopped thinking and talking about Lloyd George, of whom, as a man, he disapproved; of whom, as a 'dynamic force', he was frightened; and by whom he was clearly fascinated, to the point of obsession. One day I showed in a gentleman whom he had said he would see. He talked freely and expansively to his agreeable visitor. Next Sunday there appeared in the *People* an 'interview' which contained caustic comments on some of his colleagues in the Shadow Cabinet. The Secretariat was in a flat spin. Birkenhead, who was the principal victim, said: 'The bloody fool's done it again.' Baldwin took it with perfect equanimity and even amusement. He was not easily shaken.

On another occasion I accompanied him, on duty, to Edinburgh where he had to make an important speech. Suddenly, to my horror, I found that I had eaten all the sandwiches which had been prepared for him and myself. He had watched this process with amusement. But it never occurred to him to take remedial action while there was still

B.—B

time. I remember three things that he said, as we looked out
of the carriage window on to the smokeless towns. 'The greatest
ambition of my life is to prevent the class war becoming a
reality.' 'Protection is our only hope.' And, 'If I come back,
I intend to have Churchill by my side.' To an amazing extent
the ambition was achieved. If he had stuck to protection, we
should have been spared a lot. But, under strong pressure, he
abandoned it in order to obtain power. He was to do this
again over re-armament. The only trouble about Churchill
was that, when the time came, he gave him the wrong job.

The Labour Government of 1923–4 fell over the Campbell
case – the sudden withdrawal of a prosecution for political
subversion. It was badly handled by the Foreign Office (Sir
Eyre Crowe never forgave himself), and by the Attorney-
General, Sir Patrick Hastings. MacDonald was not to blame.
Asquith sealed the fate of the Liberal Party by his decision to
throw the Government out.

At the consequent General Election I found myself contest-
ing East Aberdeenshire. The people of Buchan are a race
apart. Like the Orcadians and the Shetlanders, they are more
Scandinavian than Scottish. They are different from the rest of
Aberdeenshire. They speak a dialect of their own, the Doric,
which it took me five years to master. It takes a long time to
get to know them, and still longer to gain their affection. But
if you do, their loyalty is quite unshakable. They have seen
me through every crisis in my life; and, indeed, life itself. I
won the 1924 election against Liberal and Labour candidates
with a minority vote. Thus we took each other on trust. I held
the seat in 1929, when the Conservatives were defeated. In the
critical election of 1945, when they were annihilated, I was
one of two Conservative candidates to keep their majority.
When I left, I had a clear majority of over 10000.

I soon found myself immersed in, and absorbed by, the
herring fishing industry. In those days it was a great industry,
and a romantic one. We were exporting over a million barrels
of cured herring a year to Russia, Germany and the Baltic
states. Big men were running it. Slater, Gordon, Dunbar,
Schultze, Sutton. The great summer fishing out of Fraserburgh and Peterhead and the great autumn fishing out of
Yarmouth and Lowestoft, to which my girls came down to gut

the fish, and which I never failed to visit, were always intensely exciting.

In those years I was very happy. It was back to Scandinavia. Because of the herring fishing, I kept in touch with Lerwick in the Shetlands; and also with Hamburg, Stettin and Riga. Fraserburgh and Peterhead (I am now very proud to be a Freeman of both) are the two towns in the British Isles nearest to Norway. It gave me much more pleasure to land in Esbjerg from Harwich than in Calais from Dover. Before the war many Buchan folk went to work on herring in Russia, and some stayed over the winter to pick up what casual work they could find. A friend of mine, a curer, told me that he once went to Moscow, and attended a service in the Cathedral on Easter Sunday. About half-time, a procession of robed and bearded, monks came down the aisle, swinging censers of incense over the congregation. Suddenly a familiar voice smote his ears. One of them was chanting 'If it does ye nae guid, it'll dee ye nae hairm.'

Now it is all over. The herring have gone. This may be due to the movement of plankton, on which they feed. But I think it is primarily due to the ruthless over-fishing of immature stocks for industrial fish-meal, particularly by the Danes. Fortunately Robert Forman, when he was Provost of Peterhead, foresaw this. He asked for my assistance and support in building up a fleet of dual-purpose craft, which could change overnight from drift-net fishing for herring to seine-net for white fish. We did it. And I am sure that this is what has saved the inshore fishing industry of the north of Scotland. If we now stand firm on limits, of which there is every sign, it may still survive. But the crash of the herring fishing industry will always remain one of the great tragedies of my life.

From a personal point of view, I not only worked harder for it than for any other, but I have now been deprived of my favourite food – the young *matje* herring. Caught in the spring, gutted, lightly salted and eaten raw, they are a delicacy beyond compare, far surpassing caviar, *foie gras* or smoked salmon. No wonder that for two centuries the Dutch, who caught most of them, put out flags and played bands when they arrived in April. Now, together with the rest, they have almost disappeared.

In my constituency I found myself confronted with the problem of religion. I had the lot. The Established Church of Scotland, the Episcopal Church (mine), the Wee Frees, the Roman Catholics, the Brethren, Jehovah's Witnesses – and all at daggers drawn. It was hardly an advertisement for Christianity. I solved it by never entering a church or a chapel of any kind for thirty-four years, except twice for funerals. There was also a strong Temperance Movement. From the outset they realized that, so far as I was concerned, there was nothing doing. But we got on well enough. They once asked me to attend one of their processions in Peterhead, and I did. The two fishermen carrying the banner in front were so drunk that they had to be held up by their wives. Afterwards I was able to say, with truth, that I had never enjoyed a procession so much in my life.

Throughout my thirty-four years as Member of Parliament for East Aberdeenshire I had only two Chairmen of my Association, Sir Garden Duff and Sir Ian Forbes-Leith; and I could have asked for no better. Both their beautiful castles, Hatton and Fyvie, were always at my disposal; and in Hatton I had my own sitting-room. Under Duff the Association saw me through the crises of Munich and the Czech assets, and under Forbes-Leith the crisis of Suez. Their friendship and unfailing support were like rock – unbreakable; and you don't often find this in life. I am glad to think that, just before they died, both were given high honours. Gardie Duff was made a Baronet; and the Queen made Ian Forbes-Leith a Knight of the Thistle, with the Garter and Order of Merit the highest of all, which she alone can bestow.

On my first arrival at the House of Commons I found a letter of congratulation from the President of Magdalen, Sir Herbert Warren, in which he said: 'Try to find one or two good lines and *stick to them*. You are young and can take long views. Go on *writing* and *reading*.' This was good advice.

Almost immediately I was chosen to be one of an Empire Parliamentary Association delegation, led by J. H. Thomas, which visited Jamaica. We sailed from Avonmouth in a small banana boat of six thousand tons, and at once ran into a tremendous Atlantic storm. There was no question of sea-sickness: it was more like mountaineering than sailing. At the

height of the storm Vernon Hartshorn, who had been a
member of the Labour Government, and a most genial one,
managed to climb up to the deck in a bowler hat, a great-coat
and snow-boots, carrying an umbrella, in order, as he said,
'to be prepared for all eventualities'.

The British Empire still existed. Four light cruisers were
anchored off Kingston, one of them wearing the flag of the
Commander-in-Chief, West Indies Station. At a banquet
given by the Governor, at which all the notables were present,
Thomas asked me to reply to the toast of the delegation. It
was the first time I had ever spoken at a major public function
of this kind, and I shall never cease to be grateful for the help
and encouragement I got from Sir Mervyn Manningham-
Buller, a member of the delegation.

I have now been a Member of Parliament continuously for
over fifty years, and one of the things I look back to with the
greatest pleasure and satisfaction is the opportunities this gave
me to see the world as a delegate of one kind of association or
another (I joined the lot): Washington, Ottawa, Quebec,
Denmark (as a delegate from the House of Commons for the
centenary of their constitution), Istanbul.

Perhaps the most memorable is the small delegation of five
sent by the Commonwealth Parliamentary Association to
Singapore, Sarawak, North Borneo, Hong Kong and Ceylon
in 1954. This was nothing less than a world tour. In Singapore
I stayed at Government House. The Governor, a charming but
punctilious man, said to me: 'You will all get gippy-tummy.'
I said: 'I don't think I shall.' He asked me why, and I replied:
'Because I never intend to have a glass of weak whisky and
water out of my hand – from dawn to dusk.' He told me that
I was absolutely right; and in fact I was the only one who did
not get gippy-tummy.

Malcolm MacDonald, Ramsay MacDonald's son, was High
Commissioner for Malaya, and therefore senior in the hierar-
chy to the Governor of Singapore They didn't get on very
well. At Government House everything was pretty formal,
and at night dinner jackets were worn. When MacDonald
invited us to dine, I asked the Governor what I should wear. He

replied: 'Pyjamas.' He was very nearly right, because no sooner had we arrived at Malcolm's much smaller house than he said to us: 'Take off your coats and ties.' The house, although small, was lovely and filled with beautiful things, including a remarkable collection of jade and two Chinese girls who, to my great disappointment, soon left us. MacDonald has had one of the most extraordinary careers of our time. Packed off to Canada as High Commissioner by Churchill in 1940, he then held a succession of important posts in Asia and in Africa, for years on end. The Chief Justice of Malaya, Charles Mathew, who was a friend of mine, told me that as High Commissioner he used to hold periodic and informal meetings of his officials. 'His predictions hardly ever came true,' he said; 'but that didn't matter in the least because he understood, better than anyone I have known, the oriental mind.' When the Labour Government fell in 1951, Churchill sent the Colonial Secretary, Oliver Lyttelton, on a tour of inspection. One of the objectives the Government had in mind was to sack Malcolm MacDonald. But when Lyttelton got back, he said to me: 'I found he was quite indispensable.' All his life he shunned publicity, and refused all honours until he was finally given the highest – the Order of Merit. He then disappeared. Robert Blake wrote a biography of Bonar Law which he called *The Unknown Prime Minister*. If anyone writes a biography of Malcolm MacDonald (and although it will be difficult I hope it will be done), it might well be called *The Unknown Pronconsul*. He was certainly a great one.

In 1925 we returned to the gold standard at the pre-war parity of exchange. This led, immediately, to a General Strike, a prolonged coal stoppage, and massive unemployment for fifteen years; and was a primary cause of the Second World War. I strongly opposed it. But I found only four supporters in the House of Commons: Sir Robert Horne, Sir Alfred Mond, Sir Frank Nelson and Sir Fredric Wise.* Snowden was passionately in favour of it. In the City only one prominent figure was against it, Mr Vincent Vickers, who resigned from the Court of the Bank of England in protest. McKenna said it would be hell, but that he could see no alternative. Keynes dithered. All the rest went along. Churchill who, as Chancellor

* Lord Strickland, later Prime Minister of Malta, was also against it.

of the Exchequer, did it, had grave misgivings, intensified by
Beaverbrook who, on this issue as on many others, was right.
But Churchill was overborne, and succumbed. He lived to
regret it. For my part I shall always believe that, with the
exception of the unilateral guarantee to Poland without
Russian support, this was perhaps the most fatal step ever
taken by this country.

I was much depressed by our failure to prevent our return
to the gold standard at the wrong parity of exchange; and in
no way surprised by the inevitable results. I was also concerned
about the herring fishing industry, although not so much as
today. Most of the British herring fleet was based on three
constituencies – my own, Banff, and Yarmouth. Our principal
market for cured herring was Russian, and the Russians had
begun to stop buying. I decided to go to Moscow, and found
that three of my Conservative colleagues in the House of
Commons were eager to come with me – Sir Frank Nelson,
Sir Thomas Moore, and my cousin R. C. Bourne, who later
became Deputy Speaker. So we formed ourselves into a private
delegation, got visas without any difficulty, and went. We
were the first Conservative Members of Parliament to visit
Russia since the Revolution. I shall describe our visit in
Chapter 8.

# 4
# Into the Treasury

I was in Moscow during the first three days of the General Strike. In view of the mounting crisis, we returned home. Baldwin was aware that I knew Ramsay MacDonald well (we had travelled back from the West Indies in the same ship and he came to dine with us at my home near Edinburgh), and asked me to act as a go-between to arrange a meeting between himself and Ramsay MacDonald with a view to the possibility of a joint statement by them both in opposition to the General Strike. This proved unnecessary, as the strike collapsed. This was Baldwin's hour, and his great chance of achieving the real peace in industry for which he longed. He did not take it. A letter from the Minister of Labour, Steel-Maitland, urging him to call a meeting of leading industrialists and trade unionists, including Bevin, under his chairmanship, remained unanswered. Instead he went off to Aix-les-Bains, leaving the miners out on strike. He had had enough. I thought at the time that this was solely due to his own physical and nervous exhaustion. Now I am not so sure. Austin Hopkinson, spokesman of the coal-owners in the House of Commons, had got at him. Hopkinson was determined to break the miners; and by going to Aix-les-Bains when he did, Baldwin, consciously or unconsciously, did just that.

Churchill, as Chancellor of the Exchequer, now found himself in charge. He made vehement efforts to obtain a just and fair settlement of the coal dispute. But owing to the obduracy of the coal-owners and of the die-hards in the Tory Party, he failed.

I now felt desperate. On October 9 1926 I wrote a letter to the Chancellor of the Exchequer from which, as it summarizes my political philosophy and also changed the whole course of my life, I must quote at length:

Dear Mr Churchill,

I must apologise for writing to you. But I am so troubled about the present trend of affairs that I would beg you to consider one or two aspects of the situation as they have struck me of late in Scotland. We are losing ground at a rate that is alarming, and the reason is not far to seek.

It is the impression, growing every day, that the Government has now divested itself of all responsibility for the conduct of our national industries in the interests of the country as a whole; that it has capitulated to the demands of one of the parties engaged in industry, and is now preparing legislative action at their behest, in order to compass the destruction of the other. In short that, despite the promise of the first months, it has become what the people of Scotland have never tolerated, and will never tolerate – a Government of reaction.

You know far better than I do, the mind of the average Scottish elector when it is not confused by side issues.

It is imbued with the spirit of true liberalism. At the last election thousands of life-long members of the Liberal Party voted for us for the first time. There are also those 'wise men who gaze without self-deception at the failings and follies of both parties; of brave and earnest men who find in neither faction fair scope for the effort that is in them; of poor men who increasingly doubt the sincerity of party philanthropy'. They, too, voted for us.

It would be difficult to exaggerate the effect of your vigorous intervention in the Mining dispute last month upon the average moderate minded person in Scotland; or the disappointment which attended the failure of your efforts. There are many who consider (I can really answer for this) that at the time you wrote to the Prime Minister the letter which you quoted in the House of Commons, you were resolved to go forward, and to compel the owners (not necessarily the Mining Association) to meet the executive of the Federation, using, if necessary, the threat of suspension of the Eight Hours Act: but that you subsequently succumbed to pressure from many quarters.

Moreover the miners' leaders assert in speech after speech that you gave them positive assurances that if they made such an offer as their last one 'the whole force and authority of His Majesty's Government' would be brought into action in their support. This has never been publicly contradicted.

To put it quite frankly, there is a widespread feeling, even amongst those who most strongly disapprove of the policy and performances of the Miners' Federation, that you made a great attempt to obtain a fair and reasonable peace in the interests of the nation; that the miners went a long way to meet you; but that the owners, supported by a section of the Conservative Party, contemptuously declined even to negotiate, and that you did not feel yourself strong enough to hold on the right course. Great hope has been replaced by great disillusionment.

Imagine the effect, in such a situation, of Hopkinson's article in the *English Review*. He points out that the owners have been following, from the start, a clearly defined policy, designed not merely from the point of view of the interests of the industry, but 'after careful consideration of the national interests involved'. He accuses the Conservative Party of being prepared to 'tear the Constitution to shreds in order to induce a few more voters to support its candidates' and refers to the 'folly and ambition of all politicians'. He accuses you personally of hatching 'plots', and of deliberate falsehood. Finally, at the conclusion of an article which, for callous cynicism and open defiance not only of the Government but of democracy itself, exceeds anything that Cook has ever imagined, he states that the present policy of the owners, for which he is largely responsible, is 'to make the position of interfering politicians so unpleasant that they will for the future think twice before they meddle with the basic industries of the country'. The calm cheek of it! Who are the owners that they should decide what is in the national interests, in opposition to the Government and the elected representatives of the people?

Hopkinson does not believe in democracy. But the Scottish people do. And they are not prepared to allow themselves to be insulted, and their prosperity wrecked by a few fanatics, whether they be owners or miners. The effect of this article has been disastrous. It proves, once and for all, that the owners have throughout treated the Government with a contempt which has at no time been accorded to it by the Federation. . . .

It is generally recognised that there are certain abuses in connection with the Trade Unions which it is the duty of the Government to remedy, but the Scarborough conference has given rise to an uneasy feeling that a massed attack on Trade Unionism is now contemplated.

There are many good Conservatives in Scotland who do not forget the speech of Mr Whitelaw, the Chairman of the LNER at the Scottish Unionist conference in Edinburgh last year, condemning any attempt at a general repeal of the Trades Disputes Act as utter folly. His warning against meddling with the political funds of the Unions was as trenchant as it was impressive, and as a result of his speech, Macquiston's motion on the subject of Trades Unions was rejected by the conference.

Surely the Government will not allow itself to be stampeded by a few English Tory agents gathered together at Scarborough for the purpose of passing some idiotic resolutions about drink in clubs and corporal punishment? The vast mass of those who support the Government do not go to conferences. Nor are their opinions to be discovered in the leading articles of the Rothermere press. But if they are inarticulate, they decide elections.

I apologise for writing at such length. My only excuse is my anxiety, and please do not think that I want a written reply.

A Scottish owner observed to me the other day, 'The sooner you bloody politicians realize that there is only one tougher set of men in the country than the Miners' Federation, and that's the owners, the better.'

How, in the face of that sort of thing, and Hopkinson's article, can the Government, having placed the weapon in the hands of the owners, stand by and allow the miners to be bludgeoned and battered back, district by district?

Bludgeoned and battered they will be, in parts of Scotland at any rate. And the instruments? Longer legal hours, cold, and starvation. No. As Lord Hermiston [Weir of Hermiston] once observed, 'There is a kind of decency to be obsairvit!'

If this is to be followed by legislative action calculated to convey the impression that the Conservative Party has utilised the power given to it by the electors to plunder the funds of the principal opposition party, and smash the Trade Unions, then, in Scotland at least, a terrible retribution awaits it at the polls. I cannot help concluding with a quotation which will be familiar to you.

'Labour in this modern movement has against it the prejudices of property, the resources of capital, and all the numerous forces – social, professional, and journalist – which those prejudices and resources can influence. It is our business, as Tory politicians, to uphold the Constitution. If under the Constitution as it now exists, and as we wish to see it preserved, the Labour interest finds that it can obtain its objects and secure its own advantage, then that interest will be reconciled to the Constitution, will find faith in it, and will maintain it. But if it should unfortunately occur that the Constitutional Party to which you and I belong, are deaf to hear and slow to meet the demands of Labour, are stubborn in opposition to those demands, and are persistent in ranging themselves in unreasoning and short-sighted support of all the present rights of property and capital, the result may be that the Labour interest may identify what it will take to be defects in the Constitutional Party with the Constitution itself, and in a moment of indiscriminate impulse may use its power to sweep both away.'

Written by one, who, in the year 1892, regarded the Miners' Eight Hours Bill as of greater importance than 'the Monarchy, the Church, the House of Lords, or the Union'.*

> Yours very sincerely,
> ROBERT BOOTHBY

To this Churchill replied with a long letter in his own handwriting which ended:

The General Strike constituted a direct challenge and is a milestone in British Politics. I shall certainly not let Hopkinson's extravagancies cloud the mirrors of thought. He is sour to himself for the sour purpose of being sourer to others – a melancholy régime.

I quite understand your pangs and anxieties, but don't let them draw you from a coherent view. Let me know when you are in London and we can have a talk.

This I did. And when I entered his room at the Treasury, he came forward with outstretched arms, and said: 'I am all on the side of the miners now. Don't leave the Conservative Party. Come and be my Parliamentary Private Secretary!' I reminded him that I had been strongly opposed to our return to the Gold Standard at the wrong parity in 1925, and had not approved of his conduct of the *British Gazette* during the General Strike. He said: 'All that is over now,' (alas, it was not), 'this will give you a great chance to see how the wheels of government work.' So I accepted his offer with gratitude, excitement and pride. After all I was only twenty-six.

Immediately I found myself generally regarded as a coming young man, if not the coming young man, in politics. All doors were open to me. At the same time I had the opportunity of watching Churchill at work, pretty closely, for three years. It was an extraordinary experience. The output was colossal. In addition to his official duties – never scamped – in the Treasury and in Parliament, he was writing the concluding volumes of *The World Crisis* and planning *My Early Life*, *Great Con-*

---

* Lord Randolph Churchill.

*temporaries* and *Marlborough*. These turned out to be his greatest
literary achievements. He was also painting pictures and laying
bricks; yet he always found time, plenty of time, to talk.

He had to think aloud. Solitary reflection was alien to his
nature. And this imposed a certain strain on his personal staff
and, still more, upon the Chiefs of Staff in the Second World
War. In the drawing-room, the bed-room, the bath-room, the
dining-room, the car, an aeroplane, a sleeping-berth on a train
or in his room at the House of Commons, the flow of his
*private* oratory never ceased. I remember on several occasions
being commanded to attend him when he was having a bath
and to make suitable notes of what he said. At intervals he
turned a somersault, exactly like a porpoise; and when his head
reappeared at the other end of the bath, he continued precisely
where he had left off. It must be admitted that there was some
danger in all this talking, unaccompanied by sustained argument for, unlike Lloyd George, he was not a good listener. The
talk was so overpowering, the improvisations – flung out with
reckless prodigality – so brilliant, that, as Harold Laski
pointed out, people were more anxious to commit to memory
the things he had said than drive him to defend them. He was
by far the most egotistical man I have ever known. He saw and
lived life in terms of himself, against the background of history
which he both made and wrote.

He was not a natural orator, in the sense that Lloyd George,
James Maxton, and Aneurin Bevan were natural orators. Once,
early on in his political career, the train of thought left him,
and his speech ground to a halt. It was an experience he never
forgot. From then on, he decided that he would never again
attempt to make a major speech without full notes. This was
the routine: he would talk endlessly to those about him on the
subject; he would then dictate his speech to a secretary. When
this came back, he would amend it in his own handwriting to
the point where it became almost unrecognizable. It then went
back to the secretaries and was amended further. Then came
the notes, usually by himself, but sometimes by Sir Edward
Marsh, whose handwriting was similar to his own, and on one
or two occasions by myself. These had to be slanted paragraph
by paragraph, from left to right across the page, including the
ifs, the buts, and the ands. From these he read his speech,

and brought this technique to a fine art. All the great speeches, including the smashers of 1940, were made in this way. That is why they could go straight on to paper as classics; that is why he was so successful on the radio – the audience couldn't see that he was reading; that is why he could never have been any good on television and knew it. He could be witty, even brilliant, in impromptu answers to supplementary questions in the Commons, but in speeches he always stuck to his guns – and his notes. He was both morally and physically, the most courageous man I have ever known, and also the most self-absorbed. He feared nothing except the House of Commons. If, as I think, fertility is the essence of genius, he had it in full measure.

I soon discovered that the Treasury was not congenial to him, and that he was basically uninterested in the problems of high finance. He was instinctively, and rightly, opposed to our return to the Gold Standard at that fatal parity, but had been overborne by the City (Montagu Norman), and by his own establishment (Sir Otto Niemeyer and Sir Richard Hopkins). Norman and he were antipathetic. Their person-alities, both strong, and their interests, were poles apart. Both, in their way, were artists; but a very different kind of artist. I remember Churchill once saying to me, after a conference of senior Treasury officials, bankers and economists: 'I wish they were admirals or generals. I speak their language, and can beat them. But after a while these fellows start talking Persian. And then I am sunk.'

Soon after I got there I asked his principal private secretary, P. J. Grigg, why, with all his gifts, Churchill was apparently so impotent at the Treasury. He replied: 'Let me tell you something that will be of use to you now that you have become a politician. There is only one man who has ever made the Treasury do what it didn't want to do. That was Lloyd George. There will never be another.'

One day Churchill came out of his room looking sombre and sad. I thought he must have had another of these meetings which he disliked so much, and said: 'What have you been doing?' 'This,' he replied; and he handed me a typed manu-script. What I read was the following:

The German unwisdom in attacking Verdun was more than cancelled in French casualties, and almost cancelled in the general strategic sphere by the heroic prodigality of the French defence. The loss in prestige which the Germans sustained through their failure to take Verdun was to be more than counter-balanced by their success in another theatre, while all the time they kept their battle front unbroken on the Somme.

But this sombre verdict, which it seems probable posterity will endorse in still more searching terms, in no way diminishes the true glory of the British Army. A young army, but the finest we have ever marshalled; improvised at the sound of the cannonade, every man a volunteer, inspired not only by love of country but by a widespread conviction that human freedom was challenged by military and Imperial tyranny, they grudged no sacrifice however unfruitful and shrank from no ordeal however destructive. Struggling forward through the mire and filth of the trenches, across the corpse-strewn crater fields, amid the flaring, crashing, blasting barrages and murderous machine-gun fire, conscious of their race, proud of their cause, they seized the most formidable soldiery in Europe by the throat, slew them and hurled them unceasingly backward. If two lives or ten lives were required by their commanders to kill one German, no word of complaint ever rose from the fighting troops. No attack however forlorn, however fatal, found them without ardour. . . . Martyrs not less than soldiers, they fulfilled the high purpose of duty with which they were imbued.

Unconquerable except by death, which they had conquered, they set up a monument of native virtue which will command the wonder, the reverence and the gratitude of our island people as long as we endure as a nation among men. . . .

The curtain falls upon the long front in France and Flanders. The soothing hands of time and nature, the swift repair of peaceful industry, have already almost effaced the crater fields and the battle lines which in a broad belt from the Vosges to the sea lately blackened the smiling fields of France. The ruins are rebuilt, the river trees are replaced by new plantations. Only the cemeteries, the monuments and stunted steeples, with here and there a mouldering trench or huge mine-crater lake, assail the traveller with the fact that twenty-five millions of soldiers fought here and twelve millions shed their blood or perished in the greatest of all human contentions less than ten years ago.

Merciful oblivion draws its veils; the crippled limp away; the mourners fall back into the sad twilight of memory. New youth is here to claim its rights, and the perennial stream flows forward even in the battle zone, as if the tale were all a dream.

Is this the end? Is it to be merely a chapter in a cruel and senseless story? Will a new generation in their turn be immolated to square the black accounts of Teuton and Gaul? Will our children bleed and gasp again in devastated lands?

Or will there spring from the very fires of conflict that reconciliation of the three giant combatants, which would unite their genius, and secure to each in safety and freedom a share in rebuilding the glory of Europe?

As I handed it back, I said: 'It is the best thing you have ever written, or ever will.' He turned away and walked slowly back to his room.

Ironically enough, in view of what was to come, it was Churchill who disarmed this country. He persuaded the Cabinet to accept a 'Ten Year Rule' that no major war was to be expected for ten years, and that this period was to be extended annually for an indefinite period. The First Lord of the Admiralty, Bridgeman, put up a stiff fight; and Balfour, with all his experience, was opposed to it. The rest of that pretty moderate Cabinet tamely accepted it. Baldwin, who as Prime Minister bore the primary responsibility for the defence of the Realm, played no part. One day I ran into the First Sea Lord, Admiral of the Fleet Lord Beatty, in a corridor of the Treasury. He stopped me and said: 'I think Winston has taken leave of his senses. This ridiculous "Ten Year Rule" is going to make this country practically defenceless. When the next international crisis comes, as come it will, we shall not be able to rebuild our strength in time.' As he walked out, he turned and said with a gesture of contempt: 'And all this is to take sixpence off the income tax.' As a result our dockyards and our arsenals were steadily dismantled. If Churchill's contrary advice had been taken in the late 1930s, the Royal Air Force might have been stronger. But when we went to war in 1939 we had no effective armour to put in the field. And Chatfield (First Sea Lord and then Minister for the Co-ordination of Defence) was to write: 'What Mr Churchill forgets invariably is that the British Fleet is *an old fleet*, largely due to his own action when he was Chancellor of the Exchequer in opposing its reconstruction.'

There were some lighter moments. During a debate on the Finance Bill in 1928, Churchill was struck down with influenza, and the Financial Secretary to the Treasury, Arthur Michael Samuel, took charge. Samuel was one of the nicest and kindest men I have ever known; but Churchill was never apt to ask ministers to join his intimate circle and practically never saw him. In fact at that time, I was much closer to the mainspring of power in the Treasury than the Financial Secretary. One evening, within minutes of refusing to do so, Samuel accepted an amendment moved by a Conservative backbencher to reduce the excise duty on cigarette-lighters made in Britain. The sum involved was small, and he regarded it as of little importance; but it was in fact an alteration in the Budget, a breach of certain trade agreements, and also raised the whole explosive question of Imperial Preference. The cry, 'Protection!' rang through the House. Members poured into the Chamber. And a stormy debate began, which lasted for two hours. Churchill kept ringing me up from his sick-bed to ask me what was happening, and became angrier and angrier as the night wore on. This is the report I sent to him next day:

I reproach myself for not having been on the second bench last night, as I might have been able to dissuade the Financial Secretary from granting the concession. At any rate I could have had a shot at stopping him. But it was the dinner hour, the chamber was practically empty, and there was no reason to suppose a hitch would occur.

Apparently the only people he consulted were Amery and Williams, who misled him about the Trade Agreement. Some of our people were irritated about the whole affair last night and there was a good deal of caustic comment in the smoking-room, but today they are disposed to regard it as a joke, although rather a bad one.

It certainly was an astonishing performance. I'm not sure that the key-note of the evening wasn't struck by the gentleman in the gallery who called the Speaker a bastard, told Arthur Michael Samuel to shut up, and threw an old hat at Colonel Woodcock MP. I have talked to – or rather been talked to by – many people today, and I am sure that no serious harm has been done. But anything like a repetition of yesterday's incidents would be very damaging.

I am afraid poor old Arthur Michael is in great distress, and one is very sorry for him.

But he made a sad hash of it. . . .

This incident put an end to Samuel's political career; and,

for my part, I much regretted it. But he took it all with perfect
equanimity and characteristic good humour. The only constructive achievement of Churchill's otherwise sterile Chancellorship was the scheme for the de-rating of factories and
farms. This involved a lot of hard work, particularly by
Harold Macmillan, who was given access to all the papers;
and continuous argument with Neville Chamberlain at the
Ministry of Health. It did some good; but it made no appeal
to the electorate and, in the event, failed to realize the expec-
tations some of us had for it. In a speech which kept him out of
office for ten years, Moore-Brabazon said that the snores of the
Government resounded through the country; in 1929, it was
soundly and deservedly defeated.

One evening, as the Chancellor's Parliamentary Private
Secretary, I was commanded to attend a State Ball at Buckingham Palace. It was the full works: resplendent uniforms; and,
for me, knee-breeches with black silk stockings and buckled
shoes. It was a marvellous spectacle which I shall never forget,
dominated by the regal figure of Queen Mary. After about half
an hour Winston came up to me white and shaken, and said:
'Get me a stiff whisky and soda, and get it quick.' When I
brought it to him, I said: 'What's the matter?' He replied:
'I have just done something that I hoped I would never have
to do. I have shaken hands with de Robeck.' De Robeck was
the admiral who had called off the naval attack on the
Dardanelles in 1915, when the Turkish forts had run out of
ammunition. There was no personal animosity. It was just that
Churchill minded the Dardanelles more than anything else in
his life.

One evening he invited William Randolph Hearst, the
American press magnate to dine, with his mistress, Marion
Davies, the film star. Mrs Churchill refused to come to dinner
so I was ordered to join them at the Embassy Club. It was an
amusing evening. Hearst was crude and shrewd, Marion
Davies pretty and fun. Churchill all out to butter up Hearst –
perhaps with an eye on journalistic contracts in the future. I
enjoyed it all; but when Churchill told Hearst that he reminded him of Lord Morley, of whom he had clearly never
heard, I thought it was a bit over the odds. After dinner
Marion Davies asked me to dance with her, and I did. When

the dance was over and I was about to take her back to the table, she said: 'Oh, don't let's go back to those two old bores.' So we danced again. Then I saw Churchill scowling at me and he signalled me to stop. Somewhat to the disappointment of Marion Davies I stopped pretty quickly.

On another night Churchill invited Charles Chaplin to dine with him at Chartwell, and asked me to accompany him in his car from London so he did not lose the way. This I did, with a charming friend of Chaplin's who later committed suicide; and I found the reminiscences of the great man fascinating. At dinner Chaplin opened the conversation by saying to Churchill: 'You made a great mistake when you went back to the Gold Standard at the wrong parity of exchange in 1925.' This was not at all what had been expected; and Churchill, who not unnaturally hated to talk about monetary policy, relapsed into moody silence as Chaplin continued to discourse upon the subject with great knowledge and, as I thought, great sense. Then, suddenly, he picked up two rolls of bread, put two forks in them, and did the famous dance from *The Gold Rush*. Immediately the atmosphere relaxed, and thereafter we spent a happy evening, with both Churchill and Chaplin at the top of their form. I have always been amazed that neither he nor Noël Coward was given an honour many years ago. When Harold Wilson became Prime Minister I joined the crowd of people clamouring for recognition for Noël. But I added: 'You should also give a knighthood to Charles Chaplin, who deserves it even more.' Sir Harold Wilson has been much criticized for his Honours Lists. But he will go down in history as the only Prime Minister who had the imagination to confer knighthoods, with the Queen's approval, upon the three Englishmen who, with Maugham, have given more pleasure to more people than any others in this century – Charles Chaplin, P. G. Wodehouse, and Noël Coward.

When Churchill joined the Conservative Party and Baldwin's Government, he and Lloyd George inevitably drifted apart. One day, after I had become his Private Parliamentary Secretary, Churchill said to me: 'I know you are a great friend of Lloyd George. I am now writing the last volume of *The World Crisis* and there are certain questions that he alone can answer. Do you think you could persuade him to come and see me?' I said: 'It is not a question of persuasion. He would be delighted.' I then went to see Lloyd George and said: 'Winston wants to see you.' He replied: 'Splendid. Fix up an appointment.' I did, for the following evening at six o'clock. Lloyd George arrived punctually and I showed him into Winston's room. They were alone together for about an hour. After that I heard Lloyd George leave by the outside door, down the corridor. I sat alone in the secretary's room. Nothing happened. No bell rang. After about ten minutes curiosity overcame me and I went in to find the Chancellor sitting in an armchair, gazing into the fire, in a kind of brown study. I said to him: 'How did it go?' He looked up and replied: 'You will be glad to hear that it could not have gone better. He answered all my questions.' Then a hard look came into his face and he went on: 'Within five minutes the old relationship between us was completely re-established. The relationship between Master and Servant. And I was the Servant.'

# INTERLUDE ONE
# Churchill

I served as Churchill's Private Parliamentary Secretary for three years (1926–9). In that time I resigned twice: once when I became associated with a City firm of stockbrokers, and the other time when I told him that not only in the interests of my constituents, but also out of personal conviction, I felt bound to advocate a policy towards Russia which was not in accordance with his own views. On both occasions my resignation was refused. In 1926 he had written to me:

> You must not mind my chaff about the Bolsheviks. It has a serious underside however. I do not want to see you get mixed up with these snakes or their servitors in this country just for the sake of herrings and so prejudice what, I dare say, will be a prosperous political career.

After the General Election Churchill deliberately went into the political wilderness and broke with his colleagues in the Shadow Cabinet over India. I played no part in this, and he never asked me to do so. I felt I did not know enough about it. He saw India through the eyes of a British subaltern at the end of the nineteenth century. He never went back there. That he completely misjudged the political situation, there can be no doubt. He really thought that Gandhi was no more than a naked *fakir* and in February 1932 he wrote me a letter in which he said: 'I always said how easy it would be to crush Gandhi and the Congress.'

Re-reading his speeches on India, I have been struck by the

recurring flashes of insight and vision they contain. If, in 1924, Baldwin had made him Viceroy instead of Chancellor of the Exchequer, there might have been a different story to tell. He would have surveyed the Indian scene from the summit of power and, kindled by his own imagination, might well have achieved solutions far superior to those we eventually got at enormous cost in slaughter. There is a revealing sentence in his chapter on Clemenceau in *Great Contemporaries* in which he quotes him as saying:

When I was in India I saw some things your people do not see. I used to go to the bazaars and to the fountains. I had a good interpreter, and lots of people came to me and talked. Your English officers are rough with the Indians; they do not mingle at all; but they defer to their political opinions. That is the wrong way round. Frenchmen would be much more intimate, but we should not allow them to dispute our principles of government.

What I think Churchill himself realized was that our final failure in India was social rather than political. Lord Willingdon, one of the greatest proconsuls we ever sent to India, once told me at Aix-les-Bains that when he went to Bombay as Governor, he invited a distinguished Indian prince, who was a friend of his, to lunch at the Yacht Club. While they were having a drink, a porter came over and said to him: 'I am sorry, Your Excellency, but the secretary has asked me to tell you that niggers are not allowed in this club.' He walked out immediately to form the Willingdon Club.

The breach between Churchill and the Conservative leaders was complete. In April 1931 he wrote to me: 'My late colleagues are more interested in doing me in than in any trifling questions connected with India or tariffs. I have a strong feeling they will not succeed.' In the House of Commons he allied himself, over India, with the Tory die-hards. I warned him that they were not his true friends, and that they would abandon him when he had served their purpose. This happened. Between the abdication and the outbreak of war, he had only three supporters in the House: Duncan Sandys, Brendan Bracken and myself.

But I never really liked Churchill. Although Keynes rightly

described *The World Crisis* as one of the most powerful tractates against war ever written, War was his element and Power his objective. In my heart I hated both. I could never take the streak of cruelty in his nature, detected in his portrait by Graham Sutherland, who once said to me in Venice: 'I painted the man I saw.' This, I am convinced, is the reason why the picture 'preyed on his mind'.

He would cry over the death of a swan or a cat. For human life he had little regard, least of all for his own. He enjoyed danger. But I have never disguised from myself the fact that this element of cruelty might have been essential for what he had to do. When he sacked or broke people, and he broke many, he never thanked and seldom saw them. He simply didn't care. And in some cases he did it with relish.

His relations with his naval, military and air commanders were fascinating. It is surprising that the American naval historian, Professor Arthur Marder, so good on the First World War, has got the Second so wrong. He has written that Churchill never interfered with his admirals. The exact opposite is true. He never stopped. When war broke out in 1939, Chatfield, who had been Beatty's Flag-Captain throughout the First World War, and was unquestionably the ablest Admiral in the Royal Navy, should have been immediately recalled as First Sea Lord. Instead he was dismissed from office by Churchill; and thereafter given absolutely nothing to do. By appointing A. V. Alexander as First Lord of the Admiralty, and keeping Pound (already a sick, and soon a dying man) as First Sea Lord, Churchill ensured that the strategic direction of the naval war remained in his own hands. He could never keep away from the Operations Room at the Admiralty, and many of the signals sent out in Pound's name were drafted by himself. In fact there was hardly a senior admiral afloat whom he did not either sack, or try to sack, including Cunningham, Tovey, Forbes, Somerville, Harwood and North. He actually sent Admiral of the Fleet Lord Cork and Orrery out to the Mediterranean to conduct a Court of Enquiry into the conduct of Admiral Somerville, commanding Force H, when he broke off an action against the Italian fleet in order to ensure the safe arrival of a large convoy at Malta; and was much disappointed when Cork reported that Somerville's dispositions had been faultless. Tovey, the Commander-in-Chief, Home Fleet, sank the *Bismarck* only because he disregarded every signal made to him by the Admiralty. One was that the Fleet Flagship (*King George V*) was to remain on the scene of action, even if it meant that she had to be towed. This would have reduced her speed to five or six knots, and would have meant that she would have been a sitting duck for the U-boats which were already gathering. Afterwards Pound was so ashamed of this signal, which had been initiated by Churchill, that he telephoned to the Commander-in-Chief when he returned to base at Scapa and apologized, saying that he would try to have it expunged from the records. He failed. Our own brilliant naval historian, Captain Stephen Roskill, is now putting all this right.

If anyone should think that I have been unfair in ascribing to Churchill a streak of cruelty, I can only quote the words of one of his closest henchmen before and during the war, Sir Desmond Morton. When Wavell rightly decided to evacuate Somaliland, and carried out a brilliant retreat, Churchill complained that his casualties had been too light. Wavell sent a telegram in which he said: 'Butchery is not the mark of a good tactician'; and that was the end of him. Morton wrote: 'I think that the first time I ever deeply disliked Winston and realized the depths of selfish brutality to which he could sink, was when he told me, not only that he was getting rid of Wavell from the Middle East, but why.' He described how Churchill had walked up and down his room, chin sunk on chest, glowering ferociously and muttering: 'I wanted to show my power', over and over again.

For my part, I do not *blame* him for this. All great men of action who have changed the course of history have been avid for power – not least Napoleon. I simply hated it; and it cannot have been fortuitous that my friendship with Lloyd George began after he had fallen from supreme power, and that my friendship with Churchill ended when he achieved it. General Lord Ismay, known to all as 'Pug', was, after Brendan Bracken, the most faithful and devoted servant Churchill ever had. By a piece of good luck he was also a close personal friend of mine. He made no claim to be a great general; but he was one of the greatest diplomats I have ever known. His services to this country during the war were incalculable. Time and again, by toning down a red ink Minute or Directive, nearly always beginning with the word 'Pray', he prevented a rupture between the Prime Minister and the Chiefs of Staff. One evening, after the war, when we were alone together, he said to me: 'I was Churchill's servant. It was my duty. And to the end of my life I shall be proud of it.' I said: 'I never was.' He replied: 'I know. Nor was it your duty.'

I then said: 'I would like to ask you one question. I was of no importance at all. I was no conceivable threat to him. Why did he bother, at intervals, to hate me?' He thought for a moment, and then replied: 'You wrote him one or two very tactless letters, which angered him; and you were apt to tell him things he didn't want to hear. But the real reason is that you are one of the very few people he has ever been fond of. That is why he bothered.' I asked him what he thought I should do now, and he said: 'Would you really like my advice?' Then he went on: 'Most of the people he sacked will never see him again. You will. Let me tell you what will happen. If he thinks you can be of use to him, he will pick you up. My advice to you is that, if you think he is right, you should do what he asks you to do; and be prepared to be dropped again when you have done it. If you think he is wrong, don't.'

It happened exactly that way. First, over Europe. Then, strangely enough, over the South Tyrol. For years I had loved the South Tyrol, and spent many happy days before the war in the beautiful valley, stretching south from Innsbruck, which had been bartered to Italy in the secret Treaty of London in order to bring her into the First World War. The people were unhappy. They did not want to change their country or their language. Even the names of the towns and villages had been changed – Bözen to Bolzano, Sterzing to Vipiteno. I thought and felt that the South Tyrol should be restored to Austria; and started a campaign for this in the summer of 1946. Churchill wrote to me to say that I had his full support. He said he had no doubt that a debate which I brought about in the House of Commons had had a definite effect: and that the credit of it belonged to me. He encouraged me to form a Committee, and in August wrote to Lord Cecil to say that he would like to join in any association that might be formed, adding: 'I am telling Bob Boothby to work on it, and that I will come along. In the vast confusion of Europe it is indeed a Touchstone. Such baffling situations as those which now confront us can only be dealt with selectively. One way is to make up one's mind which is the true point of attack on the long front of evil and bewilderment.'

The campaign got off to a very good start, with support from all parties in the House of Commons. Then Stalin issued his *Ukase* from Moscow. The South Tyrol should remain Italian. As usual, we succumbed. Since then things have gone better than I had feared; and the Italians have not behaved badly. The fact remains that the South Tyrol should be Austrian.

The next thing was heroin. Under strong American pressure, the Labour Government introduced a Bill to prohibit the manufacture of heroin in this country. I consulted my medical friends, and their opinion was unanimous. With heroin there was always the danger of addiction. But there were certain kinds of pain, particularly in cancer cases, which heroin alone could kill. If its manufacture was prohibited, there would be a great deal of avoidable suffering. This was enough for me; and I put down a motion for the rejection of the Bill. Immediately Churchill sent for me, and told me that I had his full support. He said he did not want to speak on the subject in the House of Commons if this could be avoided, but that if necessary he would do so. Then he said that I could go to the Ministry of Health and tell them that he was strongly opposed to the Bill, and would vote against it. This I did, and it was immediately withdrawn.

Finally, he supported me when I spoke in favour of a rise in the salaries of Members of Parliament. I talked to him quite often in the Smoking-Room of the House of Commons about this and that, and one day he asked me to breakfast. When I arrived, he offered me whisky. I said it was a bit too early, and he replied: 'You've lost your touch.' The question of political office never arose, because he told me one day that if I ever aspired to it, and he didn't promise anything, I would have to give up television; and I replied that I much preferred a television studio to the Post Office. He said: 'I thought you would say that.' I think that one of the reasons he hated television so much was because he couldn't do it himself. He had to read. This is all right on radio, but no good in front of a camera. He once referred to me, in the House of Commons, as 'The Hon. Member the Star of Television'. He said it not with a smile, but with a snarl. And the House didn't like it.

With him I could never avoid being tactless. One day I reminded him that he had said to me that Lloyd George should have resigned in 1918, and added: 'He was then over ten years younger than you are now. Why don't you take your own advice?' No answer. Another day, after I'd raised my majority to 12000, he came up to me and said: 'I don't know how you do it.' Before I realized what I was doing, I blurted out: 'Because they like me in the North of Scotland; whereas, although they know you saved them in 1940, they never liked you.' I awaited an onslaught. It did not come. Instead he said, very quietly: 'I never understood them. But this I will give you. No nation of its size since Ancient Greece has made a comparable impact upon the world.'

In August 1948 I spent a memorable afternoon with him in the South of France. When I got back to my hotel I wrote an account of it. I was very tired, and cannot vouch for its complete accuracy. But I feel I should record some extracts from it, if only because it still seems to be a vivid snapshot of the man.

I arrived at the Hotel Roy-Réné,* with Malcolm Bullock, at twelve o'clock. Mary Soames met us in the hall, very pretty and charming – as always; and up we went, in the lift, to a nice room where we found Clemmie and Christopher Soames, and five dry martinis. A very warm welcome from Clemmie, who seemed somewhat relieved to see us.

Suddenly the door opened, and in walked Winston, in a blue siren suit. Bowing low to Malcolm, he came across to me. 'Ah,' he said, 'red trousers. Very nice. They match your tie. I've just been dealing with the German armour at Dunkirk, in which you are so interested. At first I was inclined to accept Halder's version, which you first told me. But that has now to be modified. These German Generals say anything that suits their book. Pownall has unearthed the official German War Diary.

'Look. This is what happened. Kluge reported to Rundstedt that the armour was tired, and extended. He asked for two days in which to

* In Aix-en-Provence.

rest it. Rundstedt agreed. Then, by a piece of good luck, Hitler motored over to Rundstedt's Headquarters, and also agreed that this was necessary. In the afternoon a message came from O K W, Hitler's supreme Headquarters, ordering the armour to advance on Dunkirk. This order came from Keitel.' 'And, presumably, Halder, as Chief of Staff?' I interjected. 'Yes,' he said: 'It was disregarded by Rundstedt, despite Guderian's protests, who was fortified by Hitler's verbal agreement that the armour should be rested. That, and Calais, saved the BEF.

'I did Calais myself. I personally gave the order to stand, and fight it out to the end. I agreed to the evacuation of Boulogne with reluctance; and I think now that I ought to have ordered them to fight it out there too. But the order to Calais meant certain death for almost the entire garrison.

'It was the only time during the war that I couldn't eat. I was very nearly sick at dinner. But, together with the Gravelines line, which was steadily flooding, it gave us two vital days; and a few of our cruiser tanks actually broke out of Calais, through the German armour, and got to the Gravelines line.

'Now look at this' – producing his proofs. 'Here is a yelp from the German Commander at Dunkirk. He says the British troops are disembarking in large ships, without equipment, but unscathed. "We do not want to have to meet them again, when they have been re-equipped." Only then was the order given for the armour to move in on Dunkirk. And by then it was too late.' He put away the proofs. 'The failure to press on with their armour, and Calais, saved us. And I did Calais. Now come in to lunch.'

This was all right: langouste mayonnaise, soufflé, a couple of bottles of champagne on ice, and a bottle of Volnay, topped up with brandy.

'I find alcohol a great support in life,' he said. 'Sir Alexander Walker, who keeps me supplied with your native brew, told me that a friend of his, who died the other day, drank a bottle of whisky a day for the last ten years of his life. He was eighty-five.' 'If you ever gave it up,' I replied, 'you'd die.' Silence.

Then: 'If I become Prime Minister again, I shall give up cigars. For there will be no smoking. We cannot afford it.' 'What,' I said, 'none at all?' 'Well, only a small ration for everyone. And then a black market in coupons, organized by the Government, so that anyone who couldn't give it up would have to pay through the nose!' 'You'd better not say that before the election,' I said. 'I shan't,' he answered.

'They said,' he went on, 'that I was wrong to go to Greece in 1940. But I didn't do it simply to save the Greeks. Of course, honour and all that came in. But I wanted to form a Balkan front. I wanted Yugoslavia, and I hoped for Turkey. That, with Greece, would have given us fifty divisions. A nut for the Germans to crack. Our intervention in Greece caused the revolution in Yugoslavia which drove out Prince "Palsy"; and delayed the German invasion of Russia by six weeks. Vital weeks. So it was worth it. If you back a winner it doesn't really matter much what your reasons were at the time. They now say that I went to Greece for the wrong reasons. How do they know? The point is that it was worth it.' This I knew to be nonsense. It was not worth it. It did not lead to the formation of a Balkan front. It is by no means certain that it delayed the German invasion of Russia, the date of which had already been fixed. It gave Rommel his chance, and very nearly lost us Egypt. Finally, it was a classic example of what he himself had described, in the last volume of *The World Crisis*, as the commonest of all the great military errors: 'It is the error most easy to perceive in theory and most difficult to avoid in action. There are two enemies and two theatres; the task of the Commander is to choose in which he will prevail. To choose either, is to suffer grievously in the neglected theatre. To choose both, is to lose in both. . . . A score of good reasons can be given not only for either course, but also for the compromises which ruin them. But the path to safety nearly always lies in rejecting the compromises.' However, I had not been asked to lunch to argue, much as I would have enjoyed it. And anyway he was by now in full spate.

'My hardest time was the end of 1940, and the first six months of 1941' – with an odd look at me (it was the time of my troubles). 'I had to do eight things at once, with enough material and time for three to four. It was very exciting.'

'A bit too exciting,' I said.

'Not for me. I enjoyed it. The hornets were buzzing round my head. I like that.' I very nearly said, but didn't, that it was perhaps because everyone knew he liked it that he was no longer Prime Minister.

Then he went on: 'The Americans were not always easy to deal with. They like to concentrate on one thing. They scrap everything else – at colossal expense – to build up a single Plan. But in war nothing stands still. Everything goes on all the time. So you often lose a lot by this policy. I had the greatest difficulty in persuading them to let us capture Rome. After that, they removed nearly all Alexander's divisions for that foolish attack on the Riviera, which made no difference at all to the situation in Brittany. If they had let me have my way, we might have got to Vienna.'

And – in conclusion – 'They say I interfered during the war. I did. I interfered all the time.'

The moment then arrived for departure to Les Baux, which he

remembered from fifteen years ago, and where he thought he wanted to paint a picture. I said I could not, and would not, take my car, unless they filled it up with petrol. This was accordingly done; and all the painting apparatus collected.

Winston then appeared in snake-skin shoes, and a Mexican sombrero hat; and off we set, before a wide-eyed crowd, in three cars. Winston and Clemmie and one detective in the first. The Soameses and another detective in the second. Malcolm and I in the third – mine – without a detective.

We told them they ought to see the ruins (Roman) of St Remy on the way. But they took the wrong road, so we got there first. Somewhat dazed by the combination of tremendous heat and alcohol, I found a very nice niche in a beautiful Roman arch, where I curled myself up, and went fast asleep, dreaming of centurions. I thus missed the best scene of all.

On arrival Winston clambered out of his car, gazed for a few seconds at the ruins, and said: 'How bloody. How absolutely bloody.' 'Look at Bob asleep,' said Malcolm, hoping to divert his attention. But all he said was: 'Bloody.' Clemmie and Mary thought it was quite lovely, and decided to stay for a while. Whereupon the old boy climbed back into his car, and drove off to Les Baux; alone, except for the chauffeur and detectives.

Clemmie and Mary then looked at the ruins from every angle. Christopher confided to me, when I woke up, that he hated sight-seeing; and thanked God that he and Mary were leaving the next day for a drive along the Riviera. He called it a 'pub-crawl' but, if I knew Mary, it wouldn't be that. We all then set off for Les Baux – Clemmie, Malcolm and self in my car; Soames's following.

On arrival, the detective came up to me and said: 'There's a storm on. You'd better keep clear. It'll be over in ten minutes.' It then transpired that the painting tackle was all in the Soameses' car, so he couldn't begin. He had gone off to the top of Les Baux, in a rage. The chauffeur and detectives seized the easel and paint-box and ran up the hill after him; while I looked for, and found, a *bistro*.

By this time all the sight-seers at Les Baux had turned out to see what the hell was going on.

Presently there was an uproar. I went out and found Winston striding down the street, with the chauffeur and detectives disconsolately following him, plus all the painting apparatus. 'There's nothing to paint here,' he shouted. 'There's beer to drink here,' I shouted back. So he came into the *bistro*, which was almost pitch dark, and sat down.

'Were you really asleep in that arch?' he asked. And then: 'Don't you think the Calais story is very dramatic?' By that time the beer had arrived. 'It is cool, but not cold,' he said with truth. Two pails of ice immediately appeared. Clemmie ordered a lemonade. And peace was gradually restored. 'I hate the taste of beer,' Clemmie said. 'So do most people, to begin with,' he answered: 'It is however, a prejudice that many have been able to overcome.' The bill was then demanded. Unthinkable, said the proprietress. It was the greatest honour they had ever had. Perhaps Monsieur Churchill would sign his name in the book? Monsieur Churchill would; and did. I went out with Malcolm, wondering whether I would ever be famous enough to pay bills with my signature. 'I think,' I said, 'that we can now bugger off.' 'It's more than we can do,' said a detective, who was standing immediately behind me. I had not seen him.

The sombrero and the snake-shoes reappeared. 'Let us rendezvous at the hotel later.' But I was too tired to rendezvous any more. I killed a dog on the way back. And collapsed on to my bed, with a sty in my eye. Thus ended an astonishing afternoon.

About Lloyd George I have said enough. About Churchill I would only add that I have forgotten the cruelty; and remember only the courage and the kindness. How, in the final desperate world crisis, he saved us all; how, when I was a young man, he lit up one corridor of history after another and opened every door for me. In addition to the ruthless, there was also a childish side to his nature, which was very engaging; and from this arose his genuine love of animals, ponds and bricks. One evening, at Strasbourg, he invited the Conservative members of the delegation to the Council of Europe to dine with him at his hotel. After a few minutes I saw him glaring at me. 'What's the matter now?' I asked. He said: 'What's that in your buttonhole?' I replied: 'The Legion of Honour and I am very proud of it.' He continued to scowl. Then, suddenly, his face lit up, and he said with a smile: 'I've got something better than that.' He left the table, went up to his bed-room, and came back wearing the Médaille Militaire. With him I always felt like a toy in the hands of a mischievous boy. I never knew whether he was trying to break me to pieces, or to mend me. All I could be sure of was that it was one or the other. I once told him that he was a bully by nature, but that he could never bully me; and then slammed the door in his face. No wonder he sometimes tried to break me.

The greatest surprise of all was when one night the Chief Whip said to me: 'The Prime Minister wishes to include your name in the Coronation Honours List. You can be a Baronet, or a Knight Commander of the British Empire.' I chose the KBE not only because I thought the days of hereditary honours, apart from the Royal Family, were over but because my father had it. And I must admit that, together with the Coronation Medal, it gave added pleasure to the most memorable service I have ever attended. For this I shall always be grateful to him.

If he sometimes enjoyed hauling up under-dogs, he had no use for top-dogs other than himself. The truth is that his egotism, derived not only from his Churchill but also from his American blood, prevented him from tolerating any kind of personal challenge to his own supremacy. Hence his dismissal of Wavell. Hence his dislike of Cunningham and Tovey. It extended over the whole field. When he found that Priestley's Sunday night talks over the radio were becoming very popular, he took him off the air. When he found that Montgomery was addressing large and enthusiastic audiences of munition workers, before the invasion of Europe, he ordered him to stop. Lord Woolton told me that he had one rather disagreeable interview with him when he was Minister of Food. Churchill began by saying: 'I suppose you are very pleased with your popularity.' I asked him what he replied, and he said: 'I am pleased only because I seem to have gained the confidence of the public.' The truth is that Churchill was not keen on anyone else's popularity; and I have sometimes thought that, although it had nothing to do with power, he rather resented mine on television.

From a personal point of view, the greatest mistake of his life was to accept the resignation of Prince Louis of Battenberg, the best First Sea Lord we had had since Barham; and to replace him with Lord Fisher, who by then was senile. King George V was strongly opposed to this, and strove in vain to prevent it. But for Lloyd George, who was strong enough to bring him back to office against fierce opposition, it would have brought Churchill's political career to an end. And Churchill knew it.

The last years were sad, but not as as sad as some make out.

He knew very well that his place in history was secure. The few friends he had were gone. The only person he ever loved, his wife, didn't like the Riviera, and liked Lord Beaverbrook still less; so he often went there alone. Once he rang up a friend of mine, who had a villa in Monte Carlo, and said that he would like to come to lunch. My friend was rather apprehensive, and invited Mrs Fellowes, the Singer sewing-machine heiress, who had known him for many years, to help him out. Soon after lunch began, he closed his eyes and appeared to pass out. Mrs Fellowes then said to her host: 'What a pity that so great a man should end his life in the company of Onassis and Wendy Reves.' Suddenly, to their horror, one eye opened, and Churchill said: 'Daisy, Wendy Reves is something that you will never be. She is young, she is beautiful and she is kind.' Then the eye closed again.

Wendy Reves was the wife of his literary agent, Emery Reves. She was, and is, a delightful girl; and while he was in the South of France she took care of him. When he stayed at their villa above Menton, filled with lovely pictures, she let him do exactly what he wanted, and paint where and when he liked. If he wanted to go to the casino, she went with him and saw that he came to no harm. She once showed me the best photograph I have ever seen of him. It was inscribed 'For Wendy, with love, from Winston.' She deserves her place in history.

The last time I saw him, not long before he died, he asked me to dinner. Lady Churchill was ill in bed, so we were alone. It was a difficult evening because he was pretty far gone. He did not want to talk about the war. I tried to arouse his interest by a reference to the Battle of Jutland, but all he said was: 'I used to know a lot about that – now I have forgotten.' Finally he repeated, with a rather sad look, something that he had said to me long ago: 'The journey has been well worth making – once.' 'And then?' I asked. 'A long sleep, I expect: I deserve it.'

These were the last words he ever spoke to me.

B.—C

# 5
# The Social Scene between the Wars

Meanwhile there was, in the background, a glittering social scene. Those were the days of large houses in London and the country, butlers and footmen galore, gleaming silver, superlative food and drink, and the Embassy Club. Fortunately the unemployed were out of sight; and, I am afraid, out of mind. There were at least five great hostesses; Mrs Ronald Greville, Lady Astor, Lady Cunard, Lady Londonderry and Lady Colefax, all of whom 'took me up'.

Mrs Greville, the only daughter of an Edinburgh brewer worth millions, was a bit of an old bag, but very good to me. She married Greville for convenience; and, as far as I know, no one ever saw him. Perhaps he was dead. She regarded me as a boy from her native city who was making good; and we had an agreeable relationship on this basis. She had the shrewdness of a typical lowland Scot; and, as far as patronage was concerned, she was extremely powerful. She once said to me: 'I don't think you will ever get high office.' I asked her why and she said: 'Because I don't think you really want it. But make whatever life you choose from within Parliament, because you have the makings of a good parliamentarian.' One week-end, when I was staying at her beautiful country house, Polesden Lacey, in a party which included her two favourite Scottish celebrities, Lord Inchcape and Sir Robert Horne, as well as several others, her fat butler, of whom she was very fond, was tight; and poured some soup down one of the ladies' necks. She sent for one of the innumerable footmen, and asked for a piece of paper and pencil. On it she wrote: 'You are drunk. Leave the room immediately, M.G.' The footman gave it to the butler, who read it with evident bewilderment. Then he went to the sideboard and put it on a silver salver. After this, he tottered back to the dinner table and handed it to Sir Austen Chamberlain. He read it, and his eye-glass fell out. This was a scene that I shall never forget.*

One day, when we were walking across the drawing-room, she stopped, pointed to the carpet and said: 'This is the spot where Jack Simon fell on his knees to ask me to marry him; I refused.' Then she added, with a wink, 'I think I was right, don't you?' She was capable of saying some pretty caustic things, but I found, in the course of time, that she always told the truth. She once told a group of us that 'Rufus Reading' came down to Polesden alone in order to ask her whether he should accept the Viceroyalty of India. This was difficult to believe, and I asked the date, which she gave me. Early next morning I went downstairs in my pyjamas to look at the Visitors Book. There it was. The single signature: 'Reading'. On another occasion, after she had come back from a regal tour of the East, I asked her whether she had enjoyed it. She replied: 'George Lloyd [our High Commissioner in Egypt] was not very nice to me in Cairo. He won't last long.' He didn't.

Lady Astor's home, Cliveden, dominated by Philip Kerr and Tom Jones, was indeed the home of the so-called 'set' which advocated appeasement. But she cast her net wider than that; and, if you stayed there, you were apt to meet interesting people. The trouble was that there was never enough to drink. A glass of white wine at dinner was all you got. One week-end when the Mosleys were asked to stay, they brought a petrol tin to my bedroom. It was filled with dry martini. There is a story, which is true, that she once said to Lloyd George: 'If Waldorf [her husband] and I had known that you were living with Frances Stevenson, we would never have lent you our villa at Deauville during the Peace Conference.' Lloyd George said: 'What were you doing with my secretary Philip Kerr?' 'Absolutely nothing,' blazed back Lady Astor. 'Then,' said Lloyd George, 'you ought to be ashamed of yourself.' Lady

* This story has often been told, and sometimes applied, wrongly, to Sir John Simon. I repeat it only because I was there.

Astor had great American vitality, and a gift of quick repartee; but, as a hostess, she tried too hard to keep everyone and everything going. She would dance about in false teeth. It was not very funny.

Lady Cunard was like a bird. She had a greater capacity for keeping a dinner table alight than anyone I have known. I was at the celebrated dinner in Venice when she announced to the world that she had decided to change her name from Maud to Emerald, her favourite jewel. She quarrelled with her only daughter Nancy, an eccentric but lovable and amusing character, typical of the period. I have a letter from her, which I value, written after a lunch we had together in Paris with John Strachey: 'You do it all so well. So *gaily*. That's rare!'

It was at Lady Cunard's house that I first met Sir Thomas Beecham, and began a friendship which was to last for many years. After dinner, he strolled over to me and, stroking his beard, said in his drawling voice: 'You are just what I think a politician ought to be. You remind me of Lloyd George.' From that moment I was a devotee. He was generally accepted as Emerald Cunard's lover; but, if so, he was certainly not a faithful one. He took most of her money for his operas, and then married Betty Humby without telling her. She never recovered from the shock. Few people who knew her would regard Emerald Cunard as a pathetic figure but, in her final years, she was. Whenever I saw her she came up to me with tears in her eyes and said: 'Have you seen Thomas lately? Tell me how he is.' She loved him.

At Argyle House in Chelsea, Lady Colefax concentrated on the literary lions, and captured them. There was a ritual at lunch: bowls were brought in and put on the table: and she mixed the salads herself. I must say they were always very good. With the guests she succeeded in obtaining, there was never any difficulty about conversation. I remember one day at lunch when Eddie Marsh touched me on the shoulder and said: 'Look at that – and remember it.' Arnold Bennett, H. G. Wells and Max Beerbohm were walking downstairs arm-in-arm immediately in front of us. I was chaperoned into what was then High Society by Cynthia Mosley and Maureen Stanley, to both of whom I was devoted, and both of whom died young. By this time Tom Mosley had joined the Labour Party. Socially, it did not matter. He had married the beautiful daughter of Lord Curzon, who stormed all hearts at will.

I used often to stay with the Mosleys at their house in Denham, and twice I spent my summer holiday with them in their *palazzo* in Venice and their villa at Antibes. I loved Cimmie; and enjoyed his company. He had a powerful brain, filled with original ideas of which he was never afraid. Everyone predicted for him a brilliant political career. The only thing I could not take was his practical jokes. One evening at Denham, the cook, who was a friend of mine, warned me that the cheese savoury at dinner was going to be made of soap. I passed this on to Oliver Messel who was a guest; and he came down to dinner with a pack of cards in his pocket. After the savoury, which neither of us touched, he suddenly got up, white in the face, went behind a screen and, by coughing and scattering the cards over the parquet floor, gave the best imitation of someone being sick that I have ever heard. Lady Jowitt, who was also a guest, was actually sick. And after this there were no more soap savouries.

In Venice Tom saw himself as Byron and spent much of his time swimming in the Lagoon. I much preferred him in this rôle to that of Mussolini. Lord (Buck) De La Warr and Chips Channon were also guests at the Mosley *palazzo*. Chips Channon had a remarkable and, in some ways, unique career all his own. And, according to his diaries, brilliantly edited by Robert Rhodes James, he played a part – small but definite – in our political history. Some of the Venetian parties could be rough. I remember one, on the Lido, when a distinguished Italian aristocrat had an argument with another distinguished aristocrat sitting next to him. He concluded it by stubbing out his cigarette on the back of her hand.

At Antibes it was bathing most of the time, with excursions to the countryside. There was one memorable lunch at a restaurant, surrounded by white doves, given by Cimmie and Tom, at which the guests were Bernard Shaw, John Strachey and myself. Shaw, who had just published *The Intelligent Woman's Guide to Socialism*, was in rollicking form. I remember that John, who was taking life and himself very seriously at this time, was deeply shocked by what he regarded as Shaw's levity. Tom and I were vastly amused. But I have never been at ease in the Mediterranean. I am, essentially, Nordic; and the moment came, as it always did, when I fled to Bavaria.

Behind the whole social scene in England, and dominating it all, was Sir Philip Sassoon, the greatest host and the greatest gardener I have ever known and, in the right mood, the best company. For ten years he shaped my life. His origins were fascinating. The Sassoons were Parsees who came to England from Baghdad via Bombay, and made a lot of money on the way. His mother was a Rothschild. It was a remarkable combination, but it was no part of England. Fundamentally he was a detached and acute observer in a foreign land. He had been private secretary to Haig, as Commander-in-Chief; and Parliamentary Private Secretary to Lloyd George, as Prime Minister; and he was close to the Royal Family. I was invited, constantly, to his week-end parties at Trent and Lympne; and, for some years before the outbreak of the Second World War, I was the tenant of the French House, next door to Port Lympne, an old Tudor farm house which, with Herbert Baker, he had beautifully restored, and which had an unsurpassed view over the Romney Marsh – you could easily see Rye thirty miles away. By day the lights over the marsh never ceased to change. And by night you could see the light-houses on the French coast.

With the help of his sister, Lady Cholmondeley, and of his cousin, Mrs Hannah Gubbay, he made his week-end parties unparalleled in the world. Nothing like them had been seen before; and, surely, nothing remotely like them will ever be seen again. It was a combination of luxury, beauty, simplicity and informality, brilliantly contrived. At Trent the blue bathing pool, lit, and surrounded by a such a profusion of lilies that the scent at night became almost overpowering; the flamingoes and ducks; the banks of exquisite flowers in the garden and in the drawing-room. No pomp, no ceremony, no formality, and no white ties – just dinner jackets. But always when you went to change for dinner, a carnation and a cocktail on your dressing-table. Today it all seems like the dream of another world – the white-coated footmen, Winston Churchill arguing over the tea-cups with Bernard Shaw, Rex Whistler painting alone, an immaculate Sir Samuel Hoare

playing tennis with the professional, Osbert Sitwell and
Malcolm Bullock laughing in a corner, while Philip himself
flitted from group to group, an alert, watchful, influential, but
unobtrusive stage director.

I remember, in particular, one week-end at Trent when the
guests included the Duke and Duchess of York, soon to be
King and Queen. Philip asked me to go down on the Friday
night, and we were alone together. Early next morning I
heard the sound of cart wheels. I got up and went out in my
dressing-gown to find six horse-drawn carts coming up the
avenue, laden with flowers from Covent Garden in full bloom.
An army of gardeners was waiting to plant them out in borders
which had been carefully prepared. By the time the guests
began to arrive for lunch, they were all in.

After lunch I played a round of golf on the private course
with the Duke of York, and when we got back we found that
we could either fly over the grounds in our host's private
aeroplane, or watch an exhibition of 'stunt' golf shots by the
professional Joe Kirkwood, or just talk to a number of fascinating and fascinated guests. After dinner there was a magnificent
firework display over the lake. Then Richard Tauber sang to
us on the terrace by moonlight. Then we went to bed.

At Lympne, Sassoon gave freer reign to the exotic streak that
was in him. The walls of the dining-room were of deep blue
lapis lazuli surmounted by a Glyn Philpot frieze of white cows
driven by black men, and the chairs and tables gilded. The
'elephant' walls by Sert gave way to Sargent water-colours
against a plain white background. Rex Whistler, soon to be
killed in the war, painted the entrance-hall which, so far as I
know, still exists. The baths, in which everyone slipped, were
of marble. Outside the house were huge macracarpa hedges,
shaped in squares within each of which was a small garden. I
had a free run of the grounds; and, one day, I came across
Philip sitting reading alone in a fez. He was not in the least
disconcerted, but said: 'I never forget my oriental background.'
I asked him why he never went back to Baghdad. He replied
laconically: 'Too many cousins.'

But the chief glory of Lympne was the great autumn border
stretching from the house right down to the Marsh. Looking
down on it with me one evening, he said: 'The secret of good

gardening is clumps – never speckles; the blending of colour; and as little earth as possible.' One of his most engaging traits was his passion for showing his achievements and his possessions to others and sharing with them the pleasure they gave. Both at Trent and Lympne, when the gardens were at their zenith, the public were admitted every week; and many thousands took advantage of a privilege which was never abused.

A favourite method of producing the effect Philip wanted was his astonishing power of reckless and witty exaggeration. For example, he once said to me about Lord Berners, when he was a guest at Port Lympne, that his snores were so loud that the tiles flew off the roof like confetti. I thought this so funny that I told Berners, who immediately left. Naturally Philip was furious. Soon after the Nazis came to power, he asked me to go to Berlin in order to find out what was happening. I tried my best to dissuade him. But no. He was determined; so off we went. A German friend of mine told him that Goering was *au fond* a good apple. This delighted him and, much to the indignation of our ambassador, he himself made an appointment to see Goering the next day. The visit was a great success. And afterwards the French Air Minister, Pierre Cot, never failed to ask Philip after '*votre ami Goering*'. When we got back, Philip wrote to me: 'This is to confirm (1) that you are a good apple, (2) that I am crackers about you, (3) that I am so glad that after my shilly-shallying, beating about the bush and blowing hot and cold, I should come to the decision not to *let you down*! It was all grand, tip-top and top-hole, and must be repeated.'

The unexpected was always happening. In those days I owned an open two-seater 6½ litre Bentley, which I had bought cheap in Edinburgh from Mr McVittie or Mr Guest, who wanted to replace it with the new 8½ litre. As it turned out the 6½ litre was the best car they ever made; and, if I had only kept it, it would now be worth thousands. One day I left it outside Port Lympne when Philip was giving a party. When I came out I found that the bonnet had been opened by a grubby little Air Force mechanic in uniform, who was peering into the engine: 'I do apologize,' he said, 'but I can never resist looking at a beautiful piece of engineering when I see one.' I said that I was delighted, and that I loved it myself; and we talked for a little while about this and that. Then, to my surprise, he said: 'Now I think we will go in.' We did, and Philip introduced us. It was Lawrence of Arabia. A little later Philip said that his house was absolutely packed, and would I put up Lawrence and Victor Cazalet at the French House? I said I would be delighted, and this led to a memorable evening. Lawrence was in one of his best moods, and talked brilliantly far into the night. In fact he was the best story-teller I have ever listened to. I did not know then that they were only stories. We did not go to bed until three o'clock, and he left on his motor-bike at five. His luggage consisted of a toothbrush. I reproduce on the opposite page his letter of thanks – he called himself Shaw after he joined the Royal Air Force as an Aircraftsman.

He was first exposed by Aldington, who was vitriolically attacked in the press, and never recovered his literary reputation. More than anything else, the British hate their heroes to be exposed, or even criticized. Nelson is the classic example. They built Trafalgar Square and the monument at enormous expense, and gave a large pension to descendents whom he never knew. But they allowed Emma Hamilton – whom he bequeathed to the nation with his dying breath – to die in penury in Calais.

It has now transpired that the whole grim story in the *Seven Pillars of Wisdom* of his capture by the Turks in Deraa, where he was beaten and tortured and raped, is a myth. Perhaps some part of his subconscious wished it had happened. In fact he never went to Deraa; nor did most of his alleged exploits ever take place. He was liaison officer between Feisal and Allenby, and little more. I once asked Bernard Shaw whether Lawrence was a genius or a phoney; and he said, 'Both.' The discovery that he was a fraud has, I am afraid, only deepened my admiration for him. To have done what he said he did would have been amazing. To have invented it all, and then got away with it, seems to me an even more remarkable achievement. Churchill was completely taken in by him. So was John Buchan, who once said to me that Lawrence was the only man he would have followed to the end of the earth. To follow Lawrence he need never have gone to the end of the earth. He needn't even have ridden two hundred miles across the desert on a camel. A few miles on a motor-bike would have

Southampton

6 September 1934

Things recede so quickly as a rule;
but I've had a feeling lately that I owed you
a letter of thanks for that week-end. The
eclectic spotlessness of your French House
was like something out of Marius the
Epicurean: and the three of us were so
oddly assorted — Cazalet limpid, yourself
urbane, and myself .... I don't know what,
but in the past tense, anyhow.

I remember it as a very delightful
moment in time, and am grateful.

Yours
TEShaw

sufficed. But then Lawrence had cast himself in the rôle of a typical Buchan hero. Lloyd George was not taken in; nor was Noël Coward, who on one occasion when Lawrence came over to an air pageant at Lympne, where he was the centre of attention with all eyes upon him, said to me: 'If, as he says, he shuns publicity, why does he wear his Air Force uniform which ensures it?' As was to be expected Lawrence, who lived his life in terms of the theatre, was fascinated by it; and Coward, who liked him, was able to show him how it worked. The only comparable figure of our time is Sir Edmund Backhouse, who lived his own imaginary life on an even bigger scale. But he had not Lawrence's flair for publicity, nor his literary gifts.

I had many guests at the French House, and I now wish I had kept a visitors book. I once invited Lady Oxford, her step-daughter Lady Violet Bonham-Carter, and her daughter, Princess Bibesco, to come over from Sandwich where they were staying at the Guildford Hotel, to dine and play bridge. The day before, Margot rang me up and said she was afraid that Violet could not make it. I asked her why, and she said: 'Because she is in mourning. She has had a quarrel with Mr Falk.' This was O. T. Falk, one of the leading financiers in the City of London, whom I knew quite well. Sir Maurice Bonham-Carter, his wife Lady Violet, and Falk had the perfect *ménage-à-trois*. There was never a breath of scandal. Between them 'Bongie' Bonham-Carter and 'Foxy' Folk ran a successful business in the City, with the assistance of Keynes; and Lady Violet ran both their lives. She could easily have run the lives of ten other men if she had wished to do so.

I told Hamish Erskine, who was then working in my office, that I would like him to come down for the night in order to make up a four at bridge; and he did. When they arrived I said to Margot: 'Is she in deep mourning?' She replied: 'Jet black, with sequins. I think it is in very bad taste, and frightfully selfish.' After the first rubber of bridge Elizabeth Bibesco said she would like a drink: 'Have you got any orangeade?' said Margot. 'I have indeed,' I replied. So Elizabeth got up and went over to the drink table, which was behind a screen. To my surprise she picked up the decanter of whisky, and took a tremendous swig. She then turned round, realized that the screen was not as high as she had thought, and that I had seen. She gave me a baleful look. Then she picked up the decanter of whisky again and drained it to the last drop. As she came back to the bridge table Margot, whose back was mercifully turned, said: 'Was the orangeade good?' I said: 'Absolutely delicious.'

On another occasion 'Baffy' Dugdale, a niece of Lord Balfour, a friend of Chaim Weizmann and an ardent Zionist, and Colin Coote, later to be editor of the *Daily Telegraph*, and his wife Denise, came to stay with me. I had one bottle of priceless Château Yquem. So I told my butler and 'factotum' Williams, who ran the whole show, to bring in two bottles of white wine for dinner, both wrapped in napkins; and to give the Yquem to Colin and myself, and the other bottle of good but not comparable wine to Baffy and Denise. After the first sip Colin looked up at me with shining eyes and said: 'Nectar.' Baffy looked up suspiciously and said: 'Take the napkins off those bottles.' The game was up.

Cyril Radcliffe was also a frequent guest, and it was in the French House that he met his wife Antonia. I was surrounded by excellent golf-courses – Littlestone, Rye, Deal, Sandwich: and this was my main recreation. Noël Coward lived at Goldenhurst, only three miles away; and on alternate week-ends I used to take my political friends over to see his theatrical friends, and he used to bring them over to see mine. I am afraid that my friends got the better of the exchange. There was a famous fun-fair at Margate to which we often used to go in the evenings; and I shall never forget the excitement in my office in the City when one day a telegram arrived: 'Meet me in dreamland tonight at ten o'clock. Noël Coward.'

The decade 1925–35 was, for me, one of sheer enjoyment – life on the Lympne 'Ridge' was one of endless gaiety and entertainment, until the shadow of war began to fall. I have lingered over Philip Sassoon because he epitomized it, and because I owe to him far more enjoyment than to anyone else. He had genius of a kind. He strongly, and as it turned out rightly, disapproved of my first marriage; and after that we drifted apart. It was characteristic of the politics of the period that he was kept out of the job of First Commissioner of Works, for which he was far better qualified than any other living man, for many years. But he was there for long enough to leave his legacy – our public parks and gardens, the finest in the world. He died shortly before the war, and I was not sorry. I have no doubt he would have made a notable contribution, but he would not have been happy. War was not his element. His death, like everything else about him, was well timed.

Noël Coward understood all that was going on in Europe, and knew that, if it continued, it would be the end. He minded this more than anything in his life; but not unnaturally it bored his friends in the theatrical world, and he felt helpless. Sometimes he would come over to the French House at night to talk to me alone. He told me that he could do nothing, but that I could. I said that in the present climate of public opinion, I too was impotent. The only political support I could always depend on came from my constituency.

When, as we both foresaw, war came in 1939, he was very anxious to serve in some post where he felt he could do justice to the gifts he knew he had; and, at his request, I arranged to take him over to Chartwell to see Churchill, who invited us both to dinner. There we found a small party, and Churchill not in a very good mood. After dinner Noël cheered everyone up by sitting down at the piano and singing some of his songs to us, including *Mad Dogs and Englishmen*, Churchill's favourite. Then, as we said goodbye, came the critical question: 'What should he do in the war?' And, for him, the devastating reply: 'Go and sing to the troops.'

He was very depressed on the way home, but in fact Churchill was right. He never really liked or appreciated Coward; nor, apart from Shaw, did he ever take much interest in dramatists or the theatre – still less in music. But he knew that Coward's particular genius could only fulfil itself in his own world. During the 'phoney' war Noël was asked by Sir Campbell Stuart to join a ridiculous organization in Paris which was supposed to be some kind of Information Service, but consisted chiefly of endless and purposeless lunch, dinner and drink parties. On the two occasions when I saw him there, I told him it was a farce; and he agreed with me. He was thankful to get out of it when Stuart suggested that he should go to the United States; and, when the real war started, to go back to his real profession. He did indeed 'sing to the troops', but he did far more than that by writing films such as *In Which We Serve* and *Brief Encounter*, together with a number of other plays, when he was still at the height of his creative powers. After the war I told him that I thought that *Brief Encounter*, in the original film version, was the best thing he had ever done. He said: 'No. *Bitter Sweet*. That only comes once in life.'

I shall always be grateful to him for having introduced me to a world which made everything so much easier for me when I finally decided to embark on a career of my own on radio and television, because in the studios I felt at home from the start. More so than in the House of Commons.

# 6

# The Economic Crisis of 1931

The Labour Government of 1929–31 was, with the exception of Arthur Henderson, the Foreign Secretary, a weak one; especially on the economic side. Snowden, the Chancellor of the Exchequer, clung to the Gold Standard at the existing parity of exchange, to Free Trade, and to Economy with fanatical tenacity, even after the American crash in the autumn of 1929. He intensified the fatal policy of deflation with savage relish. The Prime Minister, MacDonald, set up a committee to solve the unemployment problem. It consisted of J. H. Thomas, Lansbury, Tom Johnston and Mosley. None of them, except Mosley, knew a thing about economics, and all they got from Snowden was a million pounds. The President of the Board of Trade, Willie Graham, a charming Scotsman, was no better. Churchill once described his speeches as without a beginning, without a middle, without a point and without end. From the Opposition benches I attacked Snowden ceaselessly, and goaded him into making some very rough replies. Churchill wrote to me: 'I should not let Snowden's remarks ruffle or influence you in the slightest degree.' And I didn't.

Meanwhile the Government was reeling towards economic disaster, and Mosley was becoming desperate. He talked to me a lot, and we found ourselves in increasing agreement. Finally, he wrote his famous Memorandum. Needless to say, it was rejected out of hand by Snowden and the Cabinet. I was with him in his room at the House of Commons when he told me that he had decided to resign; and I told him that he was quite

The start.

Lloyd George and Churchill. 'The two men of undoubted genius in British politics during the present century.'

*Top* Lloyd George at Churt. 'The fall of Lloyd George and his subsequent exclusion from office for twenty years was one of the greatest disasters that has ever befallen the British people.'

*Bottom* With Winston Churchill on his way to open the Budget, 1928. 'Morally and physically the most courageous – and by far the most egotistical – man I have ever known.'

Yalta – 'The Betrayal'. Churchill, Roosevelt and Stalin are seated, with Eden standing second from left.

The first Conservative delegation to the Council of Europe. In the front row, left to right, are Macmillan, Churchill, Maxwell Fyfe and Boothby.

*Top* With Maugham. Maugham wrote to Boothby: 'I don't myself know why . . . I happen just now to be the most widely read author in the world. I suspect it is because I was born with a dramatic instinct which makes what I write readable.'

Sir Thomas Beecham in action.

*Bottom* The opening concert of the Royal Philharmonic Orchestra at the Davis Theatre, Croydon, September 15th, 1946, conducted by Sir Thomas Beecham. 'The greatest maker of music this country has ever produced – all the stories about Beecham are true.'

right. Apart from the fall of Neville Chamberlain in 1940, his resignation speech gave rise to the most dramatic scene I have witnessed during my fifty years in Parliament. When he sat down it was clear that he had the support not only of the great majority of the Labour Party, but many other members; and the House was tense. At that moment he was the key figure in British politics. Then Lloyd George made a fatal mistake. He failed completely to appreciate the significance and importance of Mosley's speech. Instead of praising it he described it as 'an injudicious mixture of Karl Marx and Lord Rothermere'. Immediately the tension subsided. For the moment, the crisis was over.

Then Mosley himself made a fatal mistake. He took his Memorandum to a meeting of the Parliamentary Labour Party and argued his case even more brilliantly than he had done in the House of Commons. Clearly the meeting was with him. He had only to wait; but patience was never one of his virtues. Against the advice of Arthur Henderson, he pressed the matter to a division. As was to be expected, party loyalty prevailed; and he was defeated.

Tom Mosley was the only one of my friends who was against my going to Churchill as Parliamentary Private Secretary. Two years later, Baldwin was to say to my father at Aix-les-Bains: 'I am sorry that Bob has gone to Churchill;' and when my father asked why, replied: 'Because he is a bad guide for youth.' Mosley urged me strongly not to accept the offer when it came. 'You were not born to be a henchman,' he said: 'When you disagree with him, as sooner or later you will, he will regard it as personal disloyalty and kill you politically.' Now it was my turn to give Mosley advice. I told him that, as he was right and almost everyone else wrong, things were bound, in the end, to come his way. I added that, so far as politics in this country were concerned, you must be a member of a party. He said he was thinking of forming a new party of his own. I said it would be madness; and that if he remained in the Labour Party events would almost certainly bring him to the leadership. Alternatively, he could rejoin the Conservative Party; but, knowing his views, I did not see much hope there.

He had a few talks with Harold Macmillan, Oliver Stanley,

Walter Elliot and myself which led Baldwin to make a speech about people who 'hunted with packs other than their own'; but nothing came of them. Mosley went on to form his new party, of which John Strachey and Harold Nicolson became members. It cut no ice. Then Harold took him to Rome to put him off fascism. It did the precise opposite. Standing beside Mussolini in the Palazzo Venezia as the blackshirts marched by, he said to himself: 'This is just my cup of tea'; and came back to form the British Union of Fascists. Thus a brilliant political career was extinguished.

During the summer of 1931 the economic crisis steadily mounted. Gold poured out of this country, unemployment rose to vertiginous heights, and panic began to set in. There was some talk of a Labour–Liberal coalition. Then Churchill made a speech in which he said to MacDonald: 'I should be very careful, if I were he, before I invited the Right Honourable Member for Caernarvon Boroughs [Lloyd George] to come over and take charge of the Labour Government. I am sure that once he was there, with his great knowledge, his immense drive and his grip of every aspect of the administrative machinery of Government, the best course thereafter for the Prime Minister to adopt would be to make a bargain that he should be permitted to go and sit among the Liberal Party and no doubt he would find himself quite happy.' This was far too near the mark for comfort. MacDonald, who was in any case frightened of Lloyd George, sheered off.

Snowden succeeded in getting ruthless cuts in expenditure accepted by the Cabinet; but they jibbed at a cut in unemployment benefit. Whereupon MacDonald resigned, and the King called a conference of party leaders at Buckingham Palace. Meanwhile Lloyd George had been struck down by illness, and had had to undergo an emergency and serious prostate operation. Churchill had stormed off to the United States. Mosley had gone. Far from forming a Conservative administration, which he should have done, Baldwin was only persuaded – with difficulty – to return from Aix-les-Bains to London.

I do not think that MacDonald ever had any intention of deliberately betraying the Labour movement. There was no treachery on his part. When he went to the Palace his mind was in a state of confusion, which at this time was not unusual. The King, from purely patriotic motives, appealed to MacDonald to form a National Government. I have been told, on good authority, that MacDonald hesitated and that Baldwin sat silent. The men who really formed that Government were Neville Chamberlain, Hoare, Snowden, Thomas and Samuel. But a government from which Lloyd George, Churchill, Horne, Amery and Arthur Henderson were excluded could hardly be called 'National'. For my part I shall always believe that, with the only two men of authentic genius in our public life out of action – for ever, it was hoped – the chance for the political pygmies was too good to be missed. It was certainly taken. They all marched gleefully in to bring this island to the brink of destruction, and the British Empire to an end; and on 31 August Sir Samuel Hoare, the only minister on the payroll of Lord Beaverbrook, wrote to Neville Chamberlain: 'As we have said several times in the last few days, we have had some great good luck in the absence of Winston and L.G.'

In August 1931 I was staying, as usual, with Archie Sinclair at his lovely lodge, Dalnawillan, in Caithness, to shoot grouse over dogs. When the crisis became acute we reluctantly decided to travel south. At Dingwall we heard the news that the Labour Government had resigned; 'You will be a minister tomorrow,' said Archie. At Perth we were told that MacDonald had once again kissed hands as Prime Minister – this time of a 'National' Government. 'It is not I but you who will be the minister,' I said to him. And so it proved. But he did not seem elated. He kept on asking what Lloyd George's attitude was, and what had happened to Arthur Henderson. He himself became Secretary for Scotland. As Chancellor of the Exchequer in the new Government, Snowden immediately introduced a deflationary budget, rightly described by Keynes as 'replete with folly and injustice'. I attacked it in the House of Commons.

The so-called 'National' Government had been formed ostensibly for keeping us on the Gold Standard. Not for the first time the country was saved by the Royal Navy. The fleet mutinied at Invergordon; and this drove us off it. After this, it became difficult to see what precise purpose the Government served because, apart from the desirability of clinging to gold and to office for as long as possible, it had no agreed policy of any kind. Moreover, specific assurances had been given to the electorate that the Government had been formed solely to deal with the National Emergency, and would not appeal to the electorate as such.

On 20 September 1931, the Prime Minister wrote to Sir Herbert Samuel, the Home Secretary, as follows:

There was a great deal to be said from a purely political point of view for an election now, but the objections to it, both from the financial and the long-range political view, were so overwhelming that I could not have agreed to it. . . . Obviously there is not even a theoretical justification for an election now.

One week later the 'National' Government decided to hold a General Election immediately. A majority of sixty in the House of Commons was quite adequate, but they thought it would be more comfortable to have more. Unable to agree about policy, they hit upon a happy phrase – 'a doctor's mandate' – which meant absolutely nothing, and with which they secured a record majority. I fought and won this election on my own prescription. The cautious, pedestrian and wholly uninspired Labour manifesto was described by Snowden as 'Bolshevism gone mad'. Subsequently, as a viscount, he was to say even nastier things about MacDonald than he had said about his late colleagues during the election. J. H. Thomas stayed happily on at the Colonial Office: Malcolm MacDonald got a job; Baldwin was quite content to remain at the Privy Council Office where he had nothing to do. The Conservatives got the jobs they wanted; and the Liberals, as Malcolm Muggeridge unkindly remarked, 'effaced themselves like un-invited guests at a reception and took up their station near the buffet'. It was by far the worst Government this country has ever had. By comparison, the Government of Lord North was a shining example of patriotism, wisdom and courage. I once asked Lloyd George what he really thought of Herbert Samuel. He looked up, with a twinkle in his eye, and said: 'Well, I made him the first proconsul in Jerusalem since Pontius Pilate.'

In February 1932 I received the following letter:

1519 ASTOR STREET

Chicago, Ill.
February 6, 1932.

My dear Bob: –

I was delighted, on arriving here this morning, to get your long and absorbing letter.

I have had a most strenuous week, travelling every night, lecturing every day, with much weakness caused by my accident* and a bad sore throat, but with very fine meetings and very large profits. I am now back in Chicago for a second meeting.

The United States Police have played up wonderfully, and I have been guarded every moment, night and day, by groups of armed plain-clothes men. Detroit and Chicago are both places where Indian trouble was expected, but as they had about two police gun-men along-side every Indian seen no trouble arose.

I have gone the whole hog against gold. To hell with it! It has been used as a vile trap to destroy us. I would pay the rest of the American Debt in gold as long as the gold lasted, and then say – 'Hence-forward, we will only pay in goods. Pray specify what goods you desire.'

Surely it will become a public necessity to get rid of Montagu Norman. No man has ever been stultified as he has been in his fourteen years' policy.

I am very glad not to be at home just now. I shall return to find us a tariff country, and I shall accept with simple faith the new dispensation. How glad I am not to be mixed up in this slatternly show! . . .

I have a project which is taking shape in my mind, though still quite vague, which might interest you. I have always wished to see the American Presidential Election. The Republican Convention is in Chicago in the middle of June, and the Democratic Convention, which will be the exciting one, about July 1st. A five weeks' trip would do it. I have had very fine offers made to me to report the Convention for the American papers, and no doubt corresponding possibilities would be open in England.

It occurred to me you might care to come with me. We should, of course, see all the politicians of both the great Parties and be in the very centre of their affairs. I have no doubt that it could be arranged either by your writing some articles of your own, or failing that, by helping me with mine, that there would be no expense at all.

* Winston Churchill had been knocked down by a car in New York whilst looking in the wrong direction when crossing the street.

Let us see how things go on. I thought this perhaps might amuse you. It certainly will be a thing to see. Better than watching the Ramsay-Baldwin performance on the Westminster stage. *These two old tired Tims of the Commons have ceased to command my allegiance.*

Yours ever,
WINSTON S. C.

[The last sentence is in his own handwriting.]

# 7

# The United States between the Wars

My first visit to the United States was in the autumn of 1925. I was one of the British delegates to the Annual Conference of the Inter-Parliamentary Union which was held in Washington and at Ottawa. The boom still had another four years to run. I found there an exciting world well suited to my tastes at that time. First came the music. I realized that three great composers had started something entirely new – Irving Berlin, the founding father, Jerome Kern and George Gershwin. In New York, on any evening, you could hear three or four magnificent orchestras playing their music, and dance to it or just listen. Soon afterwards Richard Rodgers and Cole Porter appeared on the scene as strong runners-up. An altogether new kind of musical comedy had burst upon us. When Gershwin came to a party, always late at night, and strolled over to the piano, there was a sudden hush and an air of intense excitement, always justified. Kern was the most popular because he was the most prolific. He was filled with melody, and kept a bust of Wagner on his piano: 'When it smiles,' he said, 'I know the melody is all right.'

I think there will never again be a *renaissance* of popular music quite like this. It can certainly stand comparison with that of Vienna at the close of the nineteenth century. When you think of what has now replaced it, it makes you sad.

Ernest Hemingway dominated the literary scene. It would be difficult to exaggerate the impact which his earlier books – *A Farewell to Arms, Fiesta, Death in the Afternoon*, and the short stories – made upon my generation. Others, including *For Whom the Bell Tolls*, were to follow; but none surpassed the first ones. Both Hemingway and Gershwin were concerned with the problem of human suffering and pleasure (the motto of this book), in violent, sensual terms. Hemingway saw life as a cruel but glorious game, which you must win decently or lose with a becoming courage – this was the era of prohibition, prosperity, rackets and gangsterdom in the United States. He has had many imitators, but none who have approached him in descriptive power and literary craftsmanship. I think they helped to build up the wave of terrorism which today sweeps the world: 'I had five more drinks. Then I kicked the old man in the guts. After that I went upstairs and threw the blonde on the bed.' As J. B. Priestley wrote in *Midnight on the Desert*, this kind of thing was like receiving telegrams from some chilly, dank hell. But they were not sent by Hemingway; only by those who saw, in his style of writing and preoccupation with violence and death, a means of making money. I think his best work was done in Paris, where he was an émigré, immediately after the war. Unfortunately, I never met him, but I knew his last wife and his secretary. Neither was in the least surprised when he committed suicide. Like Gershwin he created a new era in American cultural life which dominated the world for thirty years, and is not yet extinguished – for example in Bernstein's *West Side Story*. If Gershwin had not died so young, I think he may have lived to become one of the great composers of this century. *An American in Paris* marked a significant breakthrough. In the end he was much influenced by Ravel, with whom he became friends; and he would probably have developed along these lines. It was not to be. For me *Showboat* and *Porgy and Bess* remain the best musical comedies ever written; and it took *Oklahoma*, in the same tradition, to revive our spirits after the Second World War.

Very different was the scene which greeted me on my next visit to the United States seven years later. The biggest economic crash in history had taken place. The number of unemployed was estimated at twelve million. The banks were closed. Wall Street was like a morgue. They were singing *Brother, Can You Spare a Dime?*. The collapse was total.

I went over to watch the presidential election. Barney

Baruch, perhaps the closest friend Winston Churchill ever had, and certainly one of the greatest speculators the world has seen, invited me to dine on polling day. He was one of the very few who foresaw the crash – Keynes hadn't; and had been largely responsible for financing Roosevelt's campaign. We were alone. And despite the turmoil around us I found him calm, cheerful, and, as always, interesting. After dinner he said to me: 'Now I think we will go and see Franklin.' He put on a top hat and a dark cloak, and we drove off to the Biltmore Hotel, headquarters of the Democratic Party. His tall distinguished and familiar figure opened every door. We were taken at once to a small room where Mr Roosevelt was sitting smoking a cigarette. Mrs Roosevelt was there, but only two or three others. He gave us a warm welcome, and talked about everything except the election. He was completely relaxed, and looked as if he had just returned from a holiday, instead of an exhausting political campaign. Suddenly the door was flung open and a crowd of jubilant, excited people burst in: 'Greetings, Mr President!' they shouted. Hoover had just conceded the victory. This was a moment. As I shook hands with him, the first foreigner to do so, he gave me the smile that was to become famous all over the world. There was no trace of apprehension, elation or excitement. He just sat back in his chair, and said very quietly: 'Well, gentlemen, everything seems to have gone according to plan. Now we will have a New Deal.'

When he was inaugurated as President in January 1933 he wielded a greater power than had previously been accorded to any President of the United States. Every section of the community, not excepting the Congress, turned to him, and to him alone, for leadership, guidance and salvation. Wall Street dolefully awaited punishment. He could have done anything. He could have amended the constitution. He could have introduced collective Cabinet responsibility. He could have brought into being an independent, efficient and honest Federal Civil Service. He chose instead to concentrate all power in his own hands by means of successive 'Brains Trusts'. Everyone except financiers and big industrialists was welcome at the White House; and all were listened to. They stayed as long as the policies they advocated appeared to be successful;

and when they did not, they went. I knew some of them – Rexford Tugwell, Moley and Warren – but it is not part of my purpose in this book to examine or evaluate the 'New Deal'. Like the curate's egg, it was good in parts. The best thing it did was to smash the fatuous World Economic Conference which assembled in London in June 1933, by announcing that the United States could not agree to the stabilization of exchanges and proposed to raise the price of gold. Ramsay MacDonald described this conference as the most business-like and expeditious he had ever presided over; and Maisky, one of the Soviet delegates, called it a disorderly rout. Maisky was right. The conference adjourned after a month of futile discussion, and never met again. After that there was a sharp economic recovery in the United States based upon the higher price for gold, cheap money, and deficit expenditure by the Government averaging $3 billion a year. Then, at the end of 1937, there was a sudden reversal of policy. The expansionists, including Moley and Warren, were sacked. Deficit expenditure was sharply reduced, and reserve requirements increased by twenty per cent. This was followed by a 'gold scare', which rapidly turned a recession into a major slump. Production in 1938 fell dramatically in every country of the western world except one – Germany.

The cause of this was a simple one. The 'New Deal', as such, was purely empirical; and based upon no principles whatever. This suited the President's character. He tacked this way and that, dropping his crew and picking up another one according to the way he thought the wind was blowing. Underlying it all there was no sense of purpose. And this continued until the end of his life. I once asked a leading member of the Democratic Party in the United States, who must be nameless, whether Franklin Roosevelt ever had any deep sense of purpose about anything. He hesitated, and then said: 'Only one. To remain in office.'

During my visits to the United States in the 1930s, I used to stay quite often with Harrison Williams and his beautiful wife Mona, widely known to the world through the press as 'the best-dressed woman in the world'. They had a lovely house in Long Island, and I was sometimes given a small house of my own near the swimming pool, and a car to drive myself the few hundred yards to the main house. Prior to the crash Harrison Williams had made a billion dollars by 'pyramiding', i.e. creating successive holding companies, in the North American Company, one of America's biggest utility corporations. He took the subsequent loss of half his fortune with perfect equanimity. But if you are worth a billion dollars, you can afford to do that. He was good-looking, and distinguished; but he never spoke about politics or business. His recreation was golf, and his talk consisted of genial banter. On my first visit he said to me after dinner: 'You must come and see the garden.' I said: 'I look forward to seeing it tomorrow.' 'No, now,' he said. He took me over to an apple tree which he opened; and turned on a switch. The entire garden burst into a flood of light, some of it reflected through pools of blue water.

I once asked him how and why he had built up the immense organization which he controlled: 'One day,' he replied, 'when I was a young man, I looked at myself in the glass and I came to the conclusion that I was very much like Rockefeller, so I decided to go into the business.' This was not good enough. I went on asking him questions; and then, for half an hour and for the only time, he talked seriously about public and business affairs. He said that the main problem facing the world in the second half of this century would be energy; and that this would not end with oil. It was not only his knowledge of the generation of power and the problems connected with it, and his grasp of detail, but the range of his vision which impressed me. I saw then how and why he had got where he had. And I thought what a pity it was that businessmen of his capacity and experience so seldom went into public life in the United States. Then, suddenly, the door opened and someone came in. Immediately the mask fell, and the banter was resumed.

One afternoon Mona Harrison Williams asked me to take her to the races at Belmont Park. I thought it was a point-to-point, and wore an open shirt and flannel trousers. It turned out to be the American equivalent of Ascot. When we arrived there, we found ourselves confronted by a battery of photographers: 'Hell,' said one of them; 'the best-dressed woman in the world with the worst-dressed man.'

I was staying at Oyster Bay during the presidential election of 1936. One night at dinner the wireless was switched on, and we heard Mr Roosevelt delivering his final speech of the campaign. It was an able and ruthless attack upon big business in general, and the utility men in particular. My host listened with great attention, and a faint smile, but made no comment. The conversation then turned to golf.

For the outbreak of the Second World War, the Americans in general and Roosevelt in particular must bear some responsibility. The slump which they deliberately induced, for no reason at all, in 1937, did nothing but good to Hitler and nothing but harm to the rest of the western world. Roosevelt kept on saying that commodity prices were too high. They were not. He did everything in his power to discourage investment in productive industry. In a world in which all the storm signals were hoisted, he reduced expenditure on naval and military armaments. He destroyed confidence, without which a capitalist system cannot work. On 2 November 1937 I made a speech in the House of Commons in which I pointed out that every time President Roosevelt induced a further lack of confidence, he dealt a thundering blow to the cause which he himself had most at heart – the cause of democracy and freedom; and I made an almost desperate plea for effective co-operation between the English-speaking peoples before it was too late. Such a combination, I said, could ultimately control the oceans of the world, the gold of the world, and therefore the economy of the world. As we had no arms at that moment, our only hope of salvation lay in economic strength. This had been fatally weakened at a critical moment, and the danger of war sensibly increased.

In the field of national relations, the story is even worse. Roosevelt's foreign policy, although not so shameful as Chamberlain's, was just as ineffective. The extraordinary process by which, in the words of Walter Lippmann, the partners of one great war disarmed one another in the brief period which remained before they were to be partners again in an even greater war, was not brought to an end. The Washington Treaty put an end to British sea power, upon which the world had depended for a century. The Neutrality Act prevented the United States from giving arms and raw materials to the British and French, should those two essential bastions of American defence again be the object of attack. When the victorious combination of 1918 had been dissolved and disarmed, the new combination of armed Fascist aggressor states was formed without opposition. By 1940 the policy of isolation had brought the United States to the point at which, for a whole appallingly dangerous year, the issue hung precariously upon the valour of the people of Britain, and upon the campaign which Roosevelt was obliged to wage, too late, to arouse his own country at a time of awful peril. Such was the inevitable result of the policy of 'isolationism'. To isolate his potential enemies is, indeed, the supreme object of every aggressor. The tenacity with which Hitler pursued his proclaimed policy of 'one by one' made him master of continental Europe, while the western democracies, including the United States, watched him with stagnant and fascinated wonder, as rabbits watch a weasel. The military occupation of the Rhineland separated France from her allies in Eastern Europe. The occupation of Austria isolated Czechoslovakia. The betrayal of Czechoslovakia by the West isolated Poland. The defeat of Poland isolated France. The defeat of France isolated Britain. If Britain had been defeated the United States would have been given true and total isolation for the first time. Judging by experience, isolation is not a gift which brings pleasure, satisfaction or security. About all this Roosevelt did nothing. It is only fair to add that, if he had tried, the vast majority of the American people would not have let him.

It would have been well for the Americans, and for the world, if between the two world wars they had taken to heart the sayings of two men for whom they have always professed a great admiration. The first, of their own George Washington, in a speech to the Congress in January 1790: 'To be prepared for war is one of the most effectual means of preserving peace.' The second, of our Edmund Burke, at about the same time: 'When bad men combine, the good must associate; else they will fall, one by one, an unpitied sacrifice in a contemptible struggle.'

When, in 1919, Lloyd George was, in Harold Nicolson's words, 'fighting like a terrier' to get a good Treaty of Peace, and on 1 June called in aid all the leaders of the British Empire, it was Woodrow Wilson, not Clemenceau, who prevented it. A memorandum, accepted by the whole British delegation, which from Great Britain included Austen Chamberlain, the Chancellor of the Exchequer; Lord Birkenhead, the Lord Chancellor; Mr Balfour, the Foreign Secretary; and Lord Milner, urged that we should at least meet the Germans half way; and that important concessions should be made, especially about Silesia. The meeting authorized the Prime Minister 'to use the full weight of the entire British Empire even to the point of refusing to use the services of the British Army to advance into Germany, or the services of the Royal Navy to enforce the blockade of Germany'.

Wilson would not look at it. As Churchill was subsequently to write:

If President Wilson had set himself from the beginning to make common cause with Lloyd George and Clemenceau, the whole force of these great men, the heads of the dominant nations, might have played with plenary and beneficent power over the wide scene of European tragedy. He consumed his own strength and theirs in conflict in which he was always worsted. He gained, as an antagonist and corrector, results which were pitifully poor compared to those which would have rewarded comradeship. He might have made everything swift and easy. He made everything slower and more difficult. He might have carried a settlement at a time when leadership was strong. He acquiesced in second-rate solutions when the phase of exhaustion and dispersion had supervened.

Lloyd George once told me that Clemenceau was a man with whom, when it came to the crunch, he could always do business; but that Wilson was 'absolutely impossible'. Keynes was wrong when he wrote that he was bamboozled, and subsequently could not be de-bamboozled. He was stubborn, obstinate, suspicious and, above all profoundly ignorant of Europe and of European history. In short he was, like John Foster Dulles, a narrow, rigid, Presbyterian from New England. Finally he was a sick man. When he returned to Washington, Senator Borah and others had little difficulty in tearing to pieces the Treaty of Versailles, which he had signed; or in persuading the Congress to reject, and therefore render impotent, the League of Nations. These were primary causes of the Second World War.

Twice in this century the world has had to suffer from

American Presidents who were dying. First, Woodrow Wilson in Paris. Second, Franklin Roosevelt at Yalta. In Paris Wilson's doctrine of national self-determination instead of federation, led to the creation of a number of small independent states which made little sense from a political or economic point of view, and were incapable of defending themselves against any major aggression. At Yalta Roosevelt handed over half Europe to Russian domination.

The tragedy for western civilization throughout this century has been that the United States, its undoubted leader, so rich, so powerful, and so well-meaning, has failed to produce any statesmen of the calibre of the Founding Fathers. This is undoubtedly due to the fact that far too many of the best brains in America, in the scientific, industrial, financial, academic and cultural fields where they excel, have for too long disdained the Congress; and refused to enter public life. As a result their politicians have, on the whole, been below the level of the nation they represent. Since the last war, the only two who have shown the combination of courage and vision necessary to meet the fearsome responsibilities which fell upon them, have been General Marshall, who saved Europe from economic collapse at a critical moment; and President Truman, who backed him. Adlai Stevenson might have done so; and so might Hubert Humphrey. But, as Walter Lippmann once told me, Stevenson was too amusing, and talked too much; and Humphrey killed himself politically by supporting the war in Vietnam. In the event, providence denied them both the chance. All our hopes are now precariously pinned on President Carter.

# 8

# Russia between the Wars

On my way to Moscow in the spring of 1926 in a private
delegation with Sir Frank Nelson, Sir Thomas Moore and
R. C. Bourne, I spent a night in Berlin, and another in Warsaw.
This was the period when Berlin night-life was the talk and
the wonder of the world. It was Isherwood's Berlin. We only
caught a glimpse of it, which fascinated me and shocked my
colleagues. In Warsaw it took us only a few hours to discover
that Poland was a purely feudal country, where castles with a
hundred indoor servants still existed. Free at last from foreign
domination, the whole country was imbued with a spirit of
patriotism and chauvinistic nationalism. It was filled with
horses, and remains so to this day. The Polish people were still
what they had always been, deeply romantic and recklessly
brave. The British Government, since the war, had never
handled Poland well. As Harold Nicolson wrote in his book
*Curzon: The Last Phase*:

In February 1920, the Supreme Council urged the Poles not to
advance. They did so, and were successful. The British Government
took no notice of their disobedience. In June 1920, the Poles ceased to
be successful and retreated. It was then that the British Government
expressed moral indignation regarding their action in the previous
February, ordered them to retreat one hundred and twenty-five miles
to the Curzon Line, and promised them full support if that line were
crossed by their enemies. It was crossed. But the British Government
confined their support to the despatch of a mission of enquiry . . . the
traditions of diplomacy enjoin that Great Britain should neither

threaten nor promise in circumstances in which her threats or her promises cannot, with complete certainty, be fulfilled. In the Polish crisis of 1920 there was no such certainty. Great Britain, therefore, should have indulged neither in threats nor promises. She indulged in both. And both were falsified.

In 1933, a few weeks after Hitler obtained power, Pilsudski, then Polish dictator, proposed to the profoundly shocked governments of Britain and France a preventive war against Germany. When they were denied this, the Poles signed a treaty of non-aggression with Germany. In 1938, after Czecho-slovakia had been knocked out at Munich, they seized the Czech coalfield at Teschen. None of this prevented us from giving an unconditional guarantee to Poland in 1939.

I have described elsewhere the Moscow that we saw. It was full of contradiction. The people seldom smiled. There was an inward, brooding look in their eyes – but then there always had been. There were shops, but no customers. The petty trading was done in bazaars and by means of street peddling. Except for six hundred Leyland buses the traffic, such as it was, was shoddy and ramshackle.

On the other hand the Kremlin, seen for the first time, was overwhelming. In front of the great wall which surrounds it were sentries. Behind it, the spires of a hundred churches, faintly discernible in the twilight. And above it all, illuminated by electric light, the red flag hanging listlessly. A few days after our arrival we were taken round the Kremlin. After showing our passes to the soldiers who guard the entrance with fixed bayonets day and night, and crossing a draw-bridge, we stood upon a terrace overlooking the river and over Moscow; a haze shimmered in the afternoon sun. A bell rang out; then another; and suddenly the whole air was filled with the sound of many bells merging themselves into a single vibrant note. The red flags were far out-numbered by the golden crosses on churches where the choirs still sang, the candles were still lit, and the devout still prayed.

Only in the opera house and the concert hall were you made aware of what still remained in the soul of the Russian people. There the packed audiences listened to music with a kind of savage intensity. One evening, when we went to *Prince Igor*, a

B.—D

French Communist delegation of some kind began to chatter towards the end of the first act. They were not hissed. They were just silenced by the appalling hostility which was concentrated upon them, and which you could feel. Another thing that I shall never forget was a Scriabin concert given by the Moscow Symphony Orchestra. During the *Poème de l'extase*, which was superbly played, the rhythm surging through the hall transported the audience almost to the point of intoxication. For the time being politics no longer existed, or anything else.

We saw quite a number of ministers. Residences of the Soviet leaders consisted of long, low white houses within the Kremlin which were once occupied by the officials of the Imperial Court. The interview which stands out most vividly in my mind was the one with Radek. His apartment in the Kremlin resembled that of a senior don at Oxford. He came out of a litter of books and papers to greet me with enthusiasm: 'Allow me to congratulate you on coming to the country where we eat our young,' he remarked genially, sweeping me into an armchair and handing me a cigar. He was a Jew – his real name was Radek-Sobelsohn – small and thin, with large spectacles and a fringe beard. I knew that during the final years he had been Lenin's right-hand man. In almost every extant photograph of the first Communist Dictator, his grinning features can be seen. He had once shaped the policy of the Third International, and masterminded the Congress of Baku in 1920 which condemned Britain as 'a nest of sea and land rovers', who had transformed millions of Indian workers into dumb beasts of burden; filled the prisons of Constantinople with Turkish patriots, and, in China, exploited a population of three hundred millions by poisoning them with opium. He spoke English with an accent, but with great fluency and at enormous speed. I just let him talk, confining myself to shunting him at intervals from one subject to another, upon none of which he was not prepared to express a dogmatic opinion. Among other things he said that Baldwin was grossly underestimated as a Prime Minister, but might be stultified by the reactionaries with whom he had surrounded himself; that Ramsay MacDonald was an old-fashioned doctrinaire theorist who would never do anything but hold things up; and that we ought now to hold on to India for the next fifty years because Lord Reading, the Viceroy, was shrewd enough never to take decisions. Then, rather to my surprise, he added that Lord Lloyd was the best of our proconsuls; and should do well when he became Viceroy of India, as he confidently predicted he would. He went on to say that the Washington Conference was a turning point in our history. There we surrendered both our naval supremacy, and our economic power, to the United States. We should instead have joined Europe in an economic alliance against the United States, and in the Far East co-operated effectively with Japan. 'Then,' he said, 'you might have freed yourself from the death-grip of American finance. To break your alliance with Japan at the behest of the United States is one of the most foolish things you have ever done.' He added that in the present economic organization of the world, we should be obliged to come, sooner or later, to Protection.

Darkness began to fall, and I rose to go. The tables in his room were covered with newspapers. He told me that he didn't know what he would do without *The Times*: 'It is to me a personal friend. I know the idiosyncrasies of all its leader-writers and correspondents. It is worth far more to me than the reports of all my secret agents.' I met him once again just before we left Moscow, and after the General Strike had broken out at home. 'If you are a serious student of politics, you should go back at once,' he cried. 'It is more interesting now there than here. But, make no mistake, this is not a revolution; and I have instructed our press to keep calm.' As the Soviet news-papers were already reporting the departure of the British *bourgeoisie* in battleships, I wondered what they would have said if Radek had refrained from giving them such soothing advice.

When we got back to London, again by way of Warsaw and Berlin, we published a report in which we pointed out that no single Soviet foreign trade commitment had not been punc-tually honoured, and recommended that we should give a loan, or long-term credits, or both if necessary, to the Soviet Union. We concluded by saying that, in our opinion, Russia presented a great field for the judicious investment of British capital; and that we were losing an immense opportunity:

We view with increasing anxiety, from the economic point of view, the recently concluded diplomatic agreement between Russia and Germany. We believe it to be undesirable that Germany should be the sole link between Russia and the outside world. The Soviet government informed us that they are prepared to resume negotiations with the British government immediately. We therefore suggest that HM Government should watch the situation very carefully in order that no favourable opportunity may be missed for securing between ourselves and Russia a diplomatic and commercial settlement satisfactory to both sides, for we believe that such an opportunity may well shortly present itself.

Alas, it was not the moment to advocate any kind of *rapprochement* between Britain and Russia. The General Strike was only just over, and the miners' strike was still on. The mood of the Government, even of Baldwin himself, was still one of anger, and some fear. They were bounced by the Home Secretary, Sir William Joynson-Hicks, into the egregious folly of the Arcos raid, in search of damaging documents – Arcos was the headquarters of the Soviet trade mission. Needless to say nothing was found. The relationship, political and economic, between the two countries, was strained almost to breaking point; and this became a decisive factor in the chain of events which led to the Second World War. Meanwhile, under the influence of the Bank of England, the City of London (above all Schroeders) poured money into Germany; and Germany poured it on into the USSR. By the end of 1932 credits outstanding by Germany to the Soviet Union amounted to Rm 1 000 000 000. In the event, Russia repaid all her debts to Germany in full; and Germany bilked us. It is a fearful indictment of the financial policy pursued by the City of London between the wars.

In the spring of 1934 I revisited Russia. The change that had taken place was startling. Stalin was now in undisputed control, and the great 'purge' had begun. Millions of *kulaks* (peasants who were making a living) were being murdered up and down the country. Writers, scientists and even musicians now worked under close supervision, and no 'deviation' was tolerated. I watched, for the second time, the May Day procession in the Red Square. It was almost entirely military, and lasted far too long. Stalin, pale and sombre, and smoking a pipe, stood on a platform only a few yards away from me, erected outside the shrine of Lenin, with his arm round Bukharin's shoulder. Five hundred aeroplanes roared overhead. Bukharin was soon to be imprisoned and killed. I tried, without success, to sell cured herring to the Commissar of Trade. He was interested only in machinery. In 1926 I found the atmosphere in Moscow rather exciting, and not without hope. In 1934 I found it oppressive almost beyond the point of endurance. The air was full of blood. In a letter to my mother I wrote: 'If I lived in this country, I should be on Stalin's side – simply in order to survive.' It was with feelings of enormous relief that I crossed the frontier into Finland.

At Oxford, Namier had taught me that if Britain wished to influence policy or events east of the Rhine, she must co-operate either with Germany or with Russia. In the 1930s we were confronted by a stark choice between Hitler's Germany and Stalin's Russia. There was a third alternative, advocated by Lord Beaverbrook – to disengage ourselves altogether from Europe, and confine ourselves to the Empire. I did not think this was practical. We were part of Europe, and always had been; and throughout our history we had fought to prevent the continent of Europe falling into the hands of any single power or potentate – Philip of Spain, Louis XIV, Napoleon, the Kaiser. When the Hitler menace became a reality, I chose Russia without any hesitation: and set myself to do everything I possibly could to bring about an alliance (no less) between Britain and the Soviet Union. Maisky, the Soviet Ambassador in London, knew of this, and agreed with me. We became great friends. I used to lunch with him regularly, often alone. Then I had the good luck to cross the Atlantic in the *Berengaria* with Litvinov. As we walked up and down the deck he expounded to me, with clarity and force, his own foreign policy. If it had been carried out there would have been no Second World War. In March 1938 Hitler annexed Austria. Litvinov immediately proposed that a conference of certain Powers should be held forthwith at Geneva to discuss practical measures for preventing further aggression. On 24 March 1938 Chamberlain flatly turned this down in the House of Commons. This was the occasion of Churchill's most famous pre-war peroration:

For five years I have talked to the House on these matters, not with very great success. I have watched this famous island descending incontinently, fecklessly the stairway which leads to a dark gulf. It is a fine broad stairway at the beginning, but after a bit the carpet ends. A little further on there are only flagstones, and a little further on still these break beneath your feet. Look back upon the last five years since, that is to say, Germany began to re-arm in earnest and openly to seek revenge. If we study the history of Rome and Carthage, we can understand what happened and why. It is not difficult to understand and form an intelligent view about the three Punic Wars: but if mortal catastrophe should overtake the British nation and the British Empire, historians a thousand years hence will still be baffled by the mystery of our affairs. They will never understand how it was that a victorious nation, with everything in hand, suffered themselves to be brought low and to cast away all that they had gained by measureless sacrifice and absolute victory – 'gone with the wind'.

On 19 September 1938, I went to Geneva to see the assembly of the League of Nations which was in full session. The atmosphere was very tense. Chamberlain had already flown to Berchtesgaden, and was about to fly to Godesberg. Not, be it noted, to Geneva. On 22 September Litvinov asked me to see him at his hotel. When I walked into his sitting-room, he immediately burst into bitter complaint against the British Government. Here he was representing one of the Great Powers of the world in Geneva, at a time of acute international crisis; and not one of the British representatives had even paid him a courtesy call. For all he or they knew, we might be allies in war within a few days. I enquired, in some bewilderment, whether any staff talks were taking place between our two countries. He replied: 'How can you expect staff talks when we have not even begun political talks?' I then asked him point-blank whether, in the event of a German attack upon Czechoslovakia, Russia would fight. He replied, unequivocally, that if France fulfilled her obligations to Czechoslovakia, so would the Soviet Union. He went further. He said that they had already served notice of denunciation of the treaty of non-aggression with Poland in order to enable them to pass troops through to Czechoslovakia. And he gave me precise figures of the number of aeroplanes they would place at the disposal of the Czechoslovakian Government in the event of war. I went immediately to see Lord De La Warr, who, in the inexplicable absence of the Foreign Secretary, was leading the British delegation, and suggested that he should see Litvinov without delay; and he immediately wired to London to obtain the necessary instructions. For my part, I flew back to London next morning and sought an interview with Halifax himself. He was good enough to receive me at once, and I gave him a verbal account of my conversation with Litvinov of which he took a full note. But the Prime Minister was already well on the road to Munich.

At Munich Britain and France agreed to exclude Russia from a settlement which had for her the highest strategic consequences. The annexation of the Sudetenland and the Czech fortifications by Hitler destroyed the outer bastion of the Russian defence system. 'In sacrificing Czechoslovakia to Hitler,' wrote Walter Lippmann, 'Britain and France were really sacrificing an alliance with Russia.' The Russians were not even invited to attend the Munich conference – if such it can be called. But even this insult did not prevent Litvinov from making a final effort to prevent the Second World War. After Hitler occupied Prague in March 1939, he proposed a conference of the six Powers then most immediately threatened by Nazi aggression – namely, Britain, France, the USSR, Poland, Rumania and Turkey – to be held in Bucharest. The Rumanian minister in London, Veoril Tilea, who was a great friend of mine, had already mentioned this possibility to me. One day he invited me to lunch alone, and told me that he had received instructions from his Government (in fact King Carol) to find out if anything could be done to check the growing pressure, military and economic, by Germany upon Rumania. I said that it was now pretty late in the day; but that something might still be achieved and saved if, and only if, we could get full Russian support. He entirely agreed, and went off to the Foreign Office to tell them this. Believe it or not, the British Government turned down Litvinov's proposal as, 'premature'; and the Poles, idiotically and characteristically, objected to it. When Maisky subsequently told me that this was 'the final smashing blow to any policy of collective security', I could only agree with him. On 10 March Stalin had given a grave warning to the western democracies in a speech which was described by Mr Davies, the American Ambassador in Moscow, as a significant danger signal. Stalin accused France and Britain of inciting Germany to attack the Soviet Union, and of having completely abandoned the policy of collective security. All we did in reply was to send the Strang Mission by slow boat to Russia, without the Chiefs of Staff, and without negotiating powers. This was regarded as an insult by Moscow. His fears now confirmed, Stalin altered course accordingly. Litvinov was replaced as Foreign Secretary by Molotov. The pact with Ribbentrop followed. And also, inevitably, the Second World War.

Since the war I have had only two direct contacts with Russia, but I would very much like to go back there again and see what is going on, if only because of my friendship with Litvinov and Maisky who could, between them, have prevented the Second World War, and tried their best to do so.

The first contact was when I met Khrushchev at Claridges when he visited London. 'Your salt herrings,' he said, 'are no good without vodka.' I said that I entirely agreed; and that if he would buy our herrings, we would buy his vodka. Soon afterwards a large order for cured herring reached us from Moscow. Alas, we could not fulfil it. The herring had begun to disappear from the North Sea.

The second contact was entirely non-political. At the beginning of the 1960s when, for a brief period, I was Chairman of the Royal Philharmonic Orchestra, I accompanied it to Warsaw and to Moscow. On arrival we were met at the airport by a charming man in an Embassy car. He sat by the side of the chauffeur, while Malcolm Sargent and I sat in the back. Affable as always, Malcolm leant forward and said: 'And what do you do here?' He replied: 'I am the Ambassador.' 'Oh God!' said Malcolm, 'I've done it again.' We stayed at the Embassy; and I remember when Sir Humphrey Trevelyan took me out to show me the flood-lit Kremlin on the other side of the river where the red flag still hung over it: 'It is rather exciting,' he said, 'to live under one of the two centres of world power.' We were taken to a marvellous performance of the Bolshoi Ballet. And there I met the Minister of Culture, a delightful and extremely intelligent woman. When I thanked her at the end of the evening, she said to me: 'There is one thing you can do for us. Persuade Nureyev to come back. We taught him.' I said: 'Madam, there are few things in life that I am not prepared to attempt. But this is one of them.'

# 9

# Germany between the Wars

Following the advice of Sir Herbert Warren, I concentrated, apart from the interests of my constituency (oats, beef, herring), on three subjects, economic policy, Russia and Germany.

When I first visited Germany they were recovering slowly from what can only be described as 'total inflation'. Their capital had been destroyed. They had to rebuild the country from nothing. They had to do it again after the Second World War. On both occasions they succeeded. I doubt if any other nation in the world could have done this.

For ten years, between 1925 and 1935, I went to Germany every year. I was fascinated by the personality of Walther Rathenau, a German Jew, who had provided the munitions for the First World War. He was something that only a German Jew could simultaneously be: a prophet, a philosopher, a mystic, a writer, a statesman, an industrial magnate of the highest and greatest order, and the pioneer of what has become known as 'industrial rationalization'. After the Genoa Conference of 1922 he was assassinated; and I shall come back to this in my chapter about Lloyd George. Years afterwards I talked at length about Rathenau to John Strachey; and this led him to write one of his finest essays, 'Walther Rathenau, Doctor Schacht and the German Tragedy', in *The Strangled Cry*. He died before I could meet him; but Stresemann, whom I did know, and whose wife was the leader of a gay but somewhat raffish Berlin society, might well have achieved peace in Europe, if the French had given him a chance. Briand would have done it. Poincaré would not. And Austen Chamberlain, who once said to me: 'I misinterpreted the opinion of my countrymen', threw the whole weight of British influence, which might have been decisive, behind France. When Stresemann was dying, he said to Bruce Lockhart: 'If you had given me one concession I could have carried my people. I could still do so today. But you have given me nothing, and the trifling concessions you have made have always come too late. Well, there is nothing left for us now, except brute force. The future is in the hands of the new generation, and the youth of Germany which we might have won for peace and for the reconstruction of a new Europe, we both have lost. That is my tragedy and your crime.' In the last conversation I had with him he used practically the same words.

In the 1920s and early 1930s, when I was in Germany, I got the impression of a demoralized society, desperately trying to find a way out. Among the youth, homosexuality was rampant; and, as I was very good-looking in my twenties, I was chased all over the place, and rather enjoyed it. I used to go to the *Oktoberfest* in Munich every October to listen to operas, drink tankards of foaming *Löwenbrau* beer, sing in the beer-cellars with burly Bavarians in *lederhosen* and Tyrolese hats with what looked like shaving-brushes, eat one of the thousand chickens roasting in the open on spits, and ride on the Big Dipper. I loved it all. The cold sparkling air; the lakes, especially Stahnberg; Ludwig's castles; a walk in the Englische Garten; a visit to Nymphenberg. Not until 1932 did the shadow of Hitler begin to make its presence felt. I pushed it aside.

A friend of mine, Herr Balster, was connected with the Rhenish-Westphalian Coal Syndicate; and through him I was able to establish contact with the Ruhr, upon which the gradual economic recovery of Germany was then based.

In the spring of 1928 I was invited to dine with the Thyssen brothers in Düsseldorf; and they expounded to me a plan for the formation of a European coal, iron and steel cartel in which Britain and Germany should play the leading part. They told me that they were even prepared to bring in Poland. It reflected the thought and work of Rathenau; and was, in fact, a more comprehensive and far-reaching plan than Robert Schuman's European Coal and Steel Community in 1950. It

was an agreeable and extremely interesting dinner; but when
it was over, Fritz Thyssen said to me: 'If your people won't
play, then we shall have to find some other way out.' In this I
detected a veiled threat. When I got back to London, I made a
speech in the House of Commons in which I advocated the
negotiation of a comprehensive international agreement
covering the heavy industries of western Europe; and I
followed this up with an article in the *Nation* entitled 'An
Economic Locarno'. Somewhat to my surprise, I got tremendous support from the press, both of the Right and the Left.
Beaverbrook wrote to tell me that I was making 'a great and
good name' for myself; and that he had instructed his newspapers to give me their full backing. He had not yet turned
against Europe. Nor had he forgotten that he had made his
own fortune by bringing about successful mergers in the cement
industry in Canada. It was a very different story when I
approached the coal-owners. I went first to one who was a
distant relation of mine. He said: 'We don't even talk to each
other, so why should we talk to a lot of bloody foreigners? We
don't want to meet them. We want to beat them.' The others
I spoke to were even worse. Baldwin who, as an ex-steelmaster,
might have been expected to take some interest, took none.
There was no Minister of Industry. And the coal-owners and
steelmasters of this country were not then fit to run a fish-and-
chip shop in the modern world. Their sole contribution was a
proposal by those in the central counties to levy threepence a
ton on the home consumer, in order to subsidize the Humber
export trade at the expense of Durham and Northumberland.

For a while I kept in touch with Thyssen through his
brother, who lived at the Hotel Claridge in Paris. Then I had
to tell him that, so far as Britain was concerned, there was no
hope. Subsequently he threw the whole weight and wealth of
the Ruhr behind Hitler. With the aid of six million German
unemployed, Fritz Thyssen brought Hitler to power.

Having made a remarkable economic recovery during the
latter part of the 1920s, the Germans were struck down once
again by the American crash of 1929. In 1932 I was invited to
deliver four lectures on the economic crisis, in Hamburg and
Berlin. By this time they were desperate. I have never had
bigger or better audiences. The previous year Harold Nicolson,

who was then First Secretary in the British Embassy, had told me that I ought to go to an annual ball which was held in Berlin on New Year's Eve. He said that unfortunately he could not go himself, but that a German friend of his would be delighted to take me. We went to an enormous hall, where we found over a thousand people dancing, including some of the prettiest girls I have ever seen. The band was excellent, the food and drink both good, and the atmosphere gay. It was an enjoyable evening, which I have never forgotten. When my host took me back to the Adlon Hotel, and I thanked him for his kindness, he said: 'It may interest you to know that there was not a single girl there!' After I had gone to bed I found myself wondering whether this was symptomatic of the decadence of a great nation; and decided, rightly, that it was not. The brownshirts, under Roehm, were a homosexual army; but that did not prevent them becoming the nucleus of the *Wehrmacht* which was to conquer Europe, and which very nearly conquered Russia. Homosexuals do not believe in a future. They are, therefore, not good at sustained fortitude over long periods of time. But they are reckless; and, on the spur of the moment, they can be immensely brave.

In Berlin I saw Brüning, the Chancellor, who was Snowden's German counterpart – a puritanical ascetic and a bit of a masochist, with considerable charm. His sole indulgence was black coffee and a cigar, which he offered to me. He was a willing listener to the deplorable advice tendered to him by Dr Sprague, the emissary of the Bank of England. This, of course, was to continue his policy of deflation at all costs; and was designed primarily to maintain the value of the fantastic investments made by the City to Germany, at the instigation of Mr Norman. Under various 'standstill' agreements, funds which would otherwise have left Germany accumulated in blocked accounts, producing a state of false liquidity. In the end most of the money invested in Germany by Britain was irretrievably lost; and the industrial paralysis in Germany, which was soon to bring the Nazis to power, prevailed. Brüning was a lonely, saintly man, upon whom the burden of responsibility bore heavily. Hindenburg betrayed him when his own estates in East Prussia were threatened. But, in any case, he could not have lasted long. The path which he had marked out for himself, and was resolved to pursue to the end, could only lead to disaster. And to disaster, in due course, it led.

Then I received a telephone call from my friend 'Putzi' Hanfstaengl, who was at that time Hitler's personal private secretary and court jester. He told me that the Führer had been reading my speeches with interest, and would like to see me at his headquarters in the Esplanade Hotel. The story of my interview with Hitler is well known; and I will not repeat it at any length. It is true that when I walked across the long room to a corner in which he was sitting writing, in a brown shirt with a swastika on his arm, he waited without looking up until I had reached his side, then sprang to his feet, lifted his right arm, and shouted 'Hitler!'; and that I responded by clicking my heels together, raising my right arm, and shouting back: 'Boothby!' Later this story was sometimes attributed to Maurice Bowra, who asked me whether I would mind if he did not contradict it. I said I would be delighted to share the honour with him, because I knew that if he had been in my place he would have done the same. But in his autobiography he did contradict it.

I talked with Hitler for over an hour; and it was not long before I detected the unmistakable glint of madness in his eyes. I was much impressed by his grasp of Keynesian economics at that time. He said that I was quite right about economic expansion, and the means by which it could be achieved. But he added that this was now a political crisis, and that political forces would bring him to power. 'After that,' he said, 'I shall bend economics to my will; and I have in my hands the necessary instrument, a man called Schacht.' He had no sense of humour. He asked me how I would feel if Germany had beaten us in the last war, and driven a corridor between England and Scotland. I said: 'You forget, Herr Hitler, that I come from Scotland. We should have been delighted.' He did not smile. Instead he brought his fist down with a crash on the table and said: 'So! I had no idea that the hatred between the two peoples was so great.' Perhaps this was one of the reasons why he sent Hess to Scotland in 1940, for I am sure that he did; and why he never bombed Edinburgh. I then asked him, point-blank, what he was going to do to the Jews. I thought Hanfstaengl was going to faint, but only a flicker of irritation crossed his face. After a moment he said: 'There will be no pogroms.' I think that, at the time, he probably meant it. He had already planned to take over the whole of central and eastern Europe, and intended to deport all German Jews to those countries. What I cannot bring myself to believe is that he was unaware of what Himmler ultimately did to them.

That night I thought long and earnestly about the interview. I came to the conclusion that his plans were far more advanced than I had thought. He did not then wish to attack Britain and the British Empire, or even France. What he was determined to do was to bring the whole of central and eastern Europe under German control; and for this purpose Austria, and above all Czechoslovakia, were the key points. He had not forgotten Moltke's dictum that, from a strategic point of view, the control of Bohemia was essential for the control of Europe. When I got home (and this was at the beginning of 1932), I wrote an article in which I said:

Somehow, Hitler has managed to communicate his passion to masses of desperate people. And therein lies his power. The cry *Heil Hitler!* re-echoes through Germany today. We should not underestimate the strength of the movement of which he is the living embodiment.

In the 1930s I continued to visit Germany every year, and was therefore able to watch at close quarters the growth of the Nazi movement. As I motored around I came across more and more signs outside every village: 'Jews forbidden here.' The swastika flag was everywhere apparent. Of course Wagner was called in aid. He provided perfect background music; and towards the end Hitler hardly ever made a speech without a prelude consisting of an extract from the overture to *Die Meistersinger*. Bayreuth was turned, or distorted, into a Nazi shrine. Once, when I went to a performance of *Siegfried* at the Opera House in Berlin, Goering and Goebbels were present in separate boxes. At the end of each Act it was they, not the conductor, who took the applause. And that applause was not gratifying. It was frightening. Toscanini, Klemperer and Bruno Walter would have none of it; and went to the United States.

In order to understand the Germany of the 1930s, you had

to go there often, love it, hate it, live it and *feel it*. All this I did.
You had to know a great deal about Wagner, homosexuality,
racism and anti-semitism, and the connection between them;
and to realize the magnitude of the ferment to which, in
combination, they gave rise. The way in which Hitler managed
to impart his own hysteria to the vast audiences he addressed
was not only miraculous but terrifying. No wonder he had
often to be carried out prostrate from his meetings.

One day, when I was lunching alone at the Walterspiel in
Munich, then the best restaurant in Europe, the manager, who
was a friend of mine, said to me: 'I wonder if you would do
me a great favour.' I asked him what it was, and he said:
'When I come in, and give you a sign, will you stand up?' I
said: 'That's not asking much.' He replied: 'You won't like it.'
A few minutes later he came in and gave the sign. I stood up.
Then Goering, in full uniform and covered with decorations,
waddled into the restaurant, accompanied by several staff
officers. He bowed and smiled to all of us, and then sat down
at the table next to mine. Gradually my indignation gave way
to interest. I don't think I've ever seen anyone eat and drink
so much. He had three or four courses, and drank two bottles
of hock. At frequent intervals he took a pill. When I left the
restaurant he gave me a cheerful wave of the hand.

How could I explain all that was going on in Germany to
Britain's leading politicians, and make them understand? Not
even Lloyd George and Churchill, both of whom were complete extroverts, had a clue about what was really going on
inside Germany. Neville Chamberlain had the mentality and
outlook of a competent town clerk. Gas masks in Birmingham
because of something that was happening in a small far-away
country of which we knew nothing! The very idea was pre-
posterous and intolerable. The only senior statesman in Britain
who would, I think, have understood it all, was Baldwin. He
was an introvert, with acute sensitivity. In fact, the exact
opposite of the public image he deliberately created for himself – the simple friendly squire, concerned about his workmen
and looking at his pigs. He wasn't Rudyard Kipling's cousin
for nothing. He was an extremely complicated character; and
so were at least two of his children, whom he well understood.
He knew a lot about neurosis, and what caused it, and how

dangerous it could be. But, at the critical moment, he was gone.

Who else was there to take the real measure of Hitler, and Germany, and everything they stood for? Churchill measured it in terms of aeroplanes. It was far more than that. As the fibre of the German people strengthened, under the impetus of Hitler, that of the French weakened. Lloyd George once said to me that the life-blood of France had been drained at Verdun. Churchill failed to realize that it had not been restored. Laval did.

# 10

# The Fight to Prevent the Second World War

In June 1932 a conference was held at Lausanne to discuss the financial problems confronting the world, and also the problem of reparations. At the other end of the Lake, in Geneva, there was a Disarmament Conference. I went out to report them both for the *Sunday Dispatch*. Britain was represented at Lausanne by the Prime Minister, MacDonald; Neville Chamberlain; and Runciman. They were not an inspiring trio. MacDonald asked me to go and see him, and when I arrived I purposely told him how well he was looking. The reaction was immediate. 'I am absolutely rotten.' Head buried in his hands, he said: 'Only an hour or two of sleep without sedatives.' Then I went to see Chamberlain. He was sitting on a balcony, in blazing sunshine, a black suit, and snowboots, suffering from gout – inherited, I need hardly say, from his father. Runciman spent a good deal of his time with Mrs Runciman listening to the organ in the Presbyterian Church.

Every morning MacDonald, followed by journalists, took a walk by the Lake in knickerbockers and a cap; and one day he asked me to accompany him. The walk lasted about three-quarters of an hour, and then he took me back to his hotel for breakfast. I said that I thought that his Government was not only incompetent, but extremely reactionary. To my surprise, he replied that he entirely agreed; but that he could do nothing to stop it. I was very sorry for him. I don't think he saw much of Baldwin. They certainly never worked out any political policy or strategy together. It was very different from the Lloyd George–Bonar Law régime. He was clearly unhappy, lonely, and sad. I think it would have been much better if he had not been pushed by Chamberlain, Hoare, Samuel and company into holding a General Election in 1931. If he had resigned as Prime Minister when we had to abandon the Gold Standard, he could have justifiably claimed that in forming a 'National' Government to deal with a great national emergency, he had only done what he conceived to be his duty; and he would not have laid himself open to the charge of trying to destroy the Labour movement which he had done so much to build up. He never recovered from the death of his first wife and I never felt or saw that he was enjoying life.

From Lausanne I motored along the Lake to Geneva with Nigel Ronald, Simon's private secretary. There we lunched with Lord Londonderry, Herbert Samuel and Cadogan of the Foreign Office. Samuel was happily immersed in the technical details of armaments, and said that he was making good progress. I said that I thought it might be better to pay less attention to armaments as such, and more to what caused them; but he paid no attention to this. Meanwhile, at the League of Nations itself, the Foreign Secretary, Sir John Simon, was busy justifying our refusal to take any action designed to check Japanese aggression in Manchuria. For this he earned the thanks of Mr Matsuoka. Jehol and the mainland of China followed. But our relationship with the Mikado's Empire continued, in Simon's own words, to be one of 'perfect friendship'.

In fact the conferences at Lausanne and Geneva achieved absolutely nothing. No progress was made on the economic and reparations front; and the Disarmament Conference was soon to be battered out of existence by Hitler.

With every day that passed the shortcomings of this deplorable Government became more apparent. On January 31 1934 I wrote the following letter to Baldwin:

Dear Mr Baldwin,
    I don't want to bother you with a long letter, but I am so troubled about the present course of events that I feel bound to tell you, as leader, of my uneasiness and apprehension. I occupy a more or less detached position in Scottish politics these days, and have had many

recent opportunities of estimating public opinion at gatherings of a non-partisan character. There is little enthusiasm for the National Government; and I am firmly convinced that we are now moving towards a very considerable electoral débâcle.

This seems to be to be due

(1)   to the absence of any political philosophy, or theme, or policy, adequate to the needs of the time; and

(2)   to the lack of constructive measures, and a reactionary tendency on the part of the Government which has become apparent lately. E.g. ineffective housing policy; continued and unwarranted retardation of public works; and, last but not least, the financial provisions of the Unemployed Insurance Bill.

I don't share the views of some regarding the necessity for State 'planning' of industry, although I think that some new guiding principles will have to be laid down to enable us to deal with certain industries of national importance along modern scientific lines.

But I do jib at starving the unemployed. And that is what it amounts to in some districts at the present time.

If the Government is to prosper, the people *must* be given something in which to believe.

But my immediate purpose in writing to you is simply to say that if something isn't done to mitigate the sufferings of the unemployed either in this Bill or in the Budget, I personally could not go on supporting the Government.

It isn't fair to ask people to vote down a proposal to give an extra shilling to the first two dependent children, and vote for the purchase of a Bible which no-one can read.

I have written in this sense to the Prime Minister: and apologize for the outburst.

Yours sincerely,
Robert Boothby.

Some months later I secured the adjournment of the House for a debate on national development, and made a strong plea for a more urgent housing drive. I contrasted the position in Germany, where vast housing schemes had been completed in such towns as Berlin, Munich and Hamburg with British money, with that in this country; and begged the Chancellor of the Exchequer to concentrate his efforts on two or three defined objectives, and then to do the thing on an adequate scale.

After that, the growing danger of war took hold of my mind to the exclusion of everything else. I thought, wrote and spoke about nothing else. I watched it not only from this country, but from within Germany and France. From the point of view not of physical comfort but of mental anguish, the four years from 1935 to 1939 were by far the worst of my life. For reasons which I have already given, I did not find many kindred spirits. Inside the House of Commons, apart from Churchill, only Leo Amery, Ronnie Cartland (bravest of the Young Conservatives who was to be killed in a tank battle in France in 1940, and knew it), Louis Spears, Brendan Bracken, Duncan Sandys, Derrick Gunston and Robert Bower; outside Colin Coote, who left *The Times* and later became editor of the *Daily Telegraph*, and – curiously enough – Noël Coward. He understood all that was going on, and he knew that, if it continued, it would be the end. He minded this more than anything in his life, but not unnaturally it bored his friends in the theatrical world; and he felt helpless. Sometimes he would come over to the French House at night to talk to me alone. He told me that he could do nothing, but that I could. I told him that, in the present climate of public political opinion, I too was impotent. The only political support I could always depend on came from my constituents. As early as October 1933 I said to them at Turriff that this was the critical hour for democracy: 'If those of us who believe in freedom refuse to fight for our faith under any circumstances, then assuredly we will succumb to the military forces of Fascism or Communism, and most of the things which seem to make life worth living will be swept away.' Again in October 1934, at Strichen, I said that the issue at the time was nothing less than that of freedom or tyranny, and that the whole life and soul of democracy and the freedom of the individual were being challenged today as they had not been challenged for two thousand years. The question was whether we were going to fight for freedom and liberty, or submit to tyranny and force. *At that moment* it was necessary that we should put our defences into such a state that we could defend ourselves against any hostile attack, and particularly in the air.

The climax of the personal campaign which I launched in 1934, before any dangerous or decisive step had been taken by the German Government, and continued right up to the outbreak of war, was the speech I made on Armistice Day in my home town of Corstorphine, near Edinburgh. There was a packed audience of two thousand; it was widely reported in the press; and it caused a considerable stir, nearly all of it violently hostile to myself. I must therefore quote from it at some length, because it summarizes the attitude I took, and the policy I advocated, for the next three years:

Those who gave their lives in the war did so to save freedom and to gain peace; but to-day tyranny has regained the upper hand in Europe, and the danger of war is as great as in 1914.

The cream of Britain's manhood was killed in the last war, and those who survived were never allowed to play any part in the rebuilding of Europe. The result is that there is little but brute force left.

Today Germany is governed by a group of able and ruthless men, who have persuaded the German people that they can never become great again except through armed force.

I tell you they are re-arming. And I say this – that if we go on as we are to-day, in a year or eighteen months' time they will be in a position to strike a vital blow at the very heart of the British Empire.

It is not too late to save the situation if only we learn the lessons of the past. The British Empire still stands for the things those men died to win – freedom and peace. But I would not care to share the responsibility of those who to-day are exposing us to mortal peril.

In relation to the facts of the present situation our Air Force is pitifully inadequate. If we are strong and resolute, and if we pursue a wise and constructive foreign policy, we can still save the world from war. But if we simply drift along, never taking the lead, and exposing the heart of our Empire to an attack which might pulverize it in a few hours, then everything that makes life worth living will be swept away, and then indeed we shall have finally broken faith with those who lie dead in the fields of Flanders.

This speech was received in shocked silence, except for faint cries of 'No! No!' from Lady Haig, who was sitting behind me on the platform. Afterwards nobody wanted to speak to me; and the clergymen representing five denominations refused to shake hands with me. As I walked home in sombre solitude, I said to myself: 'We are going to betray them all.' We did.

It was already clear that the League of Nations itself was beginning to collapse. Gone were the great days when it was animated and inspired by men such as Lord Robert Cecil and Aristide Briand. Briand was, after Lloyd George, the greatest orator I have ever heard, with an even better voice. Once, when he was Prime Minister of France, I was introduced to him at Geneva after he had made a spell-binding speech to the Assembly in which he anticipated the modern European movement by nearly half a century. All I could think of to say was: 'How are you?' 'Very much better,' he replied, 'since I gave up reading and writing.' His private secretary, who was standing immediately behind him added: 'The awful thing is that it's true.' His fall from power, and the death of Strese-mann; Poincaré's mad attempt to occupy the Ruhr; and the total failure of successive British Foreign Ministers – Curzon, Austen Chamberlain, Simon, and Hoare – to exercise any effective influence in Europe, gradually put an end to all hopes of Franco-German reconciliation; and therefore to real European peace. The Germans met this situation with rearmament. The French and the British, warmly supported by the League of Nations Union, with creeping paralysis.

Looking back, I believe that, after the fall of Lloyd George, there was only one British statesman who might have saved the sum of things – Baldwin. He alone had the moral authority necessary to persuade his own countrymen to resist aggression, and to provide themselves with the armaments necessary to do it. Sir John Simon and Sir Sameul Hoare most certainly had not, even if they had wished to do so. At the League of Nations Baldwin might have had an influence comparable to that of Briand. In fact he did nothing. Geneva was an hour's drive from his beloved Aix-les-Bains. He only went there once.

During this fateful year, 1934, I did not confine my acti-vities to speaking in the House of Commons and in the country. I also fought a campaign in the press. At this time Lord Rothermere was keen on rearmament; and I was invited to write two articles for the *Daily Mail*. The first was published on 12 July under the heading: 'How I Would Procure Peace.' The second entitled: 'Whither Europe?' on 10 September. They read pretty well today.

Alas, after the annexation of Austria in 1938 when the situation became hourly more dangerous, the Rothermere press, together with the whole of the rest except the *Daily Telegraph*, ratted. And the *Daily Mail* was to say in a leading article:

A group of young Members of Parliament, with Mr Robert Boothby as its most lively protagonist, is pressing the Prime Minister to make a pronouncement of policy in the event of Czechoslovakia becoming embroiled with Germany. 'Halt Hitler' might be their motto. A better one at the moment is 'Keep Out', the Government slogan.

I did not confine myself to the Right. I also turned my tiny gun on the Left. In a letter to the *New Statesman and Nation* published, with a mildly protesting leader, on 19 May 1934, I said that if their advice to the Government to make a firm, strong and prompt stand against Japanese machinations in the Far East meant anything at all, it would be necessary (1) to complete the Singapore base within a week; and (2) to send the entire Battle Fleet to the Pacific. If they were not prepared to do this they should stop vapouring about 'prompt and firm stands against Japan'. I went on to say that we were at our old games again: trying to have it all ways at once, avoiding all commitments and expenditure, shirking all responsibilities; and getting a moral kick out of lecturing the world on the subject of disarmament. When the crisis finally came, it was invariably the 'pacifist' elements that became most bellicose; and, having refused to commit themselves to any definite policy, and deceived every foreign country, finally hounded us into war with inadequate armaments. 'It happened in 1914,' I wrote, 'and, if we don't look out, it will happen again.' I concluded this letter by saying that I had just returned from a visit to Germany and Russia where they had been arming with rapidity and determination while we, in order to salve our own peculiar national conscience, had been *talking* about guns, tanks, and bombs instead of their causes. And that I wondered whether we should ever be able to summon up the courage and honesty to formulate and pronounce an unequivocal foreign policy, and provide ourselves with the forces necessary to carry it out: 'Then,' I ended, 'I bought your paper to find out what the *intelligentsia* thought. That was the last straw.'

On 28 November 1934 Churchill put down an amendment to the Address in the House of Commons in the following terms: 'But humbly represent to Your Majesty that in the present circumstances of the world, the strength of our national defences, and especially of our air defence, is no longer adequate to secure the peace, safety and freedom of Your Majesty's faithful subjects.' The signatories were Sir Robert Horne, Frederick Guest, Leopold Amery, Lord Winterton and myself. In his speech Churchill said that within a year the German Air Force would be almost as strong as our own and perhaps stronger, and in 1937 nearly double. I said that if people who believed in freedom were not prepared to defend it, freedom would surely perish in this world at the hands of those who did not believe in it. Baldwin replied that he could not agree that there was any immediate menace, or even an emergency: Germany's real strength in the air was not fifty per cent of ours. Three months later Hitler announced that his Air Force was equal to Britain's, and Baldwin apologized for having misled the House. I shall not weary the reader with any further account of my campaign against appeasement, and in favour of rearmament. I kept it up until the outbreak of war in 1939. It was like battering one's head against a stone wall. As my old tutor, Sir Lewis Namier, wrote:

The country was weary and worried. Eagles and lions would have been out of place, almost laughable: no one wanted to soar or to roar. There was no call for experiment and adventure, for bold imaginative leadership, for greatness. The country muddled along. If there were survivors of the war generation, or post-war young men fit to speak a different language, the stage was not set for them; their appeal would have sounded false and hollow, and the words would have died on their lips. . . . Sated and sophisticated, civilized, sensitive, and war-weary, the Democracies have a conscience and no faith – the most dangerous condition for individuals and nations.

All I am concerned to do here is to point out that everything I have so far described took place before any decisive blow was struck by Hitler. There was still time.

Reflecting the mood of the country, the Conservative Party was rotten at the core. The only thing they cared about was their property and their cash. The only thing they feared was that one day those nasty Communists would come and take it. The Labour and Liberal Parties were no better. With the exception of Hugh Dalton (and even he, speaking from the Front Opposition bench, announced that they would give no support of any kind to resistance to Hitler's military occupation of the Rhineland), they made violent, pacifist speeches; and voted steadily against the miserable Defence Estimates for the years 1935, 1936, 1937 and 1938. Churchill did not forget this after he came to power. When he was once asked why he did not sack more Conservative ministers, and appoint more from the Labour and Liberal Parties, he said: 'They were worse.'

In March 1935 Hitler announced conscription in Germany. This was in breach of the Treaty of Versailles. Instead of an ultimatum, he received almost universal congratulations. Three months later the Foreign Secretary, Sir Samuel Hoare, negotiated with Ribbentrop an Anglo-German naval agreement. This gave to Germany the right to build submarines, and was also in breach of the Treaty of Versailles.

In March 1936 Hitler formally denounced the treaties of Versailles and Locarno, and marched his troops into the Rhineland. I was walking down St James's Street with John Strachey when the news appeared upon the placards. We both agreed that this was the opening move of a second world war. But I found very few others who shared this view. Philip Kerr (later Lord Lothian) coined the phrase: 'They are only walking into their own back-garden': and this received wide approbation. A few days later Louis Spears* invited a few of us to meet Monsieur Flandin, the French Foreign Minister, at a small luncheon in the House of Commons. He had come to London to seek the approval of the British Government for the movement of French troops to prevent the German military occupation of the Rhineland. He asked for no more. He did not get it. For this Eden must bear his share of responsibility. We now know that, if the French Army had moved, the Germans would have immediately withdrawn; and that would almost certainly have been the end of Hitler.

I sat opposite Flandin, and well remember what he said. He told us that France could not act entirely alone; and that if the German occupation of the Rhineland was therefore to be regarded as a *fait accompli*, this completely changed the whole European situation. The French alliances in central and eastern Europe would now be valueless. They would have to make the best terms with Germany they could get, and leave the rest of Europe to her fate. From this opinion he never subsequently

* Later Major-General Sir E. L. Spears.

deviated; and that is why, partly as a result of Churchill's personal intervention, he was acquitted of the charges made against him after the war. He spoke to us quietly and placidly, but with a kind of icy passion which deeply impressed us. We were all sure that he meant precisely what he said.

There can and will be much argument about subsequent events; but about the military occupation of the Rhineland there can be none. It was the decisive moment. The response of the British Government was first to refuse to give even moral support to the French Government; and then to appoint Sir Thomas Inskip instead of Churchill as Minister for the Co-ordination of Defence. Sir Thomas said 'with all sincerity' that it never occurred to him that it was likely that he would be asked to accept these responsibilities, or that he would ever be able to discharge them if they were offered to him.

I myself kept well out of the farce of sanctions upon Italy over Abyssinia, because I knew that it could never be anything else. I said that two courses confronted us – either to declare war on Italy, defeat her, and impose our own terms; or advise the Emperor of Abyssinia to stop fighting and make what terms he could get. 'After a time,' I wrote, 'one gets sick of high moral sentiments unsupported by practical action; they cause too much misery.' I added that nothing could now restore the situation except heroic measures, and the Government possessed neither the will, the means nor the heroes to undertake them.

Equally, the policy of 'non-intervention' in the Spanish Civil War was a farce; and, in the hands of the men who were running it, could never have been anything else. We never raised a finger to help the Spanish Government, and allowed Hitler and Mussolini to win the war for Franco by the most brutal methods without protest. When Churchill rang me up from the Continent to ask whether I thought he should come back, I advised him to keep well clear of it all; and, when he came back from his holiday, to concentrate all his energies on the only thing that now mattered – his campaign for 'Arms and the Covenant'.

In September 1936 it was announced from Downing Street that the Prime Minister felt fatigued, and had retired to the country for a complete rest. The truth is that, faced by the combination of Nazi and Fascist aggression in Europe, and the crisis over the Monarchy at home, both of which were clearly pending, Baldwin had lost his nerve. About this, I said to my constituents at Fraserburgh on 18 September:

Whether we like it or not, we have already entered rough seas, and the storm signals are up. Under such conditions, there is only one place for the Captain, and that is the bridge. Stalin has recently given forcible evidence to the world that he has not left Moscow. Mussolini has not ceased to preside over his own cabinet; and we have not read in the newspapers that Hitler was too tired to attend the Nuremberg Congress.

Then, to the public as a bolt from the blue, came the Abdication crisis. My sympathies lay with the King, but I was not surprised. The truth was that he had been grossly over-worked as Prince of Wales; that he was highly strung; and that without the sustained support which he found in Mrs Simpson, he couldn't take any more. I had seen, at close quarters, the strain on his face at the funeral of King George V. When the Maltese Cross fell off the crown as the draped gun carriage turned into Palace Yard, he said: 'Christ! What's going to happen next?' Walter Elliot, who was standing next to me, murmured: 'The motto for the new reign.' I knew the King only because he had succeeded my father as Captain of the Royal and Ancient Golf Club of St Andrews in 1922. He had immense charm; but he was bohemian by nature, and did not take easily to Court life.

On the night before the Abdication was announced, my old chief, Walter Monckton, asked me to dine with him alone at Wyndham's Club. We drank champagne. As was to be expected, he had played a leading and wholly beneficial part throughout the crisis. At every stage, it was to him they all turned; and he never failed. I found him sad, but resigned. He said he was quite satisfied that there was no alternative to abdication. And then added: 'I wish to God I knew what she does to him.' I said: 'She gives him what he needs most, self-confidence.' In retrospect, I am sure that the King was right to do what he did. He had 'done enough service to the State'; and could do no more on the throne.

Nevertheless the Abdication had one disastrous consequence. Although all his demands had been met, and Baldwin had allowed him to see the King at Fort Belvedere, Churchill came down to the House of Commons one afternoon, filled with emotion and brandy. He didn't listen to what Baldwin was saying, and kept on asking a question which had already been answered. He was howled down by the entire House, and next day *The Times* came out with the headline: 'Mr Churchill's Bad Day'. In five fatal minutes the whole campaign for Arms and the Covenant crashed into ruin. Afterwards in the Smoking-Room he said to Bracken and myself that his political career was at an end. We told him that this was nonsense. But I wrote him a letter of bitter reproach, which I later regretted.* He replied that it made no difference to our old relations; but it did. He went on to say that he was absolutely satisfied that the formula devised at a dinner he gave in Chartwell was put to the King most fully, Archie Sinclair's name and his being used; and that he turned it aside on the grounds that it would not be honourable to play for time when his fundamental resolve was unchanged, and as he declared unchangeable. He added: 'It was certainly this very strict point of honour which cost him his crown.' He ended his letter by saying that he felt

---

* 'December 7th                                    The House of Commons

'Dear Winston,

'I understood last night that we had *agreed* upon a formula, and a course designed to save the King from abdication, if that is possible. I thought you were going to use all your powers – decisive, as I believe, in the present circumstances – to secure a happy issue, on the lines that were suggested.

'But this afternoon you have delivered a blow to the King, both in the House and in the country, far harder than any Baldwin ever conceived of.

'You have reduced the number of potential supporters to the minimum possible – I shd think now about seven in all.

'*And you have done it without any consultation with your best friends and supporters.* I have never said anything to you that I did not sincerely believe. And I never will.

'What happened this afternoon makes me feel that it is almost impossible for those who are most devoted to you personally, to follow you blindly (as they wd like to do) in politics. Because they cannot be sure where the hell they are going to be landed next.

'I am afraid this letter will make you very angry. But not, I hope, irretrievably angry. I could not leave what I feel unsaid.

'Yrs ever
Bob'

I was right in saying that no human effort could have altered the course of events, and that the only thing now to do was to make it easy for him to live in this country quietly as a private gentleman. 'The more firmly the new King is established the more easy it will be for the old one to come back to his house.' My only regret about the whole business is that they refused to give to the Duchess of Windsor the title of Her Royal Highness, for which he repeatedly asked. If they had done so, he would have been able to do this; and to have rendered further and valuable public service to the present Queen, for whom he had a deep admiration.

In 1937 Baldwin retired. On his last night in the House of Commons, I found him standing alone in front of the fire which then burned in the lobby. I said to him: 'This is a sad occasion.' He said: 'Not for me. It is time I went. There is only one thing I regret. I never took any interest in foreign affairs.'

Throughout 1937 I battled on for a Ministry of Supply; and in January 1938 I was the first man in public life to advocate, in my constituency, compulsory national service. The Prime Minister, Neville Chamberlain, immediately asked me what the reaction to it had been; and I was able to tell him that, apart from some loud squawks from certain Members of Parliament, I had received not a single letter of protest.

On 12 March 1938 I wrote to Mr Chamberlain begging him to announce that the Government proposed to increase our front-line air strength from the projected figure of 1700 to 3500, and that every step necessary for the acceleration of production – including the operation of all factories by day and night – would be taken immediately. The following day Hitler annexed Austria. Clearly Czechoslovakia was next on the list. If we surrendered over that, I knew that the game would be up.

In July I drove by car to Marienbad, accompanied by the Chairman of my Constituency Association, Colonel Duff, ostensibly to take off weight, but in fact to find out what was going on, and especially what the Runciman Mission, which had been sent out by Chamberlain, was up to. As we motored through Germany we had to wait at every level crossing while the goods trains clanked past. They were all loaded with munitions. As I expected, Runciman was up to no good. His mission spent most of their time visiting the private houses of the rich; and on the two occasions when I ran into him I was unable to discover what purpose he had, unless it was to undermine the morale of the Czech Government. His subsequent report proved that this was in fact the case; and after its publication, he himself never recovered.

Then Beneš, the President, asked me to come and see him at the Hrâdcany Castle in Prague, and we had a long talk. I told him that the moderate Sudeten German leaders who had come to see me in Marienbad had said that they were not asking to join the German Reich, but only what he himself had asked of the old Austrian Empire – political decentralization in a form which would enable them to develop 'as a body corporate' and manage their own affairs, while still playing a part in a federal government in Vienna. He then told me that he realized that further concessions must be made to the Sudeten Germans, and outlined the proposals he had in mind. After this he took me to the terrace outside the castle, and showed me the view over Prague – one of the most beautiful in Europe. 'We can't have that bombed,' he said. 'You may have to,' I replied. Then, suddenly, he turned to me and said: 'If Hitler attacks us, what will the French do?' I said I didn't know. 'What will you do?' I said that, alas, I couldn't answer that question either. Finally, 'What should I do?' I said: 'Fight.' On the way home I drove past the gigantic Skoda works near Pilsen, in full blast. My secretary asked me what they were making, and I said: 'Bombs for Hitler to blow you up, if we haven't got the guts to stand up to him now.'

I never had any doubt that the surrender of Czechoslovakia to Germany would lead inevitably to a second world war; and was resolved to do everything and anything I could to prevent it. When I returned to London from Prague, I went to see the Prime Minister at Downing Street and gave him a full account of my conversation with Beneš. He told me that he had definitely decided not to commit Great Britain in advance to go to war in the event of a German invasion of Czechoslovakia; and I said that I was very sorry to hear this. Otherwise he was rather more robust than I had expected. He even went so far as to say that the Germans seemed now to be attempting to impose a reign of terror upon the whole continent of Europe by means of what amounted to complete mobilization. Then he added: 'I understand that two or three years ago you talked to Herr Hitler. What impression did he make on you?' I replied: 'In Hitler you are dealing with a ferocious madman. with a destructive genius almost without parallel in history', He looked hard at me, and said: 'From what you say, I gather that you are of the opinion that the gangster element among the Nazis is now in complete control; and that they will stop at nothing.' I replied that that was my conviction. Alas, although he did not tell me so, it was not his. Soon afterwards he was to say: 'I trust Herr Hitler.'

I looked round for support, and found it in Seymour Berry, who was in charge of the *Daily Telegraph* during the temporary absence, through illness, of his father Lord Camrose. He asked me to come and see him, and I found him resolute. He suggested that I should follow up the letters I had been writing with a series of articles, which I did. The first one was published on 30 August 1938, and they continued until Munich.

The days and nights of the Munich crisis remain for me a distant nightmare, which is best forgotten. There were three groups of Members of Parliament, under Eden, Amery, and Churchill. As I have said, Churchill's consisted only of Duncan Sandys, Bracken and myself; so it could hardly be called a group. But I also belonged to the Amery group, and I shall never forget the courage and conviction with which he marshalled his arguments in favour of resistance to Hitler's threats. He had no doubt at all that, if it came to war, we should win it – and quickly. Nor had I. When Chamberlain announced that he proposed to fly to Berchtesgaden to see Hitler, some of us had deep misgivings. When he announced to a House of Commons, almost hysterical with relief, that he was going to fly back to Munich to meet Hitler and Mussolini, we knew that this almost certainly meant capitulation. I asked Lloyd George, as I always did in moments of stress, what he thought about it, but he had only one comment to make: 'In my time they came to see me.'

I cannot reproach myself for having been equivocal about my own attitude during the run-up to Munich, or for not having made my views absolutely clear both to the public and the Government.

On 11 September 1938, I wrote a letter to the First Lord of the Admiralty, Duff Cooper, in which I said:

I make no excuse for writing again, because I believe it is a matter of life or death to declare the attitude of this country in the face of naked aggression before Hitler speaks. We are morally committed, by the Runciman Mission, to support Czechoslovakia if she is now attacked.

We are also morally committed – to the hilt – to France. But the issue cuts deeper than this. In its simplest, crudest and ultimate form, it is the issue between Reason and Force, Civilization and Barbarism. If you don't make a declaration on this single point, war may still be averted by the resolution of others.

But if you don't make it and war results, then it seems to me that your responsibility is unthinkable.

This letter was read to the Cabinet.

On the night of the Munich agreement, I dined at the Other Club, and sat between Walter Elliot and Duff Cooper. It was a stormy evening. Garvin, the Editor of the *Observer*, got up and walked out when I said that one good article didn't make up for twenty lousy ones; and Churchill tried in vain to dissuade him. The press lords had arranged that the first editions of the morning papers should be brought to us; and they contained the terms of the Agreement. Duff Cooper flushed, but said nothing until he whispered in my ear: 'I shall resign tomorrow morning.' He did just that. His interview with the Prime Minister lasted only a few minutes. Both were thankful to see the last of each other. This disposes of the story that he tried to remain in the Government. Both Churchill and Duncan Sandys thought that I 'crumpled'. Of course I did. I knew it was the end. In the ensuing debate the Labour amendment typically called for a World Economic Conference. We had had one of these, and it was one too many. I had no hesitation in voting against it. But when it came to the substantive motion approving the policy of Government, I abstained. Next day I received a telegram signed by all the members of the Executive of my Association asking me to make no more speeches in the constituency until I had given them an explanation of my failure to support the Government. I travelled north at once, and did this in a speech which lasted for an hour. As usual, they supported me. The Duchess of Atholl, in neighbouring Perthshire, who also abstained, was not so fortunate. Her Association failed to give her their support; and she fought and lost a by-election.

The terms of the Munich Agreement turned out to be even worse than we had supposed. They amounted to unconditional surrender. Even Goering was shocked. He said afterwards that when he heard Hitler tell the conference at Munich (if such it could be called) that he proposed to occupy the Sudeten lands, including the Czech fortifications at once, 'we all knew what that meant'. But neither Chamberlain nor Daladier made a cheep of protest. Hitler did not even have to send an ultimatum to Czechoslovakia. Chamberlain did that for him. Ashton-Gwatkin of the Foreign Office brought it from Munich to Prague for presentation to the Czech Government. He had breakfast with our Military Attaché, Brigadier Humphrey Stronge, before he showed it to the British Minister, Basil Newton. Stronge said that Czechoslovakia could never accept such terms, as they involved, amongst other things, surrendering all the fortifications, and thereby rendering her defenceless. Ashton-Gwatkin said that they had *got* to accept, and that there was no alternative. Stronge, in his own words, was 'staggered'; and wondered what the outcome could possibly be. Later that day, after a heated argument with some of his generals and politicians, Beneš capitulated.

In 1974 Brigadier Stronge sent me a copy of a memorandum he had written regarding the state of morale and general readiness for war of the army of the Czechoslovakian Republic at the time of the Munich crisis and the period immediately preceding it. It is now in the Imperial War Museum, and the Bodleian Library; and I found it of such great interest that I urged him to expand it and publish it. He replied that he would do this, probably as a paperback or a pamphlet; and asked me whether I would write a short introductory chapter. I told him that I would be glad to do this, but unfortunately he died before the necessary arrangements could be made. I hope that, in due course, his memorandum will be published. Meanwhile it is available to historians.

I had a considerable correspondence with Brigadier Stronge, which began in July 1970 when he wrote to say that he hoped a letter of mine in *The Times* about the Munich surrender would dispose once and for all of the theory that Chamberlain had no alternative but to give in. He told me that, as Military Attaché in Prague, he came to London in June 1938 for the annual conference of military attachés and had interviews with the chief of the Imperial General Staff (Gort), the Foreign Secretary (Halifax), and the Secretary of State for War (Hore-Belisha). In each case he stressed that, in his opinion, the Czech army was resolved to fight it out with the German army, certainly if supported by their allies, and quite possibly single-handed; also that their training, equipment and morale were very good. He got the impression, however, that Halifax had expected (I suspect hoped for) a less favourable report on the Czech army, and that Gort was more interested in secondary details than factors of greater import. Hore-Belisha impressed him as the soundest man of the trio. Stronge concluded by saying that no army in Europe was ready for war in 1938; but that the Czechoslovakian army was by far the most advanced towards that state than any other. In another letter to me in August 1970, he wrote: 'The correspondence about Munich has continued unabated in *The Times* with the opponents of that shameful episode winning hands down.' On 11 September 1974, he wrote again: 'If only Beneš had done what you advised him to do, what a vast difference it would have made to subsequent world history!' And in his last letter he said that information which had become available since the war had confirmed his view that the Czech army fortifications and morale in 1938 were the best in Europe; and that it could probably have taken on the German army single-handed, which we now know was weaker in 1938 than he himself had supposed.

This brings me to the plot of the German generals in 1938. It was Nicky Kaldor, now Lord Kaldor, who first told me about it. After the war he interrogated Halder, who was the Chief of the German General Staff in 1938. The plan was to arrest the Nazi leaders in Berlin, and proclaim a military government. All the leading German generals were in, or connived at, the plot: Brauchitsch, the Commander-in-Chief; von Rundstedt; Beck; Stülpnagel; Witzleben, Commander of the Berlin Garrison; and also Graf Helldorf, who was chief of the Berlin police. Nicky Kaldor gave me full details of the plot, which I passed on to Churchill who printed them in full, without acknowledgement, in *The Gathering Storm*. Halder said that he called off the plot at the eleventh hour when Chamberlain's flight to Berchtesgaden was announced. He decided that if Hitler could get away with this he could get away with anything. Of Munich he said: 'Never in history has there been such a betrayal. A country, at least equal to ours, forced to give up the strongest defence line in Europe. How could I have foreseen it?' In his view Germany would have been defeated in three weeks in the event of war. Jodl said in evidence at the Nuremberg Trial after the war: 'I could not imagine Hitler embroiling us in a war which, in our situation then, would have led to our immediate destruction. It was impossible for five active and eight reserve divisions to hold a hundred French divisions in a West Wall which was then purely a huge construction site.' Kaldor told me that he thought at the time that Halder was telling the truth; and Professor Trevor-Roper has given the weight of his authority to the credibility of this plot, which, he wrote in *The Last Days of Hitler*, has been accepted as genuine by the authorities who examined it. J. K. Galbraith believes on the other hand that if Chamberlain had never flown to Berchtesgaden the German generals would have found some other excuse for doing nothing, as later on they always did. I simply do not know. All I am sure of is that if Baldwin had still been Prime Minister, he would never have dreamed of flying to see Hitler. Nor would he have signed the Munich Agreement. Although he never said so in public, I happen to know that he was himself opposed to Neville Chamberlain's foreign policy. On one occasion, between Munich and the outbreak of war, he roused himself to come to the House of Lords and make a speech. It was not to give thanks for Munich. It was to demand the total mobilization of British industry for a crash programme of rearmament.

On 31 March we gave a sudden, unconditional and unilateral guarantee to Poland, without any guarantee of Russian support. I was appalled. Mr Lloyd George asked whether the General Staff had agreed to this obligation to go to the defence of a country which, in no conceivable circumstances, could we reach. He got no reply. This of course made the

Second World War a certainty. But I found only two senior statesmen who agreed with me. One was Lloyd George, who opposed it for this reason; the other was Walter Elliot, who told me that he could not have remained a member of Chamberlain's Cabinet if he had not known that this was so!

1939 was a hopeless year, during which we drifted slowly, helplessly and inexorably to disaster. As so often, Shakespeare has the final comment:

> That England, being empty of defence
> Hath shook and trembled at the ill neighbourhood. . . .

On 10 March Sir Samuel Hoare denounced those of us who were still clamouring for re-armament as 'jitterbugs'. 'These timid, panic-mongers are doing the greatest harm,' he said. He went on to advocate a five-year plan worked out by five men, the three dictators and the Prime Ministers of Britain and France, who would thus make themselves the 'eternal benefactors' of the human race. Such a plan, concluded Sir Samuel Hoare, would lead to a Golden Age. Of all the political pygmies, he was the pygmiest. The only things I ever remember him saying were: 'Yees, yees, yees', or 'Quaite, quaite, quaite'. Four days after his speech the German tanks thundered into Prague.

Looking back, there can be no doubt that the Munich Agreement was one of the biggest bluffs in history. It was also the most cowardly and sordid act of betrayal ever perpetrated by a British or French Government. The fact remains that it had the full support of the British and French people. Daladier once told me in Strasbourg after the war that, when he flew back from Munich to Paris, he thought he might be lynched. On the contrary he was received with rapturous applause by vast crowds; and the same thing happened to Chamberlain in London. It is no longer arguable that the so-called 'breathing-space' given to us by Munich for rearmament did not operate wholly in Germany's favour. The two years that elapsed between Munich and the outbreak of serious war enormously increased the gap between us. Much of the armour with which France was defeated in 1940 was manufactured at the Skoda works in Czechoslovakia; and the superiority of the Luftwaffe over the Royal Air Force was at least doubled. I have heard it said that in 1938 Great Britain would have been wide open to air attack, and defenceless. But in 1938 fewer German bombers would have had to operate from bases far removed from this country, without air cover; whereas, in 1940, they were able to carry out a 'blitz' against us with a bomber force twice the size, operating from bases in Holland, Belgium and the north of France.

The handful of us who opposed the Munich surrender might have put up a better show; but we could not have altered the fatal course of events. It was ridiculous that we should split up into different groups which would have nothing to do with each other. But we did. Timid, as always, Harold Nicolson wrote to his wife that he had joined a 'hush-hush' group under Eden. 'This group,' he explained, 'is distinct from Churchill's. It was a relief to me to be with people who share my views so completely and yet who do not give the impression (as Winston does) of being more bitter than determined, and more out for a fight than for reform.' What chance did they really think they had of 'reforming' Chamberlain, Halifax, Simon, and Hoare; or, for that matter, Hitler? On the whole they were a sorry lot.

The only man in that ghastly Government who emerges with real credit, and who has never been given his due, is Lord Swinton, Secretary of State for Air from 1935 to 1938, who created Fighter Command, by setting up the Air Defence Research Committee; by giving priority to radar, against Lindemann's advice; and by ordering the Hurricanes and Spitfires off the drawing-board – which won the battle of Britain; and was sacked for his pains.

From 1935 until 1939 I watched the political leaders of Britain, in Government and in Opposition, at pretty close quarters; and I reached the conclusion, which I have not since changed, that with only two exceptions, Winston Churchill and Leopold Amery, they were all frightened men. On four occasions Hitler and his gang of bloody murderers could have been brought down, and a second world war averted, by an ultimatum: when he marched into the Rhineland; when he denounced the Treaties of Versailles and Locarno and began to re-arm; when he brutally annexed Austria; and when (with Chamberlain's support) he attacked Czechoslovakia. Every time we failed to do it. And four times is a lot. The reason for it can, I am afraid, only be ascribed to a squalid combination of cowardice and greed; and the British ministers responsible, instead of being promoted, should have been impeached.

I was led to the further conclusion that the end of the British Empire, and perhaps of this country, was in sight.

Thus we stumbled into what it became fashionable to call the 'Bore War' – without arms, without faith, and without heart.

# 11

# Into the War

Poland was completely defeated in three weeks by the German *blitzkrieg*. It took the greater part of the *Wehrmacht* to do this, leaving only a skeleton force to defend, against a vastly superior French army, a Siegfried Line which had not yet been completed. But the French refused to move, and we had practically nothing to move with.

In the middle of September, Clement Davies formed a small non-party group in the House of Commons, and asked me to be Secretary. We dined together once a week, and from time to time invited a distinguished guest to talk to us. They included Lord Trenchard, Sir Roger Keyes, Keynes and Lloyd George. Lloyd George was profoundly depressed. He said that our situation was incomparably worse than it had ever been between 1914 and 1918. Next day I lunched with him alone. I never saw him so troubled and anxious. He said we should have launched a massive attack on Germany by land and air within twelve hours of the declaration of war. Instead all we had done was to drop imbecile tracts over Germany, which could only have increased the morale of the German people. 'Why aren't we attacking now?' he said. 'If it is because we haven't got the stuff, they should never have given that insane guarantee to Poland. What are we fighting for now? The restoration of Danzig to a non-existent Poland? Or the restoration of Colonel Beck's estates in Galicia?' (Beck was the Polish Foreign Minister.) George added, rightly, that Germany was now producing far more arms than we were, and that further delay only widened the gap. If the French continued to refuse to attack, and we were unable to do so, then it might become necessary to play for time, and negotiate a peace before worse befell us. The Treaty of Amiens did not prevent the ultimate defeat of Napoleon; and, in the absence of arms, skilful diplomacy could also be a weapon of war. To my amazement he said that he had never been consulted by the Government at any time about anything. 'I wish I knew the facts,' he said. 'They tell me nothing.'

In October 1939 I went to Paris with Harold Nicolson; and there I had a long talk with Paul Reynaud, who invited me to lunch at the Ministry of Finance to meet two Senators. He opened the conversation by asking why I was not in the Government, and then said: 'I know. You have too many brilliant and energetic young men already in your Cabinet. Alas! We are not so fortunate in France!' I thought this was a promising start. He went on that our policy, jointly pursued for the last two years, had been *faible*, and always too late. 'We have still one elementary lesson to learn from the dictators,' he said, 'the power of swift and vigorous action at the right moment.'

In March, 1940, I went to Switzerland, where I found the Swiss completely sceptical about the policy and determination of Britain and France. They did not even believe that, if they themselves were attacked, we would come to their aid. I went to the frontier, and stood there within a hundred yards of the German sentries in field-grey uniform, who were quite unconcerned. From the hills on the other side a faint sound of hammering came down the wind. It was all rather ominous.

On my way through Paris I called on Pierre Laval in his office in the Champs Elysées to ask him to resume broadcasts in English on the Radio Lyons Station, which he then controlled, for the benefit of the BEF. He said he would do what he could. Then he added: 'May I speak to you seriously about the present situation?' I begged him to do so, and he went on: 'We are all agreed now that the best chance of stopping Hitler was when he sent his troops into the Rhineland; and that we failed. I know that you think that the last chance was at Munich. I disagree. The last chance was at Stresa. Austria, not

Czechoslovakia, was the essential bastion of central Europe. Only one power could have saved Austria and that was Italy. We could have had Italy. But the price was Abyssinia. It was well worth paying; and, believe me, it would have been of benefit, not harm, to the Ethiopians.' Abyssinia, he said, was the whole point of the Stresa Conference; which led me to believe, what I still believe, that he had already done a personal deal with Mussolini.

He went on: 'At Stresa your people never even mentioned Abyssinia. Simon, I understood. He is just a slick lawyer. But MacDonald? Explain to me MacDonald.' I did my best. I said that the English had an invincible reluctance to face unpalatable facts until they were rammed down their throats. For this reason MacDonald suited them admirably, because in recent years he had shared that reluctance; and almost everything he had said had been incomprehensible. In consequence anyone could interpret his remarks in any way they chose. Hence the so-called 'National' Government. 'Well,' commented Laval, 'it was unfortunate for us all that he refused to face the unpalatable fact of Abyssinia at Stresa, because Mussolini mistook his silence for agreement instead of imbecility; and his subsequent disillusion threw him into the arms of Germany, with the result that we lost Austria, and with it the whole of central Europe.

'Now, Mr Boothby,' he said, leaning forward and in a more confidential tone, 'I want to tell you that I think this war is a great mistake. If we had come to terms with Mussolini, as I wanted to do, we might have held Germany. That is no longer possible. We have given most of Europe to Hitler. Let us try to hold on to what we have got left. I am a peasant from the Auvergne. I want to keep my farm, and I want to keep France. Nothing else matters now.' I then asked what he thought we ought to do, and he replied: 'Make peace at once. Those people,' he went on, with a wave of his arm in the direction of the Quai d'Orsay, 'have no idea what they are up against. Reynaud has intelligence, and Mandel courage. The rest are no good.' So much for the French Government! 'What about the army?' I asked. He replied: 'Gamelin [the Commander-in-Chief] is absolutely useless. The troops are all underground in that wretched Maginot Line, and completely demoralized.

They should be in armour, but we haven't got any.' 'And the people of France?' I asked. He said: 'Their heart is not in this war.'

Then he said that he hoped I would forgive him if he spoke frankly: 'Quite soon the Germans are going to attack us. They will defeat us in three weeks, and we shall have to surrender. I would like to avoid that. We have already given them central and eastern Europe, and that we cannot undo. If we accept that, they might leave us alone, at least for a time; and ultimately turn east. Meanwhile, if we are to avoid immediate disaster, we have no alternative but to come to terms with them.'

When he had finished, I said to him: 'Monsieur Laval, this is certainly the most important conversation I have ever had, or am ever likely to have. Will you give me permission to repeat what you have just told me to my friends in London?'

'Yes,' he said, 'and go back tomorrow. There is no time to lose.' I walked down the Champs Elysées with my mind in a whirl. Paris was in one of her most melting moods, but she brought me no comfort that night. I could not get the little man out of my head – the swarthy complexion, the enormous intelligence, the crafty black eyes, the white tie; and the voice, soft, with a southern accent. '*Je suis payeesan.*' Ten weeks later France capitulated.

I suppose that Laval has been abused more vitriolically than any other statesman in this century; but I think this has to some extent been over-done. He was as right about France and the French army before the war as Churchill was wrong. The policy he consistently advocated for several years was rejected. When every prediction that he had made came true, he did what he could to mitigate the suffering of his fellow-country-men. No more, but no less. His death was hideous. He tried to poison himself, but they stopped that with a stomach-pump. Then the firing squad failed to kill him, and he was finished off with revolvers as he lay wounded on the ground.

On 3 April 1940, Chamberlain announced in the House of Commons, for no apparent reason, that he was ten times more confident of victory; and that Hitler had missed the bus. The complacency of the British Government remained invincible. Thousands of young men were idle. By the end of the year 1939

we still had 1 400 000 unemployed! Still no serious attempt was
made to step up our armament production. Even Churchill
was infected. At a lunch in the Admiralty, he said to me that
he had the impression that Hitler's Germany was more 'brittle'
than that of the Kaiser; and that there was no need for anyone
to think that we could not continue normal life and also win
the war.

On Sunday 14 April 1940, Churchill as First Lord of the
Admiralty, sent for me. He was accompanied by several members of the Intelligence Division. He told me that they had
reason to believe that there were large numbers of small arms,
particularly rifles, in Holland and Belgium; and asked me to
go there at once, on a secret mission, to try and get hold of
some of them. I enlisted, and at once obtained, the support of
a Belgian friend, Louis Franck, who was a partner in the firm
of Samuel Montagu & Company; and of my friend Richard
Weininger, whose banker I then was. Franck went over first,
and came back with an optimistic report that the arms were
certainly there, and that we could obtain export licences provided the goods were ostensibly purchased on behalf of a
neutral country. I asked the Foreign Office to arrange for the
necessary passport and visas to be given to Weininger, in order
that he could help me with the languages and any business
complications that might arise; and this was done. On 22 April
we flew to Brussels. There, we were warmly received by our
Military Attachés, Colonel Blake and Major MacKenzie. We
found the arms. At Liège we were offered 9000 rifles and over
a hundred machine-guns for immediate delivery f.o.b. Antwerp,
and also 1000 'Schmeisser' guns, one of the best light auto-
matics in the world. Then we went to Amsterdam, where we
were conducted to a private room in an obscure hotel. There
four Dutchmen were awaiting us. No names were disclosed.
We were given a firm offer of 200 000 to 400 000 Mauser rifles
complete with slings and bayonets, and a thousand cartridges
each. Delivery to start the following week with 50 000 rifles,
after inspection by our military authorities in Belgium, and to
be completed within three weeks. We agreed upon a price in
dollars, and they gave me an option which was to expire at the
end of four days. I had little doubt that the rifles were of Krupp
manufacture, but I knew that the offer was genuine, because

one of the Dutchmen was a representative of the Amsterdam-sche Bank, and gave us its guarantee. The tug of dollars was strong. The plan, unspoken but well understood by us all, was to ship the arms to China, and have them picked up by British destroyers in the Channel.

I travelled back from Amsterdam to Brussels, through bulb fields in full bloom, in great excitement. There I found that both Blake and MacKenzie thought the offer was genuine; and Blake said that he would drive me at once to the GHQ of the British Expeditionary Force at Arras. It was a strange experience 'advancing on the British lines' as if I were an enemy. When we reached them there was a certain amount of barbed wire, and some rather desultory digging going on. I did not think much of it. Flying Blake's flag, we were let through immediately; and, shortly afterwards, reached Arras. That night we dined in the Intelligence Mess at GHQ. I sat next to the Director of Military Intelligence, General Mason Macfarlane. He told me that we could have got a lot of arms from Germany before the war when he was Military Attaché in Berlin, but that the War Office wouldn't hear of it. He said that he had once had the opportunity of killing Hitler at close quarters, and wished he had taken it. I said that I had had a similar opportunity, and also wished I had taken it. After dinner he went on to say that Churchill's Norwegian campaign was going to be a complete flop, which was perhaps as well, as we couldn't spare the troops. I asked him why, and he said: 'Because in a very short time we shall be fighting for our lives here.' 'In Belgium, after they attack?' I said. 'No, here in Arras,' he replied. 'I hope you get these rifles. We may need them at home. I have arranged for you to be flown back to London in the Commander-in-Chief's aeroplane tomorrow.'

When I landed at Hendon, I drove straight to the Ministry of Supply. There, the Minister, Doctor Burgin, a typical Chamberlain appointment, received me without undue enthusiasm. Next day he asked me to cable for an extension of the option for a further three days. I did this with great misgiving, but received a reply of acceptance. After that I heard nothing more until the morning of 7 May, when he rang me up and told me that it had been decided by a Cabinet Committee that the rifles were not required; and that, even if they were, the

Treasury would not pay for them on the grounds that they could not spare the dollars. Upon this I wrote to Churchill:

You sent me over to Belgium at the shortest notice, and as a matter of the greatest urgency, ten days ago, in order (in Burgin's written words) 'to find and secure rifles'. I found them. This morning I was told by Burgin that no rifles are required; and that, even if they were, the Treasury would not pay for them. It would be incredible if it were not true.

I have often wondered whether the subsequent persecution of both Weininger and myself was due to fear on the part of the authorities that we might otherwise divulge the shocking truth, and thus prevent the enormous 'cover-up' operation which took place. Since the war we have both told the full story, in detail; and it has not been contradicted. But I am willing to lay long odds that there will never be an enquiry. When, in a final desperate appeal, I went to see Churchill, he talked about Norway. When Weininger went to see Simon, he talked about birds.

Long afterwards a high Treasury official told me that he had thought they had made a serious mistake in refusing to buy the rifles. It was more than that. If Guderian had not been prevented by Hitler from cutting off the BEF with his armour in front of Dunkirk, and if Goering had not switched his attack from our airfields to our cities in the Battle of Britain, those rifles might well have made the difference between victory and defeat. The pikes and sticks with which the Home Guard was armed were not an adequate substitute.

Everything drifted gradually from bad to worse; and the Norwegian campaign, botched by Churchill, brought matters to a climax. In a critical debate, arranged for 7 and 8 May 1940, Herbert Morrison announced on the second day that the Opposition intended to divide the House. The debate was on the adjournment, but it amounted to a vote of no confidence in the Government. Clement Davies immediately sent for me, and told me that he was going to try and persuade Lloyd George, who had not intended to speak, to come to the Chamber and do so. He then asked me to arrange a meeting of dissident Conservative members, and who I thought would make the best chairman. I said that Leo Amery was the obvious choice. In the event, Davies persuaded Lloyd George to make what Churchill subsequently described as 'his last decisive intervention in the House of Commons', and I had no difficulty in persuading Amery to take the chair at a meeting of Conservative MPs, several in uniform, which extended beyond the various 'groups'. At this meeting the fateful decision was taken to vote against the Government.

In the debate Amery quoted Cromwell's last speech to the Long Parliament: ' "You have sat too long here for any good you have been doing. Depart, I say, and let us be done with you. In the name of God, go!" ' Lloyd George said: 'The Prime Minister has appealed for sacrifice. . . . I say solemnly that the Prime Minister should give an example of sacrifice, because there is nothing which can contribute more to victory in this war than that he should sacrifice the seals of office.' In his speech Chamberlain turned round to the Conservative Party sitting behind him, and appealed to his friends. 'And I have friends,' he added. 'Not I,' I said; and got a withering glance with the eyes of an arrogant blackbird. Thirty-three Conservative Members, of whom I was one, voted against the Government; and many more abstained. This division was decisive. When the result was announced by the Speaker, Chamberlain turned white, got up immediately, and left the chamber alone. As I watched his solitary figure disappear behind the Speaker's chair, I felt a pang. The end, when it came, had something of the nobility of Greek tragedy.

Next day Clement Davies and I went into action in the House of Commons. He moved that the House should adjourn until 14 May instead of 21 May. In seconding this amendment I said: 'The events of yesterday proved that the Government, as at present constituted, does not possess the confidence of the House and country [ministerial cries of 'No! no!']. It is common knowledge,' I continued, 'to every member of this House, if he faces the facts, that national unity can never be achieved under the present political leadership.' That afternoon we had a meeting of our group and agreed upon a three-point policy which was issued to the press:

(1) that there must be a genuine National Government including representatives of all three parties;

(2)  that the Prime Minister, whoever he might be, should choose his colleagues on grounds of merit; and

(3)  that we would give full support to any Prime Minister who could form such a government, and none to one who could not.

Clement Davies and I wanted Churchill. The King, the Prime Minister, and a great majority of the Conservative Party wanted Halifax; and I think that, but for Davies, Attlee and Greenwood, the leaders of the Parliamentary Labour Party would have settled for Halifax. My flat in Pall Mall was opposite the Reform Club, where Clement Davies was staying; and in it he did much of his work, including several telephone calls to Attlee and Greenwood at Bournemouth, where they were attending a Labour Party conference. Then, suddenly, we found an ally in Sir Kingsley Wood, the Secretary of State for Air, who had for many years been Neville Chamberlain's closest political friend and ally. He came out in favour of Churchill. When, on 10 May, the Germans, as Laval had predicted, attacked the west, Chamberlain felt that this made it necessary for him to remain at his post. Wood told him that, on the contrary, it made it all the more necessary to have a National Government. When, at eleven o'clock on the morning of 10 May Chamberlain asked Churchill to see him with Halifax, both Wood and Brendan Bracken advised him to remain silent. After a long pause, Halifax said that he felt that as a peer his position out of the House of Commons would make it difficult for him to discharge the duties of Prime Minister in war. 'It was clear', wrote Churchill in *The Second World War*, 'that the duty would fall upon me – had in fact fallen upon me. . . . I was conscious of a profound sense of relief. At last I had the authority to give directions over the whole scene. I felt as if I were walking with destiny, and that all my past life had been but a preparation for this hour and for this trial.'

Although I think that, under the strain of the appalling danger into which we were soon to fall, the nation would have demanded Churchill as leader, he was in fact made Prime Minister by six men: Kingsley Wood, Lloyd George, Clement Davies, Amery, Brendan Bracken, and Halifax himself. Outside the political arena, Beaverbrook also played his part.

Churchill showed no undue gratitude to those of us who helped to put him there. Wood was rightly rewarded with the Chancellorship of the Exchequer; Bracken became his Parliamentary Private Secretary; Amery was marooned in the India Office which he nearly refused and, despite his experience, took no part in the direction of the war; Clement Davies got nothing at all. My own destination, as I shall tell later, was the Ministry of Food.

Churchill's main political concern after he achieved power was to reconcile himself to the Conservative Party in the House of Commons upon which that power depended. In some ways he felt a kind of resentment against those who had helped him to obtain it. He said to me: 'It took Armageddon to make me Prime Minister. But now I am there I am determined that Power shall be in no other hands but mine. There will be no more Kitcheners, Fishers or Haigs.'

# Lloyd George

For two years I had kept in close touch with Mr Lloyd George, and never found myself in disagreement with him. He told me, at the time, that our unilateral guarantee to Poland, without arms and without Russian support, was the maddest single action ever taken by a British Government; and foretold, precisely, its consequences. When Halifax went to see the Nazi leaders in Germany, he said it was like sending a curate to visit a tiger: he wouldn't know whether it was growling in anger or in fun; and in either case he wouldn't know how to reply. So it proved. Of Goering, Halifax wrote: 'I was immensely entertained at meeting the man. I remembered all the time that he had been concerned with the "clean-up" in Berlin on June 30 1934, and I wondered how many people he had been responsible for killing. Like a great schoolboy full of life and pride in all he was doing, showing it all off, and talking high politics out of the setting of green jerkin and red dagger'; and of Goebbels: 'I had expected to dislike him most intensely, but am ashamed to say I did not.' I think that, during the 'phoney' war of 1939–40 Lloyd George was the only British statesman who realized the full gravity of our situation. When the political crisis came in 1940, I told him that it was now a question of survival; and that I was convinced that Churchill alone could save us. He thought for a time, and then said: 'You are probably right. But it will be a one-man show. He has at least one great general – Wavell. I was not so fortunate. But, mark my words, he will get rid of Wavell. I will not join him. If I did, I should be the only one to stand up to him. And that would be no good for either of us. I will do my best to get rid of Chamberlain, for under him we are bound to be defeated. That is all I can do.'

After my appointment to the Ministry of Food, he said he wanted to talk to me about food production. Foolishly, I invited him to lunch at White's Club. As I should have foreseen, this caused a tremendous stir. Within the hour it had been reported to Churchill that I was plotting to make Lloyd George Prime Minister instead of himself. He may have believed it.

When, soon after this, Lloyd George received a letter from the Prime Minister asking him to join the War Cabinet, he hesitated. Then he did an extraordinary thing. He did not answer, but asked me to go and see him. I could tell at once that he was perplexed, and rather apprehensive. He didn't know how or what to reply. Eventually, after quite a long talk, he suggested that it might be better if I, not he, wrote to the Prime Minister, to tell him what his views were. Accordingly I sent the following letter to 10 Downing Street:

*SECRET*

9th July, 1940

Dear Prime Minister,

Mr Lloyd George asked me to see him this afternoon, and I think it my duty to give you a brief account of our conversation.

He began by expressing approval of the action taken with regard to the French Fleet,* and went on to say that, in his opinion, we could win a long war, and that this would be by far the greatest of our achievements. He was inclined to the view that Hitler would content himself with intensive bombing of our ports and factories for the time being; but said it was obviously right to take every conceivable precaution against invasion. His general views were robust; and he told me that he definitely refused to allow any of his grand-children to be evacuated from this country.

Turning to the political side, he said he had no personal animus against Mr Chamberlain, but considered that at the present juncture both he and Lord Halifax were a liability to this country. Evidence reached him from all quarters that the continued presence of Mr Chamberlain in the War Cabinet was a source of mingled bewilderment and irritation to the working classes, with the result that at per-

* The attack on the French fleet at Oran, 1940.

haps the most dangerous moment in our history it would be difficult
to arouse the unrestrained enthusiasm of the workers, which was so
necessary if we were to win through. He said he understood that all
the trade unions would shortly have passed resolutions similar to that
recently passed by the NUR, and that this was a very bad thing in
time of war.

Continuing, he said that he personally took the view that Lord
Halifax at the Foreign Office was a much greater liability than Mr
Chamberlain, for the reason that he was profoundly distrusted both
in the United States and in the USSR. He felt that if we were to
achieve decisive victory it would be necessary not only to build up the
productive strength of the British Empire to the maximum during the
next few months, *but that sooner rather than later both America and Russia
should be – and could be – associated with us.** So long as Mr Chamberlain
and Lord Halifax retained their present posts this would not be possible.

He then said that nothing would induce him to accept any responsibility for 'throwing them out'. It was up to them to go, if they felt it
was their duty to do so. At the same time he did not feel able to join
the present administration, not because he had a personal dislike
either of Mr Chamberlain or Lord Halifax, or because he thought
they would hamper or hinder him, or because they would adopt a
hostile attitude towards him personally, but because he felt so strongly
that any effort of the Government along the lines he had indicated
would inevitably be stultified by their continuance in their present
offices.

He said he could not understand why, in present circumstances, and
in view of the continuous attacks being made upon him, which could
be withstood in time of peace but not in time of war, Mr Chamberlain
would not agree to continue his leadership of the Conservative Party
in the House of Lords. This, coupled with the transference of Lord
Halifax to another post, would, in fact, meet the views of the critics,
and greatly contribute to the strength and unity of the country at a
critical moment.

Meanwhile he had refrained from answering your invitation to join
the War Cabinet for two reasons:

(1) Because he did not wish to commit himself in writing to
opinions which would put him in the position of having tried to force
Mr Chamberlain out of the Government against his will, and thus to
a breach with the Conservative Party and perhaps also with yourself
which might prove irreconcilable, and

(2) Because Max [Beaverbrook] had most strongly urged him not
to answer for the time being. He had sustained the definite impression

* My italics. It is a fair example of his vision.

from Max – who motored down especially to see him at Churt – that Mr Chamberlain contemplated resigning in the near future; and that premature action on his part would therefore do no good, and might do harm.

At the same time he said that he would not wish you to think that his failure to send a written reply was due to any sort of discourtesy on his part, and that if you wished to know his precise reasons for not joining your administration at the present juncture, he would send them to you immediately. He asked me to find out, on his behalf, what your desires were in regard to this matter.

The general impression I got was that *au fond* he is not only willing but anxious to serve; and that he is *not* trying to play any political game, or to make any capital out of debates in the House of Commons, etc. He believes the situation to be far too serious for that, and the flame of his patriotism still burns high. But he is, I think, convinced that the foreign policy which he believes to be essential to our ultimate success cannot be successfully carried out unless certain changes are made.

> Yours ever,
> Bob.

This was the letter I sent at Lloyd George's request. What he did not want was to write a letter of refusal himself, which might have been interpreted as an attempt on his part to drive Chamberlain and Halifax from office, and therefore antagonize the Conservative Party. But, in retrospect, I'm pretty sure in my own mind that he never wanted or intended to join Churchill's War Cabinet. When, soon afterwards, I went down to lunch at Churt, he said: 'My War Cabinet was a real Council of State. I had in it men of the calibre of Balfour, Bonar Law, Milner, Curzon and Smuts, to whom I could and did turn for advice. Hankey, Amery, Grigg, and Kerr were members of my secretariat. I listened to them all. No one in this War Cabinet or secretariat knows anything about war except Churchill. He will listen to no one but himself; and I don't trust his strategic judgement.' Then Frances Stevenson intervened. She said: 'Lord Dawson* gave his verdict yesterday. You are too old to take the strain. And that is final.' So, in the end, Lloyd George himself did write to the Prime Minister declining his invitation on grounds of age and health.

* Lloyd George's doctor.

I suppose I am the only man alive today who was for many years on terms of intimate friendship with both Lloyd George and Churchill, the two men of undoubted genius in British politics during the present century. I first met Lloyd George in the House of Commons in 1924, two years after he had fallen from power, and immediately fell under his spell. I knew that before the First World War he had been a great social reformer, and laid the foundations of the Welfare State. I knew that in an interview which he gave as Chancellor of the Exchequer, he had said:

I want things done. I want dreams, but dreams that are realizable. I want aspiration and discontent leading to a real paradise and a real earth in which men can live here and now, and fulfil the destiny of the human race. I want to make life better and kinder and safer – now at this moment. Suffering is too close to me. Misery is too near and insistent. Injustice is too obvious and glaring. Danger is too present.

And that he had meant it all. His attacks on the landed aristocracy of those days – 'a fully equipped Duke costs as much to keep up as two Dreadnoughts; and Dukes are just as great a terror, and they last longer' – only make us laugh today. But he put an end to their power, and also to the power of a purely hereditary House of Lords. When, with Masterman, he brought in the National Insurance which is now the basis of all our lives, the Treasury jibbed at putting it into operation. Immediately he created a civil service of his own to administer it.

He made only one intervention in foreign affairs before the outbreak of the First World War, but it was decisive. At the height of the Agadir crisis in 1911, when we were on the brink of war with Germany, he made a speech at the annual dinner of the bankers and merchants of the City of London in the Mansion House in which he said:

I believe it is essential and in the highest interests, not merely of this country but of the world, that Britain should at all hazards maintain her place and her prestige among the greater Powers of the world. Her potent influence has many a time been in the past, and may yet be in the future, invaluable to the cause of human liberty. It has more than once in the past redeemed continental nations, who are sometimes too apt to forget that service, from overwhelming disaster and

even from national extinction. I would make great sacrifices to pre-
serve peace. I conceive that nothing would justify a disturbance of
national goodwill except questions of the gravest national moment.
But if a situation were to be forced upon us in which peace could only
be preserved by the surrender of the great and beneficent position
Britain has won by centuries of heroism and achievement, by allowing
Britain to be treated where her interests were vitally affected as if she
were of no account in the Cabinet of nations, then I say emphatically
that peace at that price would be a humiliation intolerable to a great
country like ours to endure.

Upon this Churchill commented in *The World Crisis*:

His City audience, whose minds were obsessed with the iniquities
of the Lloyd George Budget and the fearful hardship it had inflicted
upon property and wealth – little did they dream of the future – did
not comprehend in any way the significance or the importance of
what they heard. They took it as if it had been one of the ordinary
platitudes of ministerial pronouncements upon foreign affairs. But the
chancelleries of Europe bounded together.

For the time being war was averted. Would that a similar
voice had been heard from the British Government at the time
of the Munich crisis!

Of Lloyd George as Minister of Munitions and Prime
Minister during the war, I know nothing except that he got
the munitions, and won the war. Lord Layton and Lord Salter
both told me that he was by far the greatest administrator they
had ever served. Once in the 1920s, when I was staying at a
country house in a party which included several distinguished
statesmen, somebody asked the rhetorical question, 'Can you
point to any permanent constructive achievement of Lloyd
George?' Lord Balfour, who had appeared to be asleep in a
corner, stirred in his armchair, gazing meditatively at the
ceiling, and remarked: 'He won the greatest war in history.
That really was something of an achievement.' Pressed for an
explanation, Balfour went on to say that, in his considered
opinion, we should never have inflicted the defeat that we did
upon Germany in 1918 without Lloyd George. 'That,' he
added, 'can be said of no other man.' In November 1918, Mr
Lloyd George found himself at Versailles. 'In the beautiful

forest,' he said, 'the leaves were falling, but these were not alone. Empires, Kingdoms and Kings and Crowns were falling like withered leaves before a gale.' The contrast between the spring and the fall of the leaf, he said, was the most dramatic in history. Thus Britain achieved, under his leadership, a world power greater than any since Rome. When I asked John Buchan, who was by no means his blind admirer, what he felt about him as a War Minister, he replied: 'I put him in the class of Cromwell and Chatham.'

At Versailles he strove hard for a good peace, and was thwarted by President Wilson. In 1933 Keynes was to write:

How can I convey to the reader, who does not know him, any just impression of this extraordinary figure of our time, this syren, this goat-footed bard, this half-human visitor to our age from the hagridden magic and enchanted woods of Celtic antiquity? One catches in his company that flavour of final purposelessness, inner irresponsibility, existence outside or away from our Saxon good and evil, mixed with cunning, remorselessness, love of power, that lend fascination, enthralment, and terror to the fair-seeming magicians of North European folklore. . . . Lloyd George is rooted in nothing; he is void and without content; he lives and feeds on his immediate surroundings; he is an instrument and a player at the same time which plays on the company and is played on by them too; he is a prism, as I have heard him described, which collects light and distorts it, and is most brilliant if the light comes from many quarters at once; a vampire and a medium in one.

It is one of the most brilliant and maddest pieces of prose writing I have ever read. The truth is that Keynes was sacked from the Peace Conference; and, in the words of Nicholas Davenport, 'left Paris like a woman scorned'. This was his revenge.

The basic cause of Lloyd George's downfall was the re-establishment after the war of the British party system, with a method of election unique in the world. Under it coalition governments cannot hope to survive in time of peace. The second cause was the Irish Treaty, which brought peace to Ireland for half a century, but for which he was never forgiven by the die-hard Unionists of the Conservative Party. The final cause was the failure of the Genoa Conference in 1922. Chanak, the last occasion before 1939 on which Britain stood up to a potential aggressor, shook him. His pro-Greek policy after the war had proved to be mistaken. But when he found himself deserted by his allies, face to face with a man of his own calibre, and alone, he never flinched. For two breathless days they measured each other. Then Kemal gave way and stopped. The Conservatives, and above all Baldwin, thought that we had been brought far too near the brink of war. The Cabinet was divided. Churchill wrote:

I found myself in this business with a small group of resolute men: the Prime Minister, Lord Balfour, Mr Austen Chamberlain, Lord Birkenhead, Sir Laming Worthington-Evans. . . . We made common cause. The Government might break up and we might be relieved of our burden. The nation might not support us: they could find others to advise them. The Press might howl, the Allies might bolt. We intended to force the Turk to a negotiated peace before he should set foot in Europe. The aim was modest, but the forces were small.

The aim was achieved. And that is why Chanak alone could not have brought Lloyd George down. There were other, and deeper, causes.

The Genoa Conference of 1922 was in fact the climax and the end of Lloyd George's effective political career. No such gathering had been seen since the Congress of Vienna. All the leading statesmen of Europe except Poincaré were assembled, accompanied by practically every important banker, industrialist and economist. 'It was,' wrote Count Kessler, 'an Oecumenical Council, comparable to those the medieval Church used to summon for the salvation of Christendom; and, as in the Middle Ages, a terror overhung the gathering that failure might portend catastrophe to European civilization.' Sir Robert Horne and Sir Laming Worthington-Evans, who were both there, told me afterwards that Lloyd George dominated not only the conference but, at that moment, Europe. He was at the height of his powers and vision; and his ambitions were vaulting. He was prepared to guarantee France against unprovoked German aggression, but he wanted to bring Germany back into the Concert of Europe by means of a Consortium in which the USSR would also participate. He wanted a cancellation of inter-Allied war debts as an essential prelude to any settlement of the reparations problem. He was ready to discuss rectification of Germany's frontier with Poland. He wanted agreements concerning the commerce and transport of Europe. He wanted a viable international monetary system, the absence of which has plagued us ever since, and still does. The currency resolutions of the Genoa Conference, based on a gold exchange standard, and 'continuous co-operation' between central banks of issue, drafted under his direction by Sir Basil Blackett and Sir Ralph Hawtrey, and of which the original draft is now in my possession, could have given us one. Finally, he wanted a European Pact of Non-Aggression, based on the League of Nations and with teeth in it, which he regarded as essential for the Disarmament Agreement which was always his final objective.

He made one fatal mistake. He did not see the German Foreign Minister, Rathenau, soon enough. Rathenau felt himself isolated and tried to get in touch with him through E. F. Wise, his adviser on Russian affairs. He was told that Wise had 'gone out'. When Baron von Maltzahn called on Rathenau at 2.30 a.m. on 16 April (Easter Sunday), he found him pacing up and down his room in mauve pyjamas 'with haggard looks and eyes starting out of his head'. 'I suppose you bring me my death warrant,' he said. 'No,' replied Maltzahn, 'news of quite a different character.' It was an invitation from Chicherin, the Soviet Foreign Minister, to go to Rapallo and sign a treaty. At first Rathenau hesitated, and said: 'I will go to Lloyd George and tell him the whole position, and come to terms with him.' Maltzahn then told him that this would be dishonourable, and he then decided to go to Rapallo. At lunch-time came the long-awaited invitation from Lloyd George. Maltzahn thought he would accept it. But Rathenau said: '*Le vin est tiré, il faut le boire.*' So the Treaty of Rapallo was signed; the first, but alas not the last, between Germany and Russia since the war. This gave Poincaré the chance for which he had been waiting in the wings to wreck the conference. Rathenau went home to be assassinated, and Lloyd George to be overthrown. He should of course have resigned immediately, without waiting to be turned out by the Carlton Club; but, with the notable exception of Sir Harold Wilson, Prime Ministers seldom resign when they should.

When I first entered the House of Commons in 1924 I found that, although he was the star performer, Lloyd George had no political power at all. Nevertheless, Baldwin was obsessed by him. His thoughts constantly revolved round the single question: 'What is the Goat up to?' MacDonald also feared him. They had no need to worry. He was 'up to' Committees. His private fortune was derived from a successful and perfectly legitimate speculation in the *Daily Chronicle*, and from journalism. His own much-abused Fund was spent on endless research and enquiries, and in financing Liberal candidates who usually lost their deposits. Never has there been such a waste of money, and of the time and energies of a number of able but unknown men. The public at large had never heard of Ramsay Muir, E. P. Simon, Philip Kerr, Seebohm Rowntree, Hubert Henderson or Walter Layton; and didn't care tuppence what they thought, said or wrote. Their Brown, Green and Yellow books followed each other rapidly into innumerable waste-paper baskets unread. Even the pamphlet *We Can Conquer Unemployment*, which became an election manifesto and contained a lot of good stuff, was a damp squib. By 1929 the Liberal Party was finished.

There has been a lot of criticism about the sale of honours by Lloyd George. This had gone on since the time of Walpole, and Lloyd George never took a personal interest in it. I doubt if he ever heard of Maundy Gregory, who sold them. He needed a fund for his own party, now separated from the Asquithian Liberals; and left his Chief Whip and Treasurer to get it. The Conservative Party could do nothing about it because they did the same thing, and took half the loot. The only snag was that they didn't have such luck. Their Treasurer was Lord Farquhar. He was given an Earldom for his services. But when they asked him for the money, they found that the cupboard was bare. He had spent the lot. Six months later he died bankrupt. It must be admitted that Lloyd George had some fairly tough numbers in his inner circle. One of them was Sir William Sutherland. I only met him once, at the House of Commons before I became a Member of Parliament. He stood me a drink, and said: 'You'll never guess what I've been doing. I've just created a couple of bloody Bishops.' He was a jovial buccaneer.

I sat in the House of Commons with Lloyd George for twenty years, and our friendship, which steadily grew, is one of the things I have valued most in life. As the saviour of this country in 1940, Churchill goes into a category of his own; but Lloyd George was, without doubt, the greatest man I have ever known. In the House itself, by the time I got there, he was nothing more or less than a great artist expressing himself through the medium of politics. It was pure theatre. But the theatre and the capacity audiences he attracted were both too small. The back benches on both sides applauded, while the front benches sat in glum and sometimes miserable silence. Almost always he scored a century. Only once did I see him bowled out for a duck. That was by Aneurin Bevin in a debate about the miners, and he was visibly disconcerted. But the nation saw and knew nothing of all this.

In Parliament he was rather a lonely figure. He abhorred – and who can blame him? – the company of his Liberal colleagues, whose primary objective was to get rid of him. Except for one memorable occasion, which I have already mentioned, he lost touch with Churchill. He made no effort to talk to, still less to get to know, the Labour Party. He befriended only two of the younger Conservative members, Harold Macmillan and myself. He never came to the Smoking-Room. He preferred to remain in his dressing-room until it was time to go on stage. But if you ever got him alone, or with a few friends with whom he was at ease, he was the best company in the world. And he could never keep away from the House of Commons. I once met him behind the Speaker's chair on a Friday afternoon when it was empty. I asked him what on earth he was doing, and he replied: 'To anyone with politics in his blood, this place is like a pub to a drunkard.'

In the Parliament of 1929–31, as the economic crisis mounted, it looked as if he might come back. To begin with there was much talk of a Labour–Liberal Coalition. Then Churchill made a speech (quoted on page 82, above) in which he pointed out to MacDonald the dangers of inviting a man of such great knowledge and drive as Lloyd George to share power with him. MacDonald began to turn his eyes towards Baldwin.

Then, suddenly, Lloyd George was struck down. He had to undergo a serious prostate operation. Thus, to the delight of the political pygmies, he was excluded from the so-called 'National' Government. I think that the best comment on this has been made by Dr John Campbell, in his book *Lloyd George, the Goat in the Wilderness*:*

Lloyd George's illness in 1931 has therefore a certain aptness, for though it is utterly wrong to discuss the August crisis purely in terms of Baldwin and MacDonald, Henderson and Samuel, as if Lloyd George had died the previous year, his illness gives to that interpretation a sort of retrospective truth. Had Lloyd George been fit, things might have gone very differently that summer, yet it is hard to see them turning out very differently in the end. Thus perhaps it was neater that he was ill. The tragedy of Lloyd George's failure to come back in the crisis to which events seemed to have been building up since he left office, is a true tragedy: for beneath its apparent accidental manner there is a remorseless inevitability. 1931 revealed Lloyd George finally for what he had been, in spite of all his efforts, all along: a lone outsider, an individual. He had struggled for five years to clothe his imperious personality in the garb of a Party Leader, but the dwindling Liberal Party made an incongruously disproportionate vehicle for one of his experience, capacity and ambition. The act did not fully convince himself, and the electorate still less. Bonar Law did not know how right he was when he said in 1922: 'George will always be his own party.'

It was in the last decade of his life that he gave me the privilege of his close friendship, and I went often to Churt. Gone was the Liberal Party, gone the committees. It was Lloyd George alone, but still with the magic that never left him. The mind was as powerful as ever and the vision, if anything, greater. It cut deeper than that of Churchill, who was preoccupied with air rearmament. George deplored our military and naval weakness, which he himself would never have tolerated. But he surveyed the whole European scene with the eyes of a man who had once shaped it.

In January 1937 Terence O'Connor and I lunched with him at a wayside inn on the Riviera. He talked about many of the politicians he had known. I remember that he said that Gladstone was the most courageous, Parnell the most formidable, Clemenceau – 'a rude but reasonable man' – the best to do

* Jonathan Cape, 1977.

business with, Birkenhead had the soundest judgement, and Bonar Law the one of whom he was fondest. He added that, when he was running the Government with Bonar Law, they met every morning. 'I had lots of ideas,' he said, 'which I put to him. I knew that, when he replied, every conceivable objection had been made, better than by anyone else. When I had thought about them, I reached my decision. And after that I knew that I could count on his unswerving support.' He went on to describe a drive which he once took with Bonar Law along the Riviera coast: 'I asked him,' he said, 'what he enjoyed most in life. "Scenery, music, pictures, women, literature, the theatre, politics?" All no good. After a pause he gave me a sweet sad smile and said: "I rather like a game of bridge." '

With the exception of Compton Mackenzie and Peter Ustinov, Lloyd George was the best mimic I have ever known. Apart from Jeremy Thorpe, it is now almost a lost art. He gave us an imitation of the Japanese delegates at the Peace Conference in Versailles. For three minutes he became a Japanese. When lunch was over he said: 'I will now give you my famous imitation of Asquith leaving a restaurant.' As he staggered from table to table and pillar to post, leaving his hat behind, everyone there was convulsed with laughter.

The following year, 1938, I took Vansittart, who had been kicked upstairs at the Foreign Office by Chamberlain, and was powerless, to lunch with him at Antibes. He came down the steps of his hotel to greet us, a picturesque figure in a black cape, with the wind blowing through his white locks, his face wreathed in smiles. 'It must be a relief to you,' he said to Vansittart, 'that the seat of government has now been shifted from the murky gloom of Downing Street to the salubrious breezes of Cliveden.' At lunch he was highly critical of President Roosevelt for his failure to check the economic recession in the United States, and also for his failure to rearm, 'which enormously increases the danger of the present situation'. He was far more critical of the British Government. 'They have now succeeded in quarrelling simultaneously with Germany, Japan and Italy; in alienating Russia; and in being at least two years behindhand with armaments.' Throughout his life he had held the British Foreign Office in contempt. So much so that, when he was Prime Minister, he established his own Foreign Office in the garden of 10 Downing Street; and Balfour had to beg him not to be so rude to 'poor George' (Curzon). But the irrepressible gaiety kept bursting through the underlying apprehension, which was fully shared by both his guests. On the way back Vansittart remarked grimly: 'We have no one of that calibre now.'

Lloyd George's private life was, to say the least of it, remarkable. He had two wives, two homes, and two families; and, in the words of his private secretary A. J. Sylvester, 'got clean away with it'. He was always fond of Dame Margaret, but she did not like London society, or politics above the constituency level. She did not look after him when he was first a young Member of Parliament, and then a rising minister. She preferred to live in north Wales, look after the children, and leave him to cook his own breakfast. When, before the outbreak of the First World War, Frances Stevenson became Megan's governess, they fell in love with each other. He then gave her a choice. She could become his personal private secretary and his mistress, or go; but she could not become his wife. She accepted. The consequences were pretty rough for all concerned. Throughout the period when, as Prime Minister, he was carrying a burden seldom borne by any man, his private life was devious and complicated. He swam through it all undeterred. If Dame Margaret or the children arrived unexpectedly at Churt, Frances would have to leave by the back door. But Dame Margaret seldom came to Churt, and Frances never went to Wales. In the south of France they changed places. One night I travelled out in the Blue Train with Frances. The Blue Train carrying Dame Margaret and Megan back to London passed us in the middle of the night. He took all this with perfect equanimity, and expected his intimate friends to do the same. By concealing for ten years from Megan the fact that I was a friend of Frances, I retained the friendship of both.

Many hard things have been said and written about Frances Lloyd-George. I can only record the fact that she was one of the nicest women I have ever known. As I was also a friend of Megan and Gwilym, I took immense care to keep out of the family feud, which never came to an end. When Megan died, Frances sent a wreath to the funeral. Someone close to the family said to Desmond Donnelly that they would have thrown it into the sea if they hadn't 'thought it would poison the fish'. When the statue of Lloyd George was unveiled in the lobby of the House of Commons, Frances, his widow, did not receive an invitation until some of us protested to the Speaker. Such was the domestic atmosphere in which this extraordinary man lived for many years through the greatest convulsions in our history, in which he himself played a leading part – and survived.

In March 1963 I was asked to give a Memorial Address to Lloyd George in Caernarvon. I regard this as the highest honour I have ever been given. I stayed with Michael Duff at Vaynol, and when I arrived I found a rather tense situation. The Lloyd George family had said that if Lady Lloyd-George, who had been invited, came, they would refuse to come themselves. Michael handled the situation with exquisite tact; and Frances with her usual good sense. She did not come. The large hall was packed, and it was more like a religious than a political ceremony. I was a little disconcerted when they sang six psalms in Welsh before I was called upon to speak; but, as my heart was full and I was talking about the greatest man I had ever known, it came off all right; and I was gratified to hear from Desmond Donnelly that my speech was worth travelling three hundred miles to hear.

After Lloyd George's death Frances lived with her memories and her sister, Muriel, a superlative cook, in a charming cottage with a lovely garden near Churt. I kept in touch with her, and went down there quite often with my wife, of whom she became very fond. She listened to me on the radio and television, and I have many letters from her. I once asked her whether she ever regretted having accepted Lloyd George's terms, which were harsh. She said: 'Never. My parents did. But through him I was able to play a part in great events, and to meet many of the great men of our time.' Then she added four words: 'Besides, I loved him.'

I shall never forget one summer day when I took my wife to lunch with her and her sister. Suddenly she said: 'It's Derby Day. Let's look at it on television.' I don't often bet on horses, and then only in very small amounts, but this time I said: 'Let's have some fun!' I rang up Ladbroke's and put a hundred pounds on Lester Piggott's horse. It won.

On another occasion my wife and I asked her to bring her daughter Jennifer and her children to tea in the House of Lords. It was the first time she had been there. One of the little girls upset a jug of cream over the table, and burst into tears. I said: 'Never mind. Lords are very rich. We have masses of cream here.' Immediately she cheered up. Everyone was charming to Frances, especially Lord Jellicoe and Lady Llewelyn-Davies. Only one peeress, and that a Welsh one, said to me: 'You had no right to bring that woman here.' I replied: 'She has more right to be here than you have.' After tea I took her to the lobby of the House of Commons, and said to the young policeman on duty: 'I know that visitors are not allowed in the lobby when the House is sitting. But perhaps you will make an exception for Lady Lloyd-George, who would like to look at the statue of her husband.' Immediately he opened the door and bowed her in. As she was leaving, she said to him: 'It is not good enough.' He replied: 'I'm sorry, my lady, but I never knew him.' The fact is that sculpture in this country is a lost art. In London alone those which have been erected to Lloyd George, Churchill and Smuts are appalling. Modern sculptors should find something else to do.

The two things I remember most vividly about Lloyd George, apart from his inexhaustible vitality and good humour, were his genuine concern for the poor, the old, and for the sick; and his burning zeal for disarmament. He told me often that this could never come about unless and until there was a political settlement which was felt to be just (he was never in favour of 'unilateral' disarmament); but that if it was not achieved before the end of the present century, it was unlikely that the human race would survive for very much longer. I said that I sometimes thought it might be a good thing if it didn't. He said: 'Don't say that. If you really thought it, you wouldn't be in public life doing the best you can to ensure its survival.' I was therefore very glad when Lord Noel-Baker, who should know, singled him out, with Lord Cecil and Arthur Henderson, in his maiden speech, as one of the three British statesmen who had striven hardest for disarmament. Three times he tried – in 1919, in 1922, and in 1932. Three times he nearly succeeded. He was beaten by three men – Woodrow Wilson, Poincaré and Hitler. His visit to Hitler was, of course, a mistake. For this I blame

Tom Jones, who not only encouraged it but accompanied him. But Jones, with Philip Kerr, was at the core of the Cliveden set. Rabid appeasement was never the road to disarmament. It was the road in the opposite direction.

For my part, I shall believe until the end of my life that the fall of Lloyd George and his subsequent exclusion from office for twenty years when at the height of his powers was one of the greatest disasters that has ever befallen the British people, and indeed the world.

The last time I saw Leo Amery was outside his house in Eaton Square. I said to him: 'Do you ever regret the part you played in bringing down Lloyd George and, subsequently, in putting Baldwin in his place?' He stood quite still for a few moments, and blinked. Then he looked at me and said: 'I do.'

# 12

# Britain at War

It was Lord Beaverbrook who first told me that I was to be a minister in the new Churchill administration. I hoped that I would become his Parliamentary Secretary at the Ministry of Aircraft Production – at that moment the most exciting of all. But when, next day, I was summoned to Downing Street, Churchill received me rather grumpily, and gave me one of his Graham Sutherland looks. 'I would have offered you Scotland,' he said, 'but I was advised that your divorce made that impossible.' (This was nonsense.) 'As it is,' he continued, 'I can offer you the post of Parliamentary Secretary to the Ministry of Food. Your Minister will be in the House of Lords, so you will be in charge in the House of Commons; and we will see how you get on.' At that moment of time, I would much rather have gone to the Ministry of Food than to the Scottish Office, so I accepted. Next day I woke up to find Britain really at war – at last.

I was lucky to go to the Ministry of Food. Lord Woolton was not only a great administrator, but he knew how to treat his Under-Secretary as few ministers ever do. Since I was responsible to the House of Commons for policy over the whole field, he gave instructions that I should be kept fully informed about every aspect of it. But he went further than that. He gave me specific jobs to do. For example, he said to me: 'One thing we are not short of is milk. We need a National Milk Scheme. Draft one for me, and let me have it by the end of next week. The whole resources of the Ministry are at your disposal.' I did this, and after he had made certain amendments, he told me to submit it to the Cabinet on his behalf. It was approved, and I got it through the House of Commons without opposition, and even without debate, during the evacuation from Dunkirk. Thus the National Milk Scheme, which provided ample supplies of cheap milk for children and nursing mothers, came into existence. Scientists are now generally agreed that this did more than anything else to nourish, and sustain the health of, the youth of this country throughout the war.*

On another occasion Woolton, with his usual unerring instinct, said to me: 'There is a good deal of public dissatisfaction because many people think that those who can afford it can get much more to eat in restaurants than they can at home. I want you to let me have a scheme to deal with this which will have the necessary psychological effect.' This resulted in the 'one main course only' rule in restaurants. It did not save much food, but it did allay the growing public irritation.

Then came the disaster which Laval had predicted: the fall of France. At this time the man closest to Churchill was Louis Spears.† Long afterwards I asked him whether he had ever seen the Prime Minister, who was bearing the full brunt of the mortal peril which now confronted us, daunted. He said: 'Only once. One evening I went in to the Cabinet room and found him sitting there alone, with his head in his hands. He sat quite still, and I waited. Then he looked up, and said to me: 'What have I done to deserve this?'

I then did one of the most foolish things I have ever done. I wrote a letter to the Prime Minister telling him how to run the war – what to do with Members of Parliament, where to put the troops, how to deploy the Fleet, the lot. I was immediately summoned to Downing Street, where, in the Cabinet room, he went through my letter sentence by sentence, and scorched it. After this I went to the House of Commons and drank a quadruple whisky. Next day I received a red ink Minute from the Prime Minister: 'It would be very much better if you confined yourself to the work you have undertaken to do.' This marked a further deterioration in my relationship with Churchill. When, shortly afterwards, I introduced the

---

* It was abolished by a Conservative Government after the war. Mercifully, it has now been restored.

† Major-General Sir E. L. Spears.

estimates for the Ministry of Food to the House of Commons and, in the absence of the minister, had to open and close the debate, David Margesson, the Chief Whip, told me that when he reported to the Prime Minister that I had had a great success, he replied: 'I am sorry to hear it.'

Within hours of the French capitulation, Louis Spears invited me to lunch to meet what he called 'a French Brigadier whom I have just brought over from Bordeaux'. The Brigadier was de Gaulle; and the lunch party consisted of Spears, his wife (Mary Borden), de Gaulle, Mme. de Gaulle, and myself. Spears told us about their flight, how they had run out of petrol and had to make a forced landing in the Channel Islands with two minutes to spare. De Gaulle, who was going to make a broadcast that night, told us that he thought of saying: 'France has lost a battle, but not the war.' We all thought that this was very good. Later on Spears and de Gaulle quarrelled bitterly when Spears was head of a British Mission to the Levant, and tried – rightly – to ease the French out of Syria and the Lebanon. There is no doubt that, in addition to being a brave soldier and, with Liddell Hart, the most brilliant military historian of our time, Spears was a natural intriguer. What is equally beyond doubt is that, if he had not pulled de Gaulle into that aeroplane at Bordeaux, de Gaulle would never have been heard of. Spears, and Spears alone, created de Gaulle; and in so doing made history. De Gaulle knew it, and resented it. When Spears took him to see Churchill, the latter said: 'Why have you brought this lanky, gloomy Brigadier?' Spears replied: 'Because no one else would come.'

The Battle of Britain was certainly the most critical battle for this country since the Armada. We had no hope of beating the Luftwaffe. All we had to do was to survive until the autumn, when it would be too late for the Germans to invade this country from Holland and France; and this we did. I remember lying on the banks of the Thames with a girl-friend, on a lovely Sunday afternoon in September 1940. The air was filled with a throbbing noise; and far up in the blue sky we could see tiny flashes of flame, as if a match had been struck. That was the critical day on which the battle was decided. Very soon afterwards the Germans concluded that they could not achieve the complete air control over Britain they required,

and began to close down their airports in the Netherlands and
France and turn their eyes towards the east.

The treatment of the Commander-in-Chief Fighter Command, Dowding, after he had won the most critical battle for
this country since Drake, was so atrocious that it hardly bears
description. He may well have made mistakes. His two principal Group Commanders, Keith Park and Leigh-Mallory,
disagreed about tactics; and it has been argued that he should
have knocked their heads together, and forced them to con-
form to his own views, or go. Instead he let them both fight in
the way they wished. But all criticism fades before the victory
achieved under his supreme command. The story that immediately after the battle he was sacked over the telephone by the
Secretary of State, Sir Archibald Sinclair, is untrue. That
would have been entirely out of character. On the contrary,
Sinclair sent for Dowding to offer him his personal congratulations. This, however, did not prevent Dowding's headquarters
staff from being ordered to vacate their offices within forty-
eight hours, or the immediate dismissal of Dowding himself.
After that an enquiry was set up by the Air Ministry, to which
Dowding and Keith Park were summoned. There they found
themselves confronted by an array of Air Marshals, which included Leigh-Mallory. It was more like a court-martial than
an enquiry. Dowding as was his custom, said nothing. He just
disappeared. No one now maintains that he should not have
been relieved of his command after the appalling strain to
which he had been subjected, or that Sholto Douglas was not
his obvious successor. What is almost inconceivable is that he
was never made a Marshal of the Royal Air Force. Some years
later he was given a peerage; but by then he had been forgotten.

Then came the *blitz*. After Coventry, the East End of London
had to bear the brunt. Every night, from dusk to dawn the
German bombs fell upon them. Woolton suggested that I
might go down there every morning about six o'clock when
the 'All-clear' sounded, and see what I could do to help. I
found that, as they came out of the shelters, what comforted
them most was a kiss and a cup of tea. These were easily provided. Almost overnight I got the Ministry of Food to set
up canteens all over the East End, manned by voluntary work-

ers, where the tea was free. When we took them back to their homes, often reduced to rubble, their chief concern was what had happened to the cat. I am afraid that the cat searches which I tried to organize were less successful than the canteens. A number of people, including Kingsley Martin, the Editor of *The New Statesman* and Ritchie Calder, now Lord Ritchie-Calder, came down to help. But the dominant figure was a priest called Father Grozier. He never failed. He seemed to be everywhere all the time; and his very presence brought comfort, and revived confidence and courage, to thousands of people. Like the people of Buchan, the people of the East End of London – the true cockneys – are a race apart. Most of the men were dockers, all the women cosy. Taken as a whole, they were warm, affectionate, gay, rather reckless, and almost incredibly brave. Sometimes the language was pretty rough, but it was so natural and innocent that it never jarred. One day I came across a small boy crying. I asked him what the matter was, and he said: 'They burnt my mother yesterday.' Thinking it was in an air-raid, I said: 'Was she badly burned?' He looked up at me and said, through his tears: 'Oh yes. They don't fuck about in crematoriums.' I loved them, and I am glad to have been close to them in their hour of supreme trial.

The administration formed by Churchill in 1940 has been described as the 'Great Coalition'. It may have been great, but it was not a happy Government. Most of the ministers lived in constant dread of a red ink Minute from the Prime Minister, or the sack; and some of them got both. Of them all Archie Sinclair, the Secretary of State for Air, was my closest friend. He was conscientious, a tremendous worker, and popular in the Royal Air Force; but he was never able to stand up to Churchill. Otherwise he would have played a greater part than Lindemann in the strategic direction of the air war; and would never have allowed some of his Air Marshals, including Dowding at the beginning and Harris at the end of the war, to be treated as they were. Of the Labour leaders, Arthur Greenwood was the nicest, but apt to be tight. Ernest Bevin and Herbert Morrison loathed each other. The story that when someone remarked that Morrison was his own worst enemy, Bevin said, 'Not while I'm alive he ain't', is true. Attlee was allowed to play little part in the strategic direction of the war, and not much anywhere. When he was Chairman of an important Cabinet Committee dealing with home affairs, Churchill gave orders that none of their conclusions should be brought before the full Cabinet unless they had been approved by Beaverbrook and Bracken, neither of whom had taken part in the discussions. When, for once, Attlee sent a strong note of protest to the Prime Minister, all he got in reply was: 'I shall always endeavour to profit by your advice.' He did not come into his own until he himself became Prime Minister after the war. Sir John Anderson was an outstanding but ruthless administrator. He came from Edinburgh, and was the type of lowland Scot which I knew only too well, and never much liked. He will be remembered not only for his administrative capacity, but as the man who imprisoned more people without charge or trial than any other minister in British history. Many of them were drowned when they were shipped off to Canada. Stafford Cripps had a heart of gold, but he was an ascetic, a vegetarian, a teetotaller, and by nature a schoolmaster. By way of contrast, his elder brother, Fred, who was a great friend of mine, was self-indulgent, a brilliant shot, a superb fisherman, and by nature a gambler. They were very fond of each other. In the First World War Fred won the DSO for bravery in the field, and was the lover of our most popular revue actress, Teddie Gerard. One day I went into White's Club, and found them sitting together on the fender in the hall. Fred was wearing a startling check suit, and a gaily coloured bow tie. Stafford was in jet black. Fred was pink, and Stafford blue. I said to them: 'If I did not know the impeccable character of your parents [Lord and Lady Parmoor], I would not believe you were brothers.'

One of the ablest members of the Government was Moore-Brabazon – a first-rate politician; a first-rate golfer; and in his day the best tobogganist in the world, with many Cresta cups to his credit. As Minister of Aircraft Production, he made an indiscreet speech at a dinner which he thought was private, and was immediately sacked. Afterwards he said to me: 'There were one or two things I wanted to see through, but that always happens. As it is, I am glad to be out of it. There was a thing called the Atlantic Committee, of which I was a member.

It met once a fortnight, with the Prime Minister in the chair.
He was always edgy about the Battle of the Atlantic because
he knew that, under Lindemann's influence, long-distance
bombers were being prevented from pursuing the U-boats into
the Atlantic. The bullying, especially of Archie Sinclair, was
tremendous. Now I don't have to face that any more. And I am
grateful to Churchill for giving me a peerage. Unlike some
people, I think it is a nice thing to have.' In fact, Harold
Macmillan and Duff Cooper were the lucky ones. They were
both sent to North Africa, where they ran their own shows
without interference, and ran them very well.

Then, suddenly, a bomb was dropped on me. It did not
come from the sky. It came from No. 10 Downing Street.

Despite the services he had rendered over the attempted
purchase of arms, which might have been of crucial importance to this country, Richard Weininger was interned along
with all the rest under Regulation 18B. Although I was myself
a Minister of the Crown, they had the impudence to arrest him
in my flat. Before they took him away to prison he was allowed
to ring up his secretary, Miss Frances, and put me in charge of
all his papers. The following day she rang me up and said that
Scotland Yard had telephoned to say that they were coming
round to go through his papers two days later, and asked me
whether I thought I should have a look at them first. I asked
her whether there were any love letters, and she said no. I then
said that I was very busy at the Ministry of Food, but would
try to come round to have a look at them. Next day (the day
before the CID men arrived), I telephoned to her and told her
to give them the lot. This was scarcely the act of a man with
a guilt-laden conscience. At the same time I wrote an indig-
nant letter of protest against Weininger's internment to the
Home Secretary, Sir John Anderson. When, after about a
week, I received no reply to this, I told the Home Office that
I proposed to send a copy of it to the Prime Minister. Then the
Under-Secretary of State, Osbert Peake, rang me up and asked
me not to send the letter until I had had a talk with the Home
Secretary. I agreed to do this, and telephoned Brendan
Bracken, to whom I had sent my letter, to ask him not to give
it to the Prime Minister for the time being, because I thought
it conceivable that they might have something against Weinin-

ger of which I knew nothing. He told me that he had handed
it to him five minutes ago. Anderson then thought I had gone
back on my word, and sent to the Prime Minister the file of
my private correspondence with Weininger before the war,
when I was his banker. This showed that he had guaranteed
my losses on the Stock Exchange.

The next thing that happened was the arrival at the
Ministry of Food of a tough and rather menacing letter from
the Prime Minister by special messenger. On Woolton's advice, I replied to this briefly; and said that I would be glad to
see Churchill at any time in order to give a full explanation of
my business dealings with Weininger before the war, and to
answer any questions he might wish to put to me. When I got a
summons to Downing Street, I expected to find him alone.
Instead he was sitting at the Cabinet table with the Attorney-
General on his right, and a number of civil servants. He did
not ask me for any explanation. He simply said that he had
decided to set up a Select Committee of the House of Commons
to enquire into my conduct. Then I knew that, as Mosley had
predicted, he was out for the kill.

I do not propose now to describe this. It would bore my
readers, and indeed I hardly remember it. All I know is, that
from start to finish of the proceedings, I never knew what the
charge against me was. Eventually it turned out to be failure
to disclose a financial interest in a speech I had made before the
war, and long before I was a minister, advocating the distri-
bution of the Czech assets in this country to Czech citizens,
instead of handing them over to the Nazis after the occupation
of Prague as we had previously handed over £6 million in gold
to the Nazis after Munich. For not doing this the Committee
found that my conduct had been 'derogatory' to the standards
expected by the House of its Members. The single sentence,
'I have an interest to declare', would, it seems, have cleared
me. I can only say that it never occurred to me to say it. After
the war Speaker Morrison gave a ruling from the Chair. He
said that the Rule of the House regarding disclosure of interest applied only to votes, not to speeches. There was no vote on
the Czech assets. I went immediately to see him, and he agreed
with me that this threw a new light upon the conclusions of the
Select Committee in my case. But he strongly urged me to do

nothing about it. 'Your constituents,' he said, 'have since given their verdict. Let it go at that.' I accepted his advice.

For my part I am content to rely on two quotations from Lord Robert Cecil in his autobiography, *A Great Experiment*. About the enquiry into the Jameson Raid, in which he took part as counsel, he writes: 'A Select Committee of that kind is, I believe, almost the worst possible instrument for clearing up questions of personal responsibility.' And again about the Marconi Enquiry into the conduct of Mr Lloyd George and Sir Rufus Isaacs, when he was himself a member of the committee: 'The whole incident confirmed me in the view that, for what was in the nature of a judicial enquiry, no tribunal could be worse than a Select Committee of the House of Commons.'*

After the publication of the report, I resigned immediately as a minister. Colin Coote gave me good advice, and helped me to draft my letter of resignation. But the decisive factor was Lloyd George. From him I received a peremptory message to come down at once to Churt, and I did. He greeted me by saying: 'Churchill has behaved to you like the cad he is. If I had been there, this would never have happened.' Then he paced up and down the room, with blazing eyes, shaking his head, and pausing at intervals to speak in terms of imperious authority. It was the only time I ever saw him in anger. And I confess that, although I knew the anger was on my behalf, I was pretty frightened. I knew then why A. J. P. Taylor was subsequently to describe him as the greatest ruler of England since Cromwell. He said: 'Before the war your losses on the Stock Exchange were guaranteed by a friend. So were Churchill's. And quite rightly. When the Marconi case came up before the First World War Asquith, who owed me nothing, sent for me and asked me to tell him all about it. He listened for an hour to what I had to say; then he gave his judgement, which was that I had been foolish to buy those shares, but no-

* Lloyd George was accused of having bought shares in the Canadian Marconi Company, as Chancellor of the Exchequer, on the advice of Sir Rufus Isaacs (later Lord Reading), the Attorney-General, whose brother, Godfrey Isaacs, was Chairman of the parent company which had a contract with the Post Office. A Select Committee of the House of Commons was set up, which eventually exonerated both him and Isaacs by a majority. Lloyd George actually lost money on the transaction. But the whole affair caused him much strain and anxiety for many months.

thing more than that. He would therefore give me full support. Churchill, who owed you a lot, never even saw you. Now he is trying to destroy you. You are not the first, and you won't be the last. Don't let him. If he tries it in the House of Commons, I will come up and speak myself; and he won't like it. [He repeated this later to his private secretary, Sylvester.] Meanwhile go to your constituency, and tell them the truth. If they stand by you, he won't be able to break you.' The words of his final sentence were identical to those which Lord Birkenhead had spoken to me nearly twenty years before.

Driving back to London, I reached the conclusion that the relationship between these two titans was based on mutual admiration and mutual fear, but not on mutual affection. Sure enough, when I reached my flat, I found a message from the Chief Whip (James Stuart) saying that he would like to see me as soon as possible. I asked him to come round at once, and when he arrived he said: 'The Prime Minister wants to know whether you intend to leave the House of Commons.' I said: 'Never.' The flicker of a smile crossed his face. 'I told him that would be your answer,' he said, 'and that it was a waste of my time coming to see you.'

I then went straight to my constituency and got, as usual, an overwhelming vote of confidence from my Association. When the meeting was over the wife of my Chairman, Lady Duff, said: 'Give the figures to the press.' I knew that my political fate depended upon the speech I made to the House of Commons in the debate on the Report of the Select Committee in 1940. Simon Harcourt-Smith invited me to his home in the country to compose it. My two oldest friends, Roger Senhouse and John Strachey, came to my flat to take me down to the House. At the last moment John said that he could not face it. So Roger alone took me, leaving him with a bottle of sherry. At the House I found Walter Elliot, in the uniform of a Colonel, awaiting me. He had travelled all through the night from the north of England to sit by my side. The only thing that disconcerted me when I entered the packed House (Wendell Wilkie, the Presidential candidate of the United States was in the gallery) was that James Maxton, whose regard I set great store by, scowled at me. When I had finished by speech and left the Chamber, there was a subdued but sustained cheer from both sides; and Maxton gave me one of his unforgettable smiles. In the Lobby outside, Kingsley Wood, the Chancellor of the Exchequer, came up to me and said: 'The Select Committee never heard anything like that.' I then went back to my flat with Roger Senhouse. We found John Strachey still sitting there, with the bottle empty. 'It's all right,' said Roger, 'he's saved himself.'

I had quite a number of letters from ministers. Perhaps the nicest of all was one from Ellen Wilkinson; but as they were all marked 'private' I cannot quote them. All I know is that Kingsley Wood, as Chancellor of the Exchequer, put in a strong memorandum in which he said that he could see no reason for taking any action against me; that Lord Simon, the Lord Chancellor, who was widely blamed for seeking revenge against me because of my opposition to his foreign policy before the war, had nothing to do with it; and that the final decision was taken by the Prime Minister himself. Clearly he was in one of his rougher moods, which, at that particular moment, was hardly surprising. I was told that at a lunch at Downing Street, at which Mrs Churchill, Beaverbrook and Bracken all opposed what he intended to do, he got up and left the room. He certainly held out no helping hand. He upbraided Archie Sinclair for offering me a commission in the Royal Air Force; he sent me no line of sympathy when my father died; and when Malcolm Bullock asked him what he thought I ought to do, he said: 'Join a bomb disposal squad!' On the other hand Brendan Bracken characteristically wrote to me: 'You are indeed a man of sorrows. Your father was one of the nicest men I have ever known. Alas, he died before he could see your recovery. Your mother will.'

For my part I had to take a lot, and can only claim that I managed to stick it out. My stoical philosophy saw me through. I had no illusions about death, or luck – or indeed about Churchill. I knew, for certain, that the former were part of life, and therefore unavoidable: and that Churchill alone was the Man for the Hour. The thought that I had been able to help thousands of Czech refugees to start a new life in freedom was a consolation; but the thought that I had been able to play a small part in getting him there, in the nick of time, an even greater one. Once, when I asked General Ismay why, after all this, he had not dropped me altogether, he said: 'You know that the only thing he admired in life was guts. He might have thought you had some.'

After a brief but tough training at the RAF station in Loughborough, I found myself a Pilot Officer, and was posted to an embarkation unit near Liverpool – destination Malta. Then someone changed his mind. I was ordered to report to the Air Ministry, and sent to a station in Bomber Command at Honington, where I very soon found myself Adjutant of Number 9 Bomber Squadron, with the rank of Flight Lieutenant. The motto of the squadron was: 'There's always bloody something.' There was.

I was fortunate in having as my Squadron Commanders Wasse and Inness (later to be one of Harris's right-hand men at Bomber Command Headquarters); and, in my squadron, one of the greatest of our air aces – Pickard. When I last saw him in London he was a Group Captain, covered with DSOs and DFCs. He said to me: 'I've been grounded.' I replied: 'High time.' He went on: 'Ask your friend Archie Sinclair to let me fly again. I'm no good out of the air.' They let him. He led a precision raid on a prison in France in which we knew that many British prisoners-of-war were detained, in order to blow up the walls and allow them to escape. The raid was completely successful; but, characteristically, he flew back to see what had happened, with a Messerschmitt on his tail, and was shot down.

One day I was rung up by a Wing Commander at Group Headquarters. He told me that they were putting on the first thousand-bomber raid that night, against Cologne; and that they needed every available aircraft. He added: 'According to our records here, you have twelve.' I said: 'Unfortunately we are short of a navigator, so we can only manage eleven.' About an hour later he rang up again and said: 'I have good news for you. A Warrant Officer who has already done one tour of duty has just returned from leave. He is one of the best navigators we have got. And I'm sending him over to you immediately by car. All you need to do is to introduce him to the captain of the aircraft, and take him to the briefing.' Soon afterwards there was a knock on my door, and a very smart

Warrant Officer wearing the DSM came in and saluted. I said: 'We are very glad to see you. The raid tonight is on Cologne, with which you will be familiar. I will now take you over and introduce you to your Captain.' He said: 'Thank you, sir. But I'm afraid there is a snag.' 'What do you mean?' I asked. He replied: 'I have done one tour of duty. If I do another I know I shall be killed. I have decided, therefore, never to leave the earth again. Not even in a Moth.' I said. 'You realize, Warrant Officer, that this is a very serious matter. It could mean your relegation to the rank of AC2.' He said: 'I do, and am prepared to face it.' And face it he did. I then rang up the Wing Commander at Group and thanked him for sending me the Warrant Officer. He said: 'I knew you would be pleased. With his experience you have no cause for anxiety.' 'Only one,' I said; 'he never intends to leave the earth again, not even in a Moth.'

I soon came to the conclusion that the policy of area bombing of Germany, then being pursued mainly by Wellington bombers, was not paying off, because the expenditure of our resources and, still more, of our skilled manpower, was far greater than the results achieved. Too many of our bombs were dropped in fields. German arms production was not being seriously interfered with. The best that could be said for it was that a considerable number of Goering's fighter aircraft, which might have been sent to other fronts, had to be kept in Germany. The truth is that in those days the instruments for accurate navigation did not exist. There were high hopes of one gadget, which I did not begin to understand; and which was brought to us one day in a brand-new Wellington bomber. All the navigators in the squadron went up to see how it worked. Five minutes after take-off, a wing fell off the plane, and they were all killed. After that the Station Commander sent for me and said: 'I'm now going to give you the most difficult order you have ever received. You have got to be cheerful at lunch in the Mess.'

I sometimes wondered whether I could do anything about it all; and decided, rightly, that I could do nothing. I knew that I, like everyone connected with Bomber Command, was under considerable emotional stress. Seeing the crews on most evenings at their dispersal stations, watching them take off with winking lights; and then the dawn vigil, wondering how many would return. Seven, eight, nine? Or only three or four? For the crews themselves the psychological strain was almost intolerable. For the soldiers and sailors continuously at war, battle was only an intensification of their normal life. The bomber crews who lived in great comfort, in the depths of the peaceful, beautiful English countryside, were hurled at intervals into hell, which they reached in two or three hours; and from which they returned to an excellent breakfast of bacon and eggs in a charming country house; or never returned at all.

Early in 1942, Lindemann, by then a member of the Cabinet, circulated his famous paper on strategic bombing. This said that if it was concentrated entirely on German working class houses, and 'military objectives' as such were forgotten, it would be possible to destroy fifty per cent of all the houses in the larger towns of Germany quite soon. Charming! The paper was strongly opposed by the scientists, headed by Sir Henry Tizard and Professor Blackett. Tizard calculated that Lindemann's estimate was five times too high, and Blackett that it was six times too high. But Lindemann was Churchill's man; and Lindemann prevailed. After the war the bombing survey revealed that his estimate was ten times too high. The story of the Lindemann–Tizard controversy has been well told by C. P. Snow in his book *Science and Government*; and I have not seen it seriously contradicted. But one thing remains to be said. I think the scientists underestimated the psychological effect of our bombing policy not upon the German but upon the British people. They themselves were under heavy bombardment; and between 1941 and 1944 bombing was the only method by which we could directly hit back. I am sure that it gave a tremendous boost to British morale; and that, to this extent at least, the thousands of brave and skilled young men in Bomber Command did not give their lives in vain.

As a Member of Parliament I had direct access to the Secretary of State for Air. I never sought it. But I think the Commander-in-Chief may have heard that some people (not necessarily myself, but perhaps friends of mine) were not happy about our strategic bombing policy. Anyway, to my great personal regret, but I think rightly, I was posted to

Training Command. There again I was most fortunate in my Commanding Officer, 'Turkey' Rainsford. He said that, although I was the worst Adjutant in the Royal Air Force, he would rather have me than anyone else. He went on to win the DFC as a bomber pilot, and after the war to be given the CBE for his brilliant work in organizing the Berlin air-lift; and we have remained friends ever since. He once told me that George Mackie, now Lord Mackie of Benshie, and one of a famous Aberdeenshire family who, like Pickard, was covered with DSOs and DFCs, was the bravest man he had ever known. He had flown far more sorties than he need have done, and was afraid of nothing. I asked Rainsford whether he was a good navigator. He thought for a moment, then smiled and said: 'One night he couldn't find Africa.' I was lucky again in my Station Commander, a brilliant Irishman called Taaffe. He used to take me over quite often from Luffenham to a satellite station a few miles away for drinks after dinner. Driving back one snowy evening I said to him: 'Sir, the road seems to have become very bumpy. Don't you think we ought to stop, and see where we are?' He agreed. We got out, and found ourselves in the middle of a ploughed field.

When General Legentilhomme asked me to help him in his work for the Free French, I asked Taaffe what he thought I ought to do. He then gave me the best piece of advice I have ever had. 'All we can offer you,' he said, 'is the post of Squadron-Leader Admin.; and I can imagine no more boring job. I think you should go and do what you can to help General Legentilhomme. More than that, I think you should go back to the House of Commons, where you can do better work for the country. You have the right to do so, and I will sign the necessary papers today.' Thus ended my brief but intense experience of the Royal Air Force. I look back on it with feelings of pride, emotion and profound admiration.

Meanwhile the fall of Tobruk had brought about a political crisis. Churchill had to come back from the United States to face what amounted to a vote of no confidence in his Government, moved by an influential Conservative backbencher, Sir John Wardlaw-Milne. There was a three-line whip, and I went to London to vote.

I lunched in the House of Commons. Churchill, whom I had

not seen or heard from since my case, was sitting alone in a corner of the dining-room. To my amazement he beckoned to me to come over. It was the only time during the war that I saw him looking anxious. 'This,' he said, 'is going to be a critical debate. Do you still support the Government?' I said that I did. Then: 'Do you still support me?' I said: 'I have no reason to, but there is no one else.' Then he said: 'Will you speak in the debate?' I replied that I had brought some notes. Whereupon he took me straight to the Speaker, and told him that he would like me to be called fifth in the debate. It was not one of my worst speeches. Churchill himself described it in *The Second World War* as 'powerful and helpful'. What I managed to do was to change the atmosphere of the House from one of tension to relaxation. I made them laugh. In this I was greatly assisted by Wardlaw-Milne who, in an otherwise effective speech, had suggested that the Duke of Gloucester should be made Commander-in-Chief of all our forces.

Later Churchill asked me and Oliver Lyttelton to have a drink in the Smoking-Room, and proposed a toast to 'the Pegasus wings of Bob's oratory'. He got an overwhelming majority. Next day he sent me a telegram of thanks to my Air Force station; and then didn't speak to me again for a year. I had done my job.

I worked closely with General Legentilhomme, on behalf of the Free French; and after the successful invasion of western Europe in 1944, I obtained the permission of the Speaker, rarely given, to move the adjournment of the House on 'a definite matter of urgent public importance', namely 'the refusal of His Majesty's Government to allow General de Gaulle to go to France'. Churchill, awoken from his afternoon sleep, came down to the House in a towering rage. Glaring at me across the despatch box, he said: 'If the Hon. Member insists on this debate, I shall move that the House goes into secret session.' I said that that was not my objective, and withdrew my motion. But one week later de Gaulle was allowed to land in France. There, by eluding the American armies, he reached Paris in time to lead the procession celebrating its liberation, under fire, to Notre Dame. This may well have led to his election as Prime Minister of France. So far as I was concerned, his reaction was characteristic. He never thanked me. All he did was to say to Legentilhomme: 'I see your friend Boothby has been kicking up a fuss about me in the House of Commons.'

After this fierce and final clash with Churchill, David Kirkwood came up to me with an anxious look, put his arm round my shoulder, and said: 'Bob, that man doesn't like you. Be careful. He could do you great harm.' I thanked him for his kindness and concern, but added, 'I don't think that, in the long run, he will.'

Throughout the war a few of us kept up a running fight in the House of Commons against the continued imprisonment of people without charge or trial under the monstrous Defence Regulation 18B, which reached its peak in 1940, but never stopped. We thought that that was what we were fighting to prevent. We were an oddly assorted little group, consisting of Sir Irving Albery, Sir Archibald Southby, Richard Stokes, Robert Bower, Sydney Silverman, and myself. We were unsuccessful because Herbert Morrison, who succeeded Anderson as Home Secretary, was not much better. But we tried; and kept a small lamp of freedom alight in the long dark night of total war. I myself went to see Tom Mosley in prison. The Governor said: 'I'm afraid I shall have to sit with you, but I shan't interrupt. When you want to go, blow your nose.' I said: 'I don't think I will do that, because he is an old friend.' To this he replied: 'You will, because after a time he becomes a bore about being kept in prison indefinitely; and I don't blame him.' Eventually I blew my nose.


Sometimes, when the raids were bad, I used to go to the Dorchester Hotel, more for company than safety. Everyone in London seemed to be there. And at intervals we all trooped down to the Turkish bath, which we thought was a shelter. One night when I was coming down in the lift with the Chief of the Air Staff, Portal, he said to me: 'Don't tell them. But in fact they are not under the hotel at all. They are one foot under the pavement outside. If a bomb falls on them, they will all be killed.' Another night, during the worst of the raids on the West End, when the bombs were coming down like tennis balls, I took refuge in the Ritz, and found myself lying on the floor

of the restaurant with Lord and Lady Kemsley, David Margesson (then Secretary of State for War), and Beverley Baxter.
After the raid was over the manager asked Baxter and myself
whether we would like to go up to the roof and look at the fires.
It was an astonishing sight. All Jermyn Street seemed to be
ablaze. It was the night Maples furniture store went up in
flames. I murmured to Beverley '*Götterdämmerung*'; and, rather
unfairly I thought, he used this without acknowledgement in
an article he wrote two days later.

If I had been a minister at the time of Yalta, I should have
resigned, as Harry Strauss (later Lord Conesford) did. The
betrayal of Czechoslovakia at Munich was bad enough. The
betrayal of all the countries of central Europe, including
Poland (for whom we had gone to war), was worse. I was in
America when Franklin Roosevelt died. The shock was great.
In 1940, when the United States as well as ourselves were in
dire peril, and he realized it, he gave us all the help he could.
In his final term of office as President, for which he should
never have stood, he wanted to give half Europe to Stalin, and
to bring the British Empire to an end. He succeeded in both.
But historians may judge that neither was of great benefit to
humanity.

I have said that, from 1935 to 1939, the political leaders of this
country were, with the exception of Winston Churchill and
Leo Amery, frightened men. With the shining exception of the
*Daily Telegraph*, the press too was bright yellow. Under the
leadership of *The Times* (Dawson and Barrington-Ward) Fleet
Street, from Right to Left, did everything in its power to help
Neville Chamberlain and his wretched Government turn the
whole country yellow. Even Kingsley Martin, the editor of the
*New Statesman*, who had written so vehemently about standing
up to the aggressors, buckled over Munich – and was later
ashamed of it. Churchill's supreme achievement, amounting to
a miracle, was to turn the British in 1940, within a few weeks
and single-handed, once again into a brave people; and, by so
doing, to save western civilization.

Although, under his inspired leadership, we refused to recog-
nize it, Hitler had in fact won the war by mid-summer of that

year. He was master of Europe as no one had been since Caesar. Britain alone stood against him. And, except in Africa, there was nothing we could do. Then Hitler made his first fatal mistake. I think that A. J. P. Taylor has given the true reason for his attack on Russia which, as so often happens in life, is the simplest. His generals had been apprehensive about the invasion of the Low Countries and France. He had then taken control himself. He ordered them to forget the Schlieffen Plan for a drive down the coast, to ignore the Maginot Line, to break through in the Ardennes and at Sedan, and then to march straight to Paris. He was brilliantly successful. This time he was advised by his generals that the attack on Russia would be a push-over. He would be in Moscow in three weeks; and get all the oil and grain he needed. It didn't happen that way. Leningrad, Moscow and Stalingrad all held. And, after this, his armour was defeated in the battle of Kursk.

When the Japanese attacked the American fleet at Pearl Harbor, Hitler immediately declared war on the United States. This was final proof that his undoubted genius was accompanied by insanity. A long struggle lay ahead, but there was no longer any doubt about the final outcome; and both Roosevelt and Churchill could feel absolutely sure of their political power so long as the war lasted. Sir Leslie (Dick) Plummer, who ran the business side of Beaverbrook newspapers, told me after the war that Beaverbrook himself did not think that Churchill could survive the fall of Tobruk and Singapore, and had set up a committee to plan a campaign to put forward his own claims to the succession when the time came. I said to him: 'Dick, I can believe a lot, but I can't believe that. How do you know that such a committee ever existed?' 'Because I was its chairman,' he replied.

Churchill was shaken by the sinking of the *Prince of Wales* and *Repulse*, for which he was personally responsible; and his political power gradually diminished as that of Stalin and Roosevelt increased. But as Prime Minister he was never seriously threatened until after Germany had been defeated. He once talked to me, when the war was over and he was out of power, about the position he would ultimately occupy in history; and I said that nothing could take from him the fact that he had saved Britain in 1940. He then said, rather sadly:

'Historians are apt to judge war ministers less by the victories achieved under their direction than by the political results which flowed from them. Judged by that standard, I am not sure that I shall be held to have done very well.'

# INTERLUDE THREE
# Musicians and Writers

In 1945 I spent most of my time in the United States. First I was asked to do a lecture tour; and from that I went on as a journalist, to represent the *News of the World* at the conference in San Francisco which set up the United Nations Organization.

I crossed the Atlantic to the United States in the *Queen Mary*. We were still at war; and she was being used to bring American troops over to Europe, and to take wounded officers and men back to the United States. We left Clydebank at twenty-nine knots, and for the first hundred miles were escorted by *Sunderland* aircraft. There were only about half-a-dozen passengers, who included Sir Thomas Beecham and his wife Betty Humby; Malcolm Sargent; Katherine Cornell, the famous American actress; and myself. We sat at the same table and had one good meal (breakfast, lunch and dinner combined) a day. As we sat down to the first, Beecham opened the conversation by saying to Malcolm Sargent; 'I know you've been doctored, but why have they never made you a knight?' This was a sore point, because the knighthood had been too long delayed; and I said to myself, like Bette Davis: 'Fasten your seat-belt; this is going to be a bumpy ride.' But after that it was sunshine all the way. We took about seven days to reach New York, because we moved at high speed all over the Atlantic. One day we would find ourselves in freezing cold near the Arctic. Next day we would be in tropical heat, surrounded by flying fish. The night before we got to New York, we had a brains trust. I was the question-master, and I put one of my own. 'To what extent was Richard Wagner responsible for the Nazi movement?' In all my life I have not heard two more brilliant speeches than those which were made by Beecham and Sargent. Needless to say, Wagner was completely exonerated. Not only *Meistersinger, Tristan,* and *Lohengrin,* but the *Ring* itself, were the antithesis of everything the Nazis stood for. The packed audience of wounded American soldiers, most of whom had never heard of Wagner, sat spell-bound.

In New York Malcolm Sargent, who had come over to con-duct the NBC Orchestra, took me one evening to see Toscanini. He said he would like to play to us a record he had just finished of Debussy's *La Mer.* He put it on and, when it was over, both Malcolm and I were in tears. Toscanini looked at us sharply, and said: 'Cheer up! I will cheer you up.' He then went over to the gramophone and put on a rousing Sousa march. 'I love them,' he said. Beecham went off to conduct concerts in vari-ous states. It was sometimes said of him that Beethoven was beyond his compass. But a few days later I read an article in the *New York Times* by Virgil Thomson, a severe critic if ever there was one, in which he wrote: 'Last night Sir Thomas Beecham brought some kind of a brass band from Rochester to the Carnegie Hall, and gave the finest performance of the *Eroica* I have ever heard.'

This seems to be a convenient place at which to digress from the main story and to remember the musicians and writers whom I have known well. There has never been a time when music was not important to me.

When I was a small boy at a private school in Rottingdean the music master, a man called Holmyard, who was also the brilliant organist of one of the largest churches in Brighton, took me aside one day and said: 'You have just about the best treble voice I have ever heard. Take no credit for it. You did not make it, it was given to you. You've also been given a very good ear. This means that you have no need to learn to play an instrument – you already have one, and perhaps the best. It also means that you will be able to read a score with the minimum of effort. As you are both lazy and conceited, it all adds up to the fact that music will play a great part in your life.' At the lovely parish church in Rottingdean I led the choir, and much enjoyed reducing the old girls in the pew to tears with *Oh! For the Wings of a Dove* before I went back to suck a bulls-eye. At Eton I won the school singing prize with a song called *Rose in the Bud* and Roger Quilter's setting of *Now Sleeps the Crimson Petal*.

Few people now alive can have heard Paderewski play the piano, or Enrico Caruso sing. Thanks to my mother, I heard both. I was interested to read a comment recently made by Artur Rubinstein, our greatest living pianist, about Paderewski. He said that, technically, he was not a very good pianist; but that he was something far more than that. He was a very great man. And it came through.

Beecham once said to me that there has never been a voice to approach Caruso's. As a boy I heard him sing *Ché gelida manina*. It remains the most unforgettable experience of my life. The world stood still. I can hear it now: *Aspetti Signorina*. He had the sob in his voice that the Italians alone have. Gigli had it, and Gobbi. So have the gondoliers in Venice, and the fishermen in the Bay of Naples.

Opera has played a great part in my life. *Die Meistersinger* is my favourite, because every time I get something new from it. I must have heard it about thirty times. The best performance I have ever heard was in Munich, under Knappertsbusch. *Tristan* is another. The greatest Isolde – greater than Flagstad – I have ever heard was Leider, in Bayreuth; and the finest Tristan Frank Mullings, a name now forgotten. I was delighted to find that Thomas Beecham agreed with me about this. He said:

The value of Mullings's interpretation of Tristan was that while the music was sung with greater vitality and tenderness than by any other artist I have heard, the whole part was endowed with a high nobility, an almost priestly exaltation of mood, and a complete absence of any wallowing in the sty of merely fleshly obsession. The general effect was one of rapt absorption in an other-worldly fantasy, hopeless of realization on this earth; and this I believe to have been Wagner's own conception.

The greatest piece of acting I have ever seen, on the operatic or any other stage, was by Callas in *Tosca* – when, suddenly, she sees the knife on the writing-table with which she is going to kill Scarpia. Rather to my surprise I bumped into Eddie Sackville-West, a severe musical highbrow, as we were leaving the opera house. He said: 'We shall never see anything like that again.'

At one time I believe I was considered for appointment as a director of Covent Garden. Anyway, I was invited one evening by the Chairman, Lord Drogheda, to his box. It was for a performance of *Götterdämmerung* by the Leipzig opera, under a conductor whose name I now forget. When it was over he asked me whether I had enjoyed it. I said: 'Enormously. I have just seen a man do something that I have always wanted to do more than anything else in life – conduct the last act of *Götterdämmerung* when I was drunk.' I was not offered a directorship. But afterwards Sir David Webster, the General Administrator of Covent Garden, said to me: 'You should not have said that. But in fact you were right. He drank a bottle of hock before it started, and another one between each act.'

For twenty years my musical life was dominated, and indeed governed, by Sir Thomas Beecham. I had access to all his rehearsals; and dined with him frequently – sometimes alone. He explained to me why on the one hand I loved Sibelius and on the other Grieg, in a single word – Nordic; and went on to tell me why this led inevitably to Debussy and Delius. I was delighted when I found that Grieg came from my constituency, East Aberdeenshire. His original name was Greig; his family changed it to Grieg only when they went to Norway. His ancestors are buried in the churchyard of the village of Rathen.

Of Delius, Beecham once said to me: 'Opinions are bound to differ, and widely. For myself I cannot say other than that I regard him as the last great apostle in our time of romance, emotion and beauty in music. There is in him so much melody that you have to keep a tight hold on the melodic line in order to control it.' When he was taking a rehearsal for the Delius Festival which he had organized, a bar in the score was obscure. He stopped the orchestra, turned round, and said: 'Frederick, what note do you want played here?' Delius who was sitting, blind and paralysed, in the front row, said: 'I haven't the faintest idea.'

All the stories about Beecham are true. I witnessed many of them, and am now happy to leave them to Archie Newman.* But there are two which I must record, because I think they are not generally known. One day I met him and said: 'That was a terrible thing that happened to Malcolm Sargent.' He said: 'What is it? I haven't read the newspapers.' I replied: 'His convoy was ambushed and shot up yesterday by the Arabs on its way from Jerusalem to Tel Aviv. The tyres were punctured, but they escaped unhurt.' The familiar twinkle came into his eye, and he said: 'How interesting! I had no idea the Arabs were so musical.' But he had a far greater regard, and indeed affection for Sargent than Malcolm himself ever realized. He once said to me: 'Don't tell him this, because he might take it amiss; but I think he will go down in history as one of the greatest choir-masters we have ever produced; and that is what, as a nation, we are best at. I can do it sometimes – for instance in the last act of *Die Meistersinger*. He can do it always. He makes them sing like blazes.'

On another occasion, when he was conducting *Siegfried* at Covent Garden, he gave a superb performance of the first two acts, but conducted the third at breakneck speed, so that the singers could not keep up. Next day he was severely taken to task by Neville Cardus, the music critic, his great friend and ultimate biographer. Characteristically, he gave orders that Cardus should not be allowed in to any more of his performances; and this lasted for several months. Next time I saw him I asked him what had really happened. He stroked his beard, and said: 'Wagner was apt to go on too long. I knew that many of my audience were commuters, with last trains to catch. So, at the beginning of the last act, I said to myself: "Whoops! I'll get the buggers home." And I did.'

I enjoyed talking to Beecham more than anyone except Lloyd George. His favourite niece Audrey lived next door to me at Lympne when she was a little girl. I loved her, but she never knew it. She is now the distinguished head of the Nightingale College in the University of Nottingham. Only once did Beecham talk to me with sadness. It was about Puccini, for

* *Beecham Stories*, Robson Books, 1978.

whom he had a tremendous affection and regard. He told me
that, despite all his success, he was at heart an unhappy man;
and that he was the most *effective* opera composer because 'he
speaks to us personally in a way we all understand'.

When all is said and done, Beecham was the greatest maker
of music this country has ever produced.

'I like,' he would say, 'a good tune. Your American friends
could write them. Now we don't get them any more. Modern
music is a cacophony of raucous dissonance.' There have been
moments when I have thought that, with the exception of
Walton, he was right. Once, when I went to a concert at the
Albert Hall, they played a piece of very modern music in the
second half, and brought every kind of instrument on to the
platform, including a coal-scuttle and a pair of tongs. On my
way out I passed a box in which a member of the orchestra was
standing alone with a trumpet. I said to him: 'What are you
doing here?' He replied: 'God alone knows.'

Towards the end, when Beecham shuffled on to the platform
in what looked like snowboots, and appeared to collapse into
the conductor's chair, I sometimes said to myself: 'At last he's
finished.' A minute later he sprang to his feet, called the orchestra to attention, and the magic began. Once, at the Edinburgh
Festival, he did something that I have never seen before or
since in a concert hall. He played Delius's *In a Summer Garden*.
At the end there was no applause. The ravishing sound he
produced reduced his Usher Hall audience to stricken silence.
Sargent and Barbirolli caught Delius, and Sir Charles Groves
and Sir Alexander Gibson still catch him; but Beecham was
part of him. Now that he is gone, I don't think we shall ever
hear the authentic voice of Delius again.

The last time I heard Barbirolli conduct, shortly before he
died, was in the courtyard of the Palace of Monaco. Afterwards
I took my wife round to see him. He said: 'Did you enjoy the
concert?' My wife replied 'Immensely.' 'In that case,' he said,
'I will give you a present,' and he handed her his baton. It is
one of our most treasured possessions.

After Beecham died, it was found that he had expressed a
wish that I should become Chairman of the Royal Philharmonic Orchestra, and I did. It was hard going. I found myself
wondering, and sometimes I still wonder, whether any city –

even London – could sustain indefinitely five major symphony orchestras. Then we were approached by Covent Garden, who were undermanned and overworked, with the idea of amalgamation. A massive orchestra, which would play at Covent Garden and also give symphony concerts, and collar all the recording, on the lines of the Vienna Philharmonic. To begin with I was attracted by the idea; but the orchestra would have none of it, and in retrospect I think they were right. Nevertheless the situation was pretty desperate until one night I had an inspiration. I had known the Queen Mother for many years, and I knew that she was a lover of music and had a great admiration for the Royal Philharmonic Orchestra. I asked her if she would become Patron of the orchestra; and rather to my surprise, but to my absolute delight, she accepted. The Conservative Home Secretary, Henry Brooke, had announced to the House of Commons that the orchestra had no right to use the title Royal. On the recommendation of a Labour Home Secretary, Roy Jenkins, the Queen restored it. As for the Queen Mother, she saved the orchestra. Of all the manifold public services she has rendered to the country, this is not the least. Today it is generally acknowledged to be one of the great orchestras of the world.

As Holmyard predicted, music has played a great, perhaps the predominant, part in my life. But I have had my fill of it, and can take no more. With Sibelius, Elgar, Debussy, Delius, Kern and Gershwin, I stop. Together with the great romantic composers of the nineteenth century, they will see me out. But before I end this chapter I must tell an enchanting story, which I hope is not apocryphal. When Elgar composed his violin concerto he asked Yehudi Menuhin, then a boy, to come down to the west country and play it with an orchestra conducted by himself. They played it straight through, without a break. Then Elgar said: 'That'll do. Now we can go to the races.'

My closest friends in the literary world have been Somerset Maugham and Compton Mackenzie, known to all his friends as Monty. They didn't like each other much. From Capri, Monty tried to stop Maugham getting married to Syrie Barnado. Years later, he said to me: 'It was the only time in his life that Willie behaved like a gentleman; and the result was fatal.' During the war I went to stay with Monty Macken-zie in his island home at Barra, in the Hebrides. I sent him a telegram to say that I was bringing a mutual girl-friend of ours called Araminta. The postmistress in Barra had never heard the name Araminta, and changed it to Armaments. When the boat came alongside at the pier in Northbay, we found Monty, who was commanding the Home Guard, awaiting us with his troops in uniform, and an ammunition cart. I told him that, if the Germans landed, Araminta would be worth more than all the rifles I could have brought.

Monty led an extraordinary life. He wrote most of the night, slept for most of the morning, and talked for the rest of the day. He once said to me: 'Your incorrigible habit is sleep.' I stayed at Suidheachan for Christmas and the New Year during what was, for me, the critical winter of 1940–1. In the morning I used to go and spear scallops, and in the evening tramp for cockles, both of which were plentiful; and which his secretary and subsequent wife, Chrissie, cooked beautifully. One evening he picked up his book, *Extraordinary Women*, and began to read it aloud. It was about lesbianism in Capri. Suddenly, he put it down, convulsed with laughter, and said: 'I had no idea I was so brilliant.' He had several hundred gramophone records, which he constantly played; and, sitting on the Aga stove in the kitchen, I found twelve Siamese cats.

As against Maugham, Monty was hopeless about money. He wrote a book called *Whisky Galore*, based on fact, which was subsequently made into a film, in which he himself played a part. It swept the world. If he had asked for a royalty, he would have become a very rich man. Instead he sold all his rights for a few thousand pounds. It was in the aftermath of the sinking of *The Politician* in a fog, laden with whisky, that I went to Barra. The crofters had dived for it for days, except on Sundays; and were still rather tight. I found, rather to my surprise, that it was a purely Catholic island. On Christmas Eve Monty took me to dine with the senior Father. The outside of his house looked like a typical Scottish manse, but the inside was very different. We started with the best dry martinis I have ever drunk, and went on to the best Veuve Cliquot I have ever tasted. As he raised his glass over the latter, our host said:

'You must sometimes be glad, Mr Boothby that the Reformation never reached this part of the Outer Hebrides.' I was also invited by another Father, one of the most renowned Gaelic scholars in Scotland, to come and have a drink. When I arrived he said: 'I've sent for a bottle of "the Boy" [whisky], and it'll be here in ten minutes. Meanwhile we'll have to put up with Communion wine.' He then went over to a shrine in the corner, and took out from under a statuette of the Virgin Mary a decanter of wine. He poured out two glasses, and as he brought them over, he looked at me. 'Don't be alarmed,' he said. 'It's not The Host yet.' This is the nearest I ever came to submission to Rome.

Monty's literary career had its ups and downs. It started with a blaze before the First World War. *Sinister Street*, by far the best account of Edwardian Oxford, *Sylvia Scarlett*, *Guy and Pauline*, and *Carnival*, when he was held by many (including Henry James), to be the rising star among British novelists. Then, with the war, there came a pause; and after it *Gallipoli Memories*, *Athenian Memories*, and *Greek Memories*. The last gave rise to a famous case, which has been well described by Montgomery Hyde in his book *Crime Has Its Heroes* (Constable). He was charged under the Official Secrets Act with having revealed the name of the Head of the Secret Service during the war, then known as 'C'. The real reason was because he had attacked Sir Basil Thomson, who was Director of Intelligence at Scotland Yard from 1919 to 1922. The magistrate at the Guildhall was about to dismiss the case when he was reminded by the Clerk of the Court that the Attorney-General had issued his *fiat*, which meant that the case must be tried by the High Court. The Attorney-General was Sir Thomas Inskip, and he made a fool of himself. At the subsequent trial before Mr Justice Hawke, when Monty was brilliantly defended by Sir Henry Curtis-Bennett and St John Hutchinson, Sir Ian Hamilton himself gave evidence on Monty's behalf, and Inskip was constantly interrupted by an increasingly irritated judge. Finally Monty was given a derisory fine of £100.

Long after the Second World War, when he was Prime Minister in the 1950s, Churchill, who knew that Monty was a great friend of mine, told me that he had been reading *Gallipoli Memories* again, and that he much admired Mackenzie's work. I said: 'You know why he has never been given an honour?

Because of that ridiculous case when he was charged with re- vealing the name of "C" ten years after he was dead.' 'I don't believe it,' he said. But the following day he said to me: 'I have made enquiries, and found that what you told me about Compton Mackenzie is true.' He was knighted in the next Honours List, together with my old tutor Lewis Namier; and after the Investiture at Buckingham Palace I gave a small celebration party for them both. There could hardly have been a more incongruous couple, but they got on like a house on fire. At the end Lewis Namier said: 'And now the knights must go home to wash the dishes.'

The writer who has exercised a greater influence over me than any other is William Somerset Maugham; and the reason for this is that he made me see life as he himself saw it. I never stayed with him at the Villa Mauresque because he was a dis- ciplinarian, who insisted on punctuality; but I went there often over many years, and he always came to see me when he was in London. He was fortunate in having two secretaries through- out his life who were, for him, quite invaluable – Gerald Haxton and Alan Searle. Haxton was a rather brash American, apt to be drunk, but a marvellous 'mixer'. Maugham was small, shy and stammered. Haxton was the vital contact man. He made everyone talk, while Maugham sat in a corner and listened, with pencil and notebook. The great short stories of Malaya, China and the Pacific owe much to him. Once, when they were travelling in a coastal boat from Penang to Singapore, they went to the ship's bar, where a number of planters and solicitors were getting drunk. Maugham got fed up, and went to bed. Haxton stayed on. At two o'clock in the morning he burst into Maugham's cabin and said: 'They've just told me a marvellous story.' Maugham said: 'You're drunk. It'll have to wait until the morning. Go to bed.' 'It can't wait,' said Haxton, 'because by the morning I shall have forgotten it.' Wearily Maugham sat up in his bunk, and stretched out for his notebook and pencil. The story was *The Letter*.

Almost all the short stories are based on fact. For example, *The Painted Veil* is true, only the names being changed. For some years after the Second World War, Maugham did not go back to the Far East because of the resentment he had caused among those who had been the subjects – some said the victims – of his writing; but when, finally, he went, he was given a hero's welcome. They were proud of having provided the setting and the characters for some of the greatest short stories that have ever been written. He once said to me: 'I suppose I have seen more of what used to be the British Empire than anyone else – and, what's more, I have made a fortune out of it. It was not an inglorious moment in history.' I said: 'Who ran it?' He replied: 'The Scots.'

For years we corresponded freely; and I have many letters from him. In this book I shall quote only part of one, in his own handwriting from Bangkok on 9 January 1960.* On the question of why he happened 'just now to be the most widely read author in the world' he wrote:

I don't myself know why. I suspect it is because I was born with a dramatic instinct which makes what I write readable. And then of course the simple way I write makes it a convenient way to learn English with the result that for quite a long time boys and girls throughout the East have been learning the language by means of my stories. Though they read them for scholastic reasons, I am assured that they find this not only a task, but also a pleasure. It was good of you to write so warmly about my work. I was pleased and touched. Yours always, Willie.

I spent Christmas after the abdication of King Edward VIII with my parents in Monte Carlo. By then he was Duke of Windsor, awaiting Mrs Simpson's decree of divorce to become absolute, in Austria. Maugham rang me up to ask me to lunch at the Villa Mauresque on Christmas Day. I told him I was with my parents, and he said: 'You can dine with them. You are very g-g-greedy and I have got a s-s-s-sucking pig. Also I need you. I will send a car to fetch you.' When I arrived I found a small party; and was offered one of his excellent cocktails. 'Have another,' he said. I said: 'No thanks.' He replied: 'You'd b-b-better.' At that moment the door opened, and Mrs Simpson and her aunt Mrs Merryman were announced. I just had time to say to Willie: 'How dare you!' before I was introduced. At lunch I found myself sitting next to Mrs Merryman, the famous Aunt Bessie. She opened the conversation by

* See illustration on next page.

*Erawan Hotel*

BANGKOK, THAILAND
CABLE ADDRESS: ERAWAN
TEL. 58051-69

because I was born with a dramatic instinct which makes what I write readable. And then of course the simple way I write makes it a convenient way to learn English with the result that for quite a long time boys & girls throughout the East have been learning the language by means of my stories. Though they read them for scholastic reasons I am assured that they find this not only a task, but also a pleasure. It was good of you to write so warmly about my books. I was pleased & touched.

Yours always

[signature]

saying: 'You know, Wallis and I have been having a very tough time lately.' All I could think of to say was: 'I seem to have read something about it in the newspapers.' After lunch we played bridge. I cannot remember who my partner was, but we were playing against Mrs Simpson and Maugham. When the first hand was dealt, Mrs Simpson declared one no trump, my partner said no, Maugham said three no trumps, and I said no. As he put down his hand he said: 'I'm afraid I am not very good, partner. I've only got a couple of k-k-kings.' Never able to resist a wisecrack, Mrs Simpson flashed back: 'What's the use of them? They only abdicate.' Maugham said: 'I d-d-don't think that's in v-v-very good t-t-t-taste.' In the event, she was a marvellous wife to the Duke. I met them on occasion over the years, and once crossed the Atlantic with them, when they were good enough to ask me to lunch twice. A close friend told me that in his latter years, except when he was playing golf, the Duke could hardly bear to have her out of his sight.

It was only in the final years of his long life that Willie Maugham began to lose his formidable intellectual power. Niehans had ensured by his injections that the body would keep going; but the mind began to fade. Otherwise he would never have written his last book. This was a cause of sadness to his friends. But there were some funny moments. One day at a lunch-party he was giving at the Villa Mauresque he suddenly said: 'Who is that old bitch sitting at the end of the table?' There was an embarrassed silence. Relentlessly he pointed to her, and said: 'The one in green.' Another time he was invited to lunch with a famous Riviera hostess. When they arrived he said to Alan Searle, 'Where are we?' 'We've come to lunch with Lady B.,' said Alan. He said to the chauffeur, 'Drive on!' One day Eric Dunstan invited him to lunch at his villa at Antibes. After he had sat down, he turned to his host and said: 'Tell me, what's become of Eric Dunstan?'

I was in the South of France when he died, and drove to the Villa Mauresque to see Alan the following day. I found him alone, and we had a long talk. He was calm and resigned, although he knew that the remarkable life he had led for so many years had come finally to an end. He was good enough to say to me: 'In some ways your friendship with Willie was unique. There were no complications. He knew that you much admired his work, and greatly appreciated what you wrote about it. He was very fond of you, and always at ease. Did you notice that, when we were alone together, the stammer practically disappeared? But, most important of all, he knew that you were genuinely fond of him. Not very many people were.' He told me that Maugham was upstairs, and asked me whether I would like to see him. I said no; and when he asked me why, I replied: 'Because nothing in life looks so dead as the dead.'

We know, because it has been observed, that the body does not survive death; and in disembodied survival I am uninterested, because it would not be the survival of the individual. In *The Summing Up* Maugham wrote:

If then one puts aside the existence of God and the possibility of survival as too doubtful to have any effect on one's behaviour, one has to make up one's mind what is the meaning and use of life. If death ends all, if I have neither to hope for good to come nor to fear evil, I must ask myself what I am here for and how in these circumstances I must conduct myself. Now the answer to one of these questions is plain, but it is so unpalatable that most men will not face it. There is no reason for life and life has no meaning.

Ever since I first read this, I have been trying to escape from it; and I have not succeeded. All I have learnt from a long life is that the only thing that brings any kind of abiding personal happiness is compassion.

These are the authors I have known best. But I cannot conclude this part of my book without mentioning the one I have loved most. I salute the giants. I cannot forget that my grandfather was a friend of Thackeray, about whom he wrote a delightful essay, or read the concluding paragraph of perhaps the greatest novel ever written without emotion: 'Ah! *Vanitas Vanitatum!* Which of us is happy in this world? Which of us has his desire? or, having it, is satisfied? – Come children, let us shut up the box and the puppets, for our play is played out.' My favourite novelist remains Turgenev. As a young man he thought that his gift had left him. He went to Rome. There he wrote a story called *Asya*, which was subsequently published in a volume called *The Torrents of Spring*. After that he never looked back.

As characters, Bazarov in *Fathers and Sons* and Lavretsky in *A House of Gentlefolk* remain for me two of the most interesting in fiction; and *Asya* the most moving short story – beating Maupassant's *Boule de Suif*, Chekhov's *The Lady with the Dog*, and Galsworthy's *The Apple Tree* by a short head. I was delighted when Moura Budberg, one of the most remarkable and discerning women I have ever known, as well as the best friend, told me that she agreed with me about Turgenev. 'He is also my favourite,' she said; 'but I'm afraid the poor darling was a coward. He fled from his estates in Russia to Paris, and then sat on Mme Viardot's hearthrug for the rest of his life.'

# 13
# Aftermath of War

During my lecture tour of the United States in 1945, a conference was held at Bretton Woods to decree the future international monetary system of the free world. The leading parts were being played by Mr Vinson, the United States Secretary to the Treasury, Keynes and Mr Harry Dexter White. I thought that the proposals which gradually leaked out were absolutely idiotic, and wrote two letters to the *New York Times* to say so. Both were published with a supporting leading article; and I received two long telegrams of anguish from our Ambassador in Washington, Lord Halifax. When, eventually, I reached Washington, I found that everyone was absolutely furious with me. This of course was not because I myself counted for much. It was because I had the formidable support of the *New York Times*; and they knew it.

Distant rumbles swept across the Atlantic from Anderson, the Chancellor of the Exchequer, and from Eden, the Foreign Secretary. I stayed with my friend Bill Wasserman and his wife; and they invited the Vice-President, Henry Wallace, to lunch. That morning he rang up to say that he had received instructions from his Government that he could not meet me; and the cook walked out. I said to Bill: 'What are you having for lunch?' He replied: 'Roast goose.' I said: 'I can do that. Tell the Vice-President that he can come to lunch because I won't be there. I will go to the kitchen and cook it.' He said:

'That's not a bad idea.' I said: 'Right. But you know what the newspapers will say tomorrow? "Boothby cooks Wallace's goose."' As usual, I lunched alone.

Two days later I was summoned to the British Embassy to see the British Ambassador. Isaiah Berlin, now Sir Isaiah Berlin ОМ, then the most brilliant member of the Embassy staff, rang me up and said: 'At present I can't be seen with you in public. But there is a small fish restaurant on the quay where the lobsters are excellent, and we shall not be noticed. Come there by yourself at one o'clock.' The lunch was delicious, and Isaiah was at the top of his form. He gave me a marvellous *vignette* of Halifax the man – a virtuoso display of his insight into character – which I hope one day he will publish. Then he went on to tell me what our interview would be like: 'The first ten minutes will be very sticky,' he said, 'because he is as angry as he is capable of being – which isn't much. I know it will be difficult for you, but try to be humble. The signal that the tension has begun to relax will be when he asks his horrible little dog to jump into his lap.' When I was shown into his room he was sitting at his desk, looking both grave and sad. I began by saying: '*Peccavi*,' hoping to impress him with my knowledge of Latin. He replied: 'You have indeed.' But when, after about ten minutes, he asked his dog to jump into his lap, I burst out laughing. For this I received a well-deserved look of reproach. Later I gave my reasons for opposing the Bretton Woods Agreement and the American loan to the House of Commons, and there is no need to repeat them now at any length. At Bretton Woods they fixed exchange rates in a world of chaos. The theoretical price paid for this was adequate monetary reserves, and they were not provided. Keynes tried to do it through the invention of a phoney currency which he called 'Bancor'. White defeated him. The price of monetary gold, which was made the basis of international credit, was fixed at an absurdly low level – the level that Roosevelt had fixed in 1933. The price of every other commodity in the world was allowed to soar. 'The truth is,' I said, 'that free multinational trade, fixed exchange rates, and a fixed price for monetary gold without any regard to reality, cannot be made to mix in the modern world.' Of the American loan, I was later to say:

We are now financing the world dollar deficit. The convertibility
of sterling is imposing upon us an unbearable burden which we are
simply not capable of carrying. . . . All these arrangements will be
short-lived. They will all fall to the ground and will have to be
abandoned. . . . It is sheer, stark insanity, in our present position, to
embark upon this ludicrous course.

Bretton Woods is now in ashes. The American loan was
washed away in a month; and we have been living on tick ever
since. Today I assert, not only with conviction but with vehe-
mence, that over Bretton Woods and the American loan,
Keynes was utterly wrong, and I was absolutely right. In his
review of my book *My Yesterday – Your Tomorrow*, Nicholas
Davenport, the famous economic correspondent of the *Spectator*,
wrote: 'Boothby was always ahead of his time, and always
right.' From this conclusion I cannot dissent.

Instead of doubling the price of monetary gold, as they
should have done, the Americans went on, after the war, to
demonetize it altogether. This, they said, was necessary because
an increase in the price of bullion would be of benefit to South
Africa and the Soviet Union. In fact it was a mortal blow to
the western democracies. The dollar has proved to be no substitute for gold; and no alternative international measuring-rod
of value has been found. As a result we have today no viable
international monetary system in the free world.

I travelled from New York to San Francisco on a special train
which contained most of the world's press. It was the most
enjoyable journey I have ever had. We were all tight all the
time. So much so that, when we reached Chicago, we were put
in a siding in a stockyard and not allowed to get out. In San
Francisco we found most of the leading allied statesmen trying
to draft a charter for the projected United Nations. On the
whole, Smuts was the most successful. Stettinius represented
the United States, Eden Britain and Molotov Russia. As a
result of my campaign against Bretton Woods, about which he
hadn't a clue, Eden cut me dead in an elevator in San Francisco; and thereafter had nothing to do with me.

During the conference Stalin collected half Europe; but no
one seemed to notice until, one evening, Molotov blandly told
Stettinius and Eden in the corridor of our hotel that sixteen

members of the Polish Government in Warsaw, who had gone to Moscow at the request of the American and British Governments to negotiate a treaty of peace, were all in prison. I was immediately behind them: and they were visibly shaken.

That night I wrote a despatch for my paper in which I said:

There is only one way out of the present *impasse*, and that is for Great Britain and the United States to formulate clear-cut policies and carry them out with resolution. We have already lost ground that will be difficult, if not impossible, to recapture. We have now to decide where to stand, and there stand. So far as Europe is concerned, the Western Democracies, including Scandinavia, constitute for us an essential minimum; and our continuing failure to form a regional group of those countries which fringe the Atlantic is greatly to be deplored. . . . The alternative is a dangerous and increasing sense of insecurity, and a return to the situation with which we are all horribly familiar.

Michael Foot was also at San Francisco, as a journalist. One day he said to me: 'What are we doing here?' I said: 'Reaping the bitter fruits of Yalta. And Eden and Stettinius are appropriate recipients.'

Soon afterwards Jan Masaryk, the Czech Foreign Minister, who was an old friend of mine, rang me up and asked me to dine with him alone. When I arrived at the restaurant, I could see he was much upset. Our dinner consisted of aspirin and champagne. He told me that he had been ordered by his Government to announce that they recognized the puppet 'Lublin' Government which had been established by the Soviet Union in Poland; and that he could not bring himself to do it. I besought him to resign and to stay in the United States, at least for the time being; but he replied: 'I love my country too much to do that.' My last words to him were: 'Jan, if you go back to Prague, you go to your death.' He did.

Next time I went to the United States was after the war, when I was sent, again by the *News of the World*, this time to report the signing of the NATO Treaty in Washington. As President Truman and Ernest Bevin came on to the floodlit stage to append their signatures, the band of the American Marines struck up a familiar tune. A distinguished American journalist who was sitting next to me seized my arm and said:

'Christ! What do you think they're playing?' It was Gershwin's
*It Ain't Necessarily So*. That night I dined with an old friend,
Felix Frankfurter, then a Justice of the Supreme Court. When
I described the signing of the Treaty, he was so amused that he
rang up his friend, Dean Acheson, the Secretary of State, to
congratulate him on his choice of music for the ceremony.
Acheson said: 'That's only one of Bob Boothby's bad taste
jokes.' But five minutes later the telephone rang again. It was
Acheson. He said: 'I have just made enquiries, and I find that
it's true. But there's nothing I can do about it now.'

I returned from the United States in 1945 to find that the
'Great Coalition' had broken up, and that Churchill had
formed a 'caretaker' Government pending a General Election.
The *personnel* of this Government came under widespread criticism, and some of the newspapers described it as a Noël Coward
farce. I myself was under no illusions about the election. I had
no doubt that the Conservative Party was going to be heavily
defeated. I fought a personal and solitary campaign against a
good Labour candidate. I neither sought nor received any
support from the Conservative leaders. As usual I wrote my
own Election Address in which I put forward my own policy;
and this was endorsed by the Unionist Association in my
constituency. The torrent of nonsense which poured out daily
from the Conservative Central Office in London went straight
into the wastepaper basket.

As I drove around the lovely familiar countryside of Buchan,
alone with my faithful organizer Archie Campbell (widely
known, through his journalistic activities, as 'The Buchan
Farmer'), I said to him: 'I wonder if we can manage this.' He
said he was sure we could; and, as the days went by, I began
to share his view. My meetings were packed; and even staunch
Socialists wanted to know what I had to say. At my eve-of-the-
poll meeting in Fraserburgh, an elderly lady in pince-nez got
up and said: 'I would like to ask the candidate a personal
question.' I thought to myself: 'My God! What's coming now?'
but said: 'Certainly.' She then said: 'I read in my *Daily Mirror*
this morning that you are engaged to a Danish film star, who
was greatly admired by Hitler, after what' – she added severely

– 'my *Daily Mirror* describes as a whirlwind courtship in an orange grove in California. Is this true?' I think in fact, I was engaged to a Danish film star, but I replied: 'Madam, I can truthfully tell you that I don't know whether I am engaged or not. You had better ask the Editor of the *Daily Mirror*. But, without any disloyalty to my fellow-candidates in this election, I must now ask *you* a question. Take a look at them in the north of Scotland, and tell me which of them, with the exception of myself, is capable of conducting a whirlwind courtship in an orange grove?' As I sat down to a storm of laughter and applause, Archie Campbell leant forward and whispered in my ear: 'That's worth a thousand votes.'

An amusing incident occurred on polling day. It is customary for all the candidates to visit all the polling stations; and in county constituencies this takes up to ten hours. I started at Turriff at eight o'clock in the morning and as I was leaving the school, the Returning Officer came over and said: 'I am not supposed to speak to you, but I must tell you that all your trouser-buttons are undone. I don't know whether this will win or lose you votes; but I think that, before you go round the constituency, you ought to know it.'

In the event, I was one of only two Conservative candidates to hold their majority. In fact, I increased mine, until the Service vote was counted later. This, as I expected, was ninety per cent Labour. The landslide defeat of the Conservative Party throughout the country was overwhelming; and was certainly not diminished by its propaganda machine, or by the idiotic speeches of its leaders, including Churchill himself although he still held the personal regard and gratitude of the nation. When I reached the House of Commons I found a telegram awaiting me: 'We all congratulate you most heartily, and are thankful that in the midst of the Red Ruin that remains you erect one pillar of sound Conservative principle, of prosperity, of temperance and of morality – Duff Cooper, the Earl of Carlisle, Lord Stanley of Alderley and the Earl of Birkenhead.' As far as I was concerned, the farming vote had remained steady, and the Service vote had gone against me; but the decisive factor was the fishermen's vote, which was solid. I had worked hard for them during the war.

In the entirely different circumstances of the new Parliament,

I found myself in a position of some political power. I was invited by the Conservative Whips to open the debate in the Commons on Dalton's first Budget on the second day, and described it as 'pedestrian'. Then, suddenly, the Bretton Woods Agreement and the American Loan were simultaneously thrown at our heads; and I decided to move the rejection of both on second reading. This gave rise to a good deal of agitation on both sides of the House. Shortly before the debate, Churchill said to me: 'I make no complaint of what you propose to do, because I know it is the result of sincere convictions, long held. But I must warn you that I shall advise the Opposition to abstain.' The debate itself was tense, and dramatic. I described Keynes as a siren, beckoning us to our doom from the murky depths of Bretton Woods; and can still see him sitting in the gallery, with his head between his hands. I ended by saying: 'We have heard a lot about mandates recently, especially from the Chancellor of the Exchequer. It may be that the Government have a mandate to nationalize the gas works. I do not deny it. And on the question of whether this will be good for the gas works, or the public, I would not venture to dogmatize. But there is one mandate which His Majesty's Government never got from the people of this country, and that was to sell the British Empire for a packet of cigarettes.' And with that I threw a packet on to the floor of the House. The result of the division was a surprise to all. I got over a hundred members into my lobby, including several Labour supporters of the Government. Churchill was much upset. He thought that his leadership had been challenged by his own party, which it had; and, at one moment, threatened to resign. But he could not, and did not, take it out on me.

For the rest of the Parliament of 1945-9, which carried through a considerable social revolution, I was allowed to take an independent line, which suited my constituents, and did not trouble the Conservative leaders. In general I supported the social and industrial measures proposed by the Government, and actually voted in favour of the nationalization of the Bank of England, without any complaint from the Conservative Whips. On one subject alone did I come into bitter conflict with the administration, and that was Palestine.

For many years Dr Chaim Weizmann had been a close and

valued friend of mine, in good times and in bad. I watched him
build up the Zionist Organization and the Jewish Agency in
London; and later I watched him at work in New York, when
his influence was largely responsible for the necessary majority
in favour of partition in the United Nations Assembly, which
led to the establishment of the State of Israel. He had mesmeric
charm; and greatness of a kind that I have not encountered in
any other man. As Dick Crossman said: 'Without the personality of Weizmann there would have been no Balfour Declaration and no British Mandate.' In 1947 Attlee and Ernest Bevin,
the Foreign Secretary, decided to throw up the mandate; and
leave the Jews to fight it out alone in Palestine, at odds of ten
to one against them. I regarded this as an act of betrayal on our
part. But, with one notable exception, Dick Crossman, I found
no support among the gentiles on either side of the House.
Churchill had supported the Jewish cause in the past, and was
known to be in favour of it; but neither he nor Eden played an
active part in the House of Commons. It was not easy to do this
when the King David Hotel in Jerusalem was blown up, and
British sergeants were being killed by the Irgun terrorists; and,
for a while, the going was very rough. It was worse than
Munich. One evening when Dick Crossman and I were sitting
in the Smoking-Room being cut right, left and centre, I said
to him: 'Look here, I don't want office and if I did I wouldn't
get it; but you are putting your whole political career in
jeopardy.' He said: 'I know. I shan't get office from this lot,
and probably never will. But I am going on, because I know
that we are right.' On many subjects a mercurial and erratic
politician, on this one he was not. They were right to plant a
forest in Israel in his memory.

When, to Bevin's discomfiture, the Jews won their war of
independence, world opinion began gradually to shift in their
favour; and today the State of Israel is pretty firmly established.
But we do not know what the future holds. In the peroration of
the Memorial Address to Chaim Weizmann which I was invited to give at Rehovoth in 1960, I said:

I am not, like Chaim, a prophet, a mystic, or a dreamer of dreams
that come true. All I can do is to quote his last words to Meyer
Weisgal and beg of you to heed them: 'I have loyal friends, more than

*Left* On a dual-purpose craft (a fishing boat which Boothby helped to invent).
*Right* At work in Hatton Castle.

*Bottom* Buchan in daylight.

The 'In the News' team: Left to right, W. J. Brown, Boothby, Dingle and Michael Foot, and A. J. P. Taylor. 'The programme was an immense success . . . Understandably the politicians couldn't take this.'

'Face to Face' with John Freeman. 'A daunting experience – but the "Face to Face" programmes are certainly the best that have ever been seen on television.'

Caxton Hall at last!

Buchan at twilight.

I deserve. Tell them not to permit the destruction of the thing we have laboured to build. We Jews can do something very good, something which can be an honour to us all and to mankind. But we mustn't spoil it. We are an impetuous people, and we spoil and sometimes destroy what has taken generations to build up.'

He often spoke to me on this theme, about which he was deeply apprehensive. Today we can only hope that his apprehensions will prove to be unjustified; and that, in the long run, his wisdom and vision will prevail, and bring peace to the Middle East.

By 1949 it was clear that the Labour Government was in the process of disintegration. They were all exhausted. Ernest Bevin and Stafford Cripps were dying. Herbert Morrison was not popular, and misplaced when Attlee sent him to succeed Bevin at the Foreign Office. Hugh Dalton, who had left the Treasury owing to a piece of sheer bad luck, and never complained, had clearly had enough of looking after national parks. Aneurin Bevan alone was fresh to the point of ebullience although, as Minister of Health, he had had to bear the heaviest legislative burden of all; and he was discontented. Shinwell who, as Minister of Defence, had rightly wanted to retain National Service, was not allowed to do it. The only hope for Labour lay in a clean sweep, and the appearance of new faces on the Government front bench; and this could only have been achieved through a combination of Hugh Gaitskell and Aneurin Bevan. A government with Gaitskell as Prime Minister and Bevan as Foreign Secretary had the makings of a good government; but it was not possible. I had the good fortune to be a great friend of both, and appreciated to the full their respective qualities. But these were too divergent for any kind of reconciliation. Bevan thought Gaitskell was a cold fish, and once described him as a desiccated calculating machine. In this he was wrong. He was in fact an emotional man. Gaitskell regarded Bevan as intellectually inferior to himself; and, as a politician, dangerously far to the Left, and disloyal. In this he was also wrong. I have never known anyone in my life who had a clearer grasp of the fallacies of Marxism than Nye. But in character they were entirely different, and I never thought there was any chance of friendship between them. After Bevan resigned, their relationship degenerated into a personal feud; and that could only mean the temporary eclipse of the Labour Party. They could never have been friends, but events might ultimately have forced them into political alliance. The premature death of both was a great loss to this country.

By 1951, when the Conservatives were returned to power, I was myself a member of the Consultative Assembly of the Council of Europe, and completely absorbed in the politics of Strasbourg. Thereafter I took little interest in domestic affairs, apart from those of my own constituency, for which I was returned at successive elections with increasing majorities. I had little truck with the Conservative leadership. They had no use for me; and, with one or two exceptions, I had not much use for them. But I had only one more clash with them. That was over Suez. It is not worth recalling the details of that idiotic escapade, because they are now too boring. If Eden had had the sense and the modesty to ask his Ambassador in Cairo, Sir Humphrey Trevelyan, to negotiate directly with Nasser, the whole business might have been settled in half an hour. Trevelyan, now Lord Trevelyan, was one of the most brilliant Ambassadors we have ever had. He knew Nasser well; and, like Archie Clark-Kerr, he understood the oriental mind, which he once described as often conspiratorial but seldom treacherous. Despite his warning messages to London, he was never even consulted! Instead Eden lost his head, his patience, his temper, and finally his nerve. But he was ill. We shall probably never know the full truth about Suez, because vital documents are said to have been destroyed. All that is certain is that both we and the French encouraged the Israelis to attack Egypt and, when they were on the brink of victory, stopped them. We then said that our objective was 'to separaate the combatants'. That is no reason for going to war, although what we should have done if the Israelis had got to Cairo, God alone knows. Lord Fisher once said that the essence of war is surprise and speed. We had neither. Selwyn Lloyd's book on Suez* proves only that he was himself a very nice man, and that he was deceived by Dulles; but it does not convince. Owing to the utter folly and ineptitude of our policy from start to finish, I was one of eight Conservative Members of Parlia-

* *Suez 1956; A Personal Account,* Jonathan Cape 1978.

ment who abstained in the vote of confidence in the Government; and, once again owing to my constituents, the only one who survived politically. Two years later, a young member of the Israeli Foreign Service said to me, in Tel Aviv: 'You'll never guess where I was when you landed at Port Said. Sitting in the sunshine on a little hill above the town of Ismailia, your ultimate military objective. We had only to walk down the hill to take it. But what happened? You sent us an ultimatum ordering us to return immediately to the Sinai Desert.'

Eden once said to me: 'The difference between us is that you are a European animal, whereas I am an Atlantic animal.' In fact this was not true. He never understood the Americans, and they never understood him. He was apt to call everyone 'My dear'. I rather liked this. But Dulles didn't. Nor did Acheson, who once said at a diplomatic reception: 'If that man calls me his dear again, I'll leave the house.' With the best intentions in the world, Eden brought about the worst relationship between Britain and the United States in this century. It took Macmillan two years to restore it.

In the autumn of 1949 I celebrated my Silver Jubilee as Member of Parliament for East Aberdeenshire. They gave me a tremendous dinner in Aberdeen, and presented me with a bronze bust of myself which bore a fortunate resemblance to the head of an Aberdeen Angus bull. Walter Elliot came up to propose my health; and I received many messages of congratulations, including a telegram from Churchill 'on this auspicious occasion'. The letter which gave me the greatest pleasure came from Harold Nicolson:

My dear Bob,
    Congratulations on your semi-jubilee. It is a fine thing to have been 25 years in Parliament before the age of 50, and I don't wonder that you feel proud of it. But what you ought really to feel proud of is the strength of character which enabled you to emerge stronger than ever through an ordeal which would have shattered most people's courage. Being a cowardly man myself I admire courage almost more than any other quality, especially courage which entails not a momentary reaction to a sudden danger, but prolonged fortitude of will.

In 1954, I made a speech to the Hardwicke Society in which I said that the present law regarding homosexuality was iniquitous, and that the clause in the Act which made indecency between consenting male adults in private a crime should be removed from the Statute Book. This had been inserted as an amendment to a Bill to make 'further provision for the protection of women and girls', moved in committee by Mr Labouchère in 1886, which was passed without discussion. The press reported my speech widely, and this led me to put down some questions in the House of Commons, and to write to the Home Secretary, Sir David Maxwell-Fyfe. When I next saw him, he said: 'I am not going down to history as the man who made sodomy legal.' It was an unpromising start; and his wife, Sylvia, said to me: 'You will never persuade him.' But I persisted, and eventually he asked me to write him a memorandum on the subject. This I did and, after considering it for some time, he wrote and told me that he had decided 'with reluctance', to refer the matter to a committee presided over by Sir John Wolfenden. Later he said to me: 'I thought that, if I was going to do it at all, I would appoint the best man I could find; and I hope you will agree that I have.' I said that indeed I did. I regard the Wolfenden Report as wholly admirable; and, for my part, I have no wish to change it. I am sure that for many people it has removed much unhappiness, and even fear. All I am now trying to do, with the approval of the Lord Chancellor, and the Law Officers on both sides of the border, is to have its recommendations applied to Scotland as well as England and Wales. I was thankful, and slightly surprised, when Parliament implemented them so quickly. Lord Wolfenden, one of our greatest public servants, once said to me: 'I have only one grudge against you. You have ensured that, for the rest of my life, my name will be associated with homosexuality.'

I have known many homosexuals in the course of my life, in this country and abroad; and some of them are my friends. All I would say about them is this. To regard them as wicked and 'abnormal', and therefore as criminal and beyond the pale, is not only foolish but insane. From Plato and Socrates, through Caesar, and down the centuries, they have played a large part in the development of European culture, and therefore of western civilization. As artists they can depict and interpret emotion, and deep emotion at that, perhaps better than anyone else; but in their own lives they shrink from it. With rare exceptions they are by nature promiscuous. They like to pick each other up, casually, in bars, clubs and Turkish baths. They enjoy sex in its cruder manifestations; but the enjoyment is transient. When it is over, all they want to do is to say goodbye. Tom Driberg once told me that sex was only enjoyable with someone you had never met before, and would never meet again. I replied: '*À chacun son goût*.' As I have already said, they don't believe in a past, or in a future. They live for the day, and even for the hour. Many of them are attracted by the ritual of the Church, and by the personality of Jesus – no nonsense about the family there; but few of them are religious in depth. They call themselves 'gay', and so they are, for they are nearly always good company; but basically they are not happy. Homosexuality is equally prevalent among what used to be called 'the higher and lower orders'; and sometimes these are attracted to each other. This is known in homosexual circles as 'plain sewing'. They are addicted to blackmail, and to theft, but seldom to cruelty. It is because they have played, and always will, an important part in shaping all our lives, from which there is no escape, that I have done and written so much about them. My trouble is that, to a considerable extent, and much against my will, I share their general outlook on life.

Early one morning in July 1957 I rang up my doctor, Stephen Blaikie, and told him that I had had the most frightful indigestion all night. I said that, although I had taken twelve of the pills that Gilbert Harding was recommending on television, it was getting worse; and had now gone down to my arms. He said: 'You can't have indigestion in your arms. Sit down in your arm-chair, and sit still.' Ten minutes later he was with me, giving me two injections. An hour later I was with Walter Somerville, the famous heart specialist. Three hours later I was in bed in the King Edward VII Hospital. I was told that, although I had not had a full infarct, they were going to treat me as if I had; and that I was not to move. Fortunately, on my way in, I had asked the hall porter to switch the telephone on to my room; and no one thought of telling him to switch it off.

It was Goodwood Week, and I had intended to go to the races. I persuaded the nurses to turn on the television, and was therefore able to watch them. When they were out of the room I telephoned every day to Ladbroke's, and put £2 mixed doubles on sixteen horses at Goodwood and another race meeting. All of them won. If I had then known that there was such a thing as an 'accumulator', I would have made a lot of money. As it was, I made enough to pay all the expenses of the nursing home. Although I know I owe most to the skill and care of the doctors and nurses, I think this played an appreciable part in my recovery.

I was in hospital for five weeks and subsequently had one or two more mild attacks. So that, when they told me that life in the House of Commons had become too strenuous for me, I was not surprised. I knew that, when one of my old friends, Bill Allen, wrote to me from Ireland: 'You *must* slow down your activities. You are too greedy for life – both work and play. You should now aim at playing the elder statesman for a couple more decades and treat yourself with more consideration,' he was right. I was about to resign from the House of Commons when the Prime Minister, Harold Macmillan, sent for me and offered me a peerage. He said: 'You can be the last of the old, or the first of the new.' He had no doubt which I should choose, and nor had I.

So my name appeared in the first list of Life Peers created under the new Act; and, as it begins with *B*, I can justifiably claim to be the first of all.

There was an amusing sequel, in the shape of a tremendous row between Garter King of Arms (England) and Lord Lyon (Scotland) about my coat-of-arms. Garter claimed, rightly, that I was English by origin. Lyon claimed that as my father and I had been born in Scotland, my mother and grandmother were both Scottish, and I myself had represented a Scottish constituency for thirty-four years, I was *de facto* Scottish. It was like *Alice in Wonderland*. One day I went to see Garter King of Arms. He picked up the telephone, and said: 'Give me Lyon.' Then: 'Is that you, Lyon? It's Garter speaking. I've just been talking to Rouge-Croix about Lord Boothby.' I managed to look grave. A few days later I had a letter from Lyon (Sir Thomas Innes) saying: 'Lyon will fight, and Lyon will win.' Lyon won. So I got a Scottish coat-of-arms with the title of Baron Boothby, of Buchan and Rattray Head. My supporters are a Buchan farmer, dressed like Archie Campbell, and a fisherman.

The light-house at Rattray Head, half way between Peter-head and Fraserburgh, guides the fishermen round a difficult corner of the coast, and my choice was designed to record my long association with the inshore fishing industry.

It was a tremendous wrench to leave the constituency after thirty-four years. They gave me the Freedom of all four burghs – and I have been told by the Librarian of the House of Commons that they can find no precedent for this for a county Member of Parliament. I am content to record the fact that the people of Buchan have been the essential background to my whole life, and that they have seen me through every crisis. Their affection and loyalty, once gained, are as strong and un-shakeable as the rocks around their coast. To them I owe everything. I took my wife there on our honeymoon and, after a good look at her, they said: 'She's a' richt.' I went back to open the new harbour at Peterhead, and a complex at Mintlaw of Buchan Meat Producers, a great agricultural co-operative enterprise which I helped Joe Mitchell to bring into being. Now I cannot bring myself to go back again. There are too many ghosts.

# 14
# Europe after the War

In 1946 Churchill sent for me and said that he had decided to form a committee for what he called a 'United Europe', and invited me to be a member of it. Immediately afterwards he made his famous Zurich speech in which he said that western Europe was in a desperate state, as indeed it was, and proposed as a 'sovereign remedy' the re-creation of the European family, or as much of it as we could, through a structure under which it could dwell in peace, in safety and in freedom. 'We must build,' he said, 'a kind of United States of Europe'; adding that we were geographically and historically a part of Europe, with a full part to play as a member of the European family. This was what I had advocated in despatches from the San Francisco conference in 1945, and I accepted his invitation with enthusiasm. Churchill himself took the chair at our meetings. Duncan Sandys was the driving force; Edward Beddington-Behrens an invaluable treasurer; and the *éminence grise* was Joseph Retinger, a Pole who had been Sikorski's political adviser. He had parachuted into Poland during the war at the age of sixty, and was an ardent European, and one of the most remarkable men I have ever known. Between us we organized an international conference at The Hague in 1948, at which a resolution was passed which led directly to the establishment of the Council of Europe at Strasbourg in 1949.

Immediately before the Hague Conference, on 5 May 1948, I made a speech in the House of Commons, in which I said:

It seems to me that the supreme object of our policy should surely be to build a democratic world order so strong that no State or combination of States would dare to challenge it. . . . Such a democratic world order can only be built up by the creation of a United States of Western Europe, in some form or other, in close association with the British Commonwealth, and with the United States of America, upon whose material strength the entire structure must in the first phase depend. . . . The process must be one of spiritual growth, as well as material progress; and the end must be a series of organic acts of union. I see no other way. The choice that confronts Hon. Members is fundamental. I do not think it is obscure. It is the choice between international anarchy and the rule of law; between the rebirth or the doom of our Western civilization.

Churchill appointed me as one of the five delegates from the Conservative Party to the first meeting of the Consultative Assembly in 1949. He himself led the delegation.

That summer I had been lent a lovely villa near Cadenabbia on the Lake of Como; and, as Churchill was himself in Italy at the time, he asked me to travel with him from Chiasso to Strasbourg. The journey lasted for most of the day. We had the usual sumptuous lunch, specially prepared for him, with plenty of champagne. To begin with we talked about the economic plight of Europe, and economic policy generally. After a while he said: 'You mustn't think that you know everything about economics, and that no one else knows anything.' I said: 'I sometimes do.' When we reached Basel, a number of photographers with cameras carrying lenses, any one of which could have contained a machine-gun, jumped into the train, and pointed them straight at him. He showed no trace of fear. But after they had gone, he sent for the chief of police and gave him a dressing-down which he was not likely to forget. On the way from Basel to Strasbourg I asked him what he really meant by 'a kind of United States of Europe'. He refused to be drawn. All he said was: 'We are not making a machine, we are growing a living plant.' And then, changing the metaphor, he added: 'We have lit a fire which will either blaze or go out; or perhaps the embers will die down and then, after a while, begin to glow again.'

In the opening debate of the Assembly I made a speech, to which Churchill listened, in which I said that absolute State sovereignty was one of the principal causes of evil in the modern world, and that the only solution to this problem lay in some merging or pooling of national sovereignty. I went on to say that I felt most strongly that in the Assembly and the Committee of Ministers, we had the instruments with which an organic European union could be forged. We must co-ordinate our monetary and fiscal policies. We must plan investment in our basic industries on a European scale, and encourage specialization. We must also negotiate reciprocal trade and payment agreements on a preferential basis. This would require the establishment of a number of permanent functional European authorities. But it would also require frequent and major decisions of policy; and therefore, unless we established at the same time an executive international political authority, the functional authorities would be powerless, because they themselves could not decide policy, or give the necessary orders. From this speech Churchill did not dissent.

I was much influenced at this time by Field-Marshal Lord Montgomery who, I had discovered, was apt to get to the heart of any matter which engaged his attention. He had said, when he was Deputy Commander of the NATO forces in Europe: 'The task before the nations of the West is primarily political. Economic fusion and military strength will not be obtained until the political association between the group of nations concerned has first been defined.' Ten years later, when I went to the House of Lords and we became friends, he was often to repeat this to me. He said: 'You want western European unity. So do I. But we will never get it by means of a talking-shop in Strasbourg and an international bureaucracy without political power.'

That is precisely what we have got today. And that is why we have not got European unity. The political association has never been defined; and until it is, we can never hope to achieve the 'imposing confederation' which de Gaulle envisaged shortly before his death. At Strasbourg in 1949–51 we got the Assembly to pass a resolution demanding the creation of a European Political Authority 'with limited functions but defined powers'. I described this in a speech as, 'not so much the surrender as the joint exercise, by common consent, of certain defined sovereign powers'. But nothing came of it.

In 1949 Britain could have had the leadership of a united western Europe on her own terms. De Gaulle was not there to oppose it. They were all clamouring for it. After all, we had at that time tremendous prestige, because we were the only one of the countries concerned which had not been conquered and occupied. What happened? Coldly and deliberately we set out to destroy the Council of Europe, and everything it stood for. First of all, Bevin refused to join the Coal and Steel Community Robert Schuman devised. This was a damaging blow. Then, in 1950, Churchill made a speech to the Consultative Assembly, in which he demanded the immediate creation of a European Army, under a unified command with a single Defence Minister, 'in which we should all bear a worthy and honourable part'. I think that, at that moment, he had himself in mind as the Minister. The speech was widely acclaimed as marking a considerable advance on the part of Britain. Herbert Morrison, the Foreign Secretary, went so far as to say that a purely functional approach was not necessarily the solution for all time, and that some collective European authority of a democratic character might in due course develop specific powers to decide certain matters direct. 'New ideas,' he said, 'do not frighten me.' But his days at the Foreign Office were numbered. In 1950 I circulated a memorandum for the European Movement which gave rise to such interest that, although it had no effect, I think it is worth reproducing.*

In 1951 the Conservatives were returned to power; and for a moment, but only for a moment, this brought fresh hope to the Council of Europe. In the autumn a debate took place at Strasbourg between a powerful delegation from the Congress of the United States headed by Senators Benton, Green, Hickenlooper, Humphrey and McMahon, and a delegation from the Consultative Assembly. Despite strong opposition from the Foreign Office, Churchill appointed me to represent the Conservative Party, and by implication the Government, in this debate. I found that all the members of the American delegation were strongly in favour of European unity.

In my report to the Foreign Secretary, Anthony Eden, I said:

* See Appendix 2, pages 262–5.

I am disturbed and depressed by the present position here, which has approached demoralization. . . . In politics you can play with people's careers and even their lives; but you cannot, with impunity, play with their faiths. Today the youth of many continental countries in Europe believe, passionately, in the ideal of European union. That is their faith; and many of them have no other. I fear the consequence of dissillusionment, especially in France and Germany. . . . I feel that it would be a good thing if the Consultative Assembly were given something to do, other than brooding introspectively over its present sense of frustration, and impending fate.

This report can only have encouraged Eden and the British Foreign Office to do what they now proceeded to do: kill the Council of Europe, and the whole concept of European union.

One week later the Home Secretary, Sir David Maxwell-Fyfe, came out to a plenary session of the Consultative Assembly to give the views of His Majesty's Government about a proposed European Defence Community which had been drafted by a committee presided over by M. Pleven, which we had refused to join. He said:

I cannot promise you that our eventual association with the European Defence Community would amount to final and unconditional participation because this, as I have said, is a matter which must be left for inter-governmental discussion. But I can assure you of our determination that no genuine method shall fail for lack of thorough examination which one gives to the needs of trusted comrades.

At a subsequent press conference that evening, at which I was present, he added: 'It is quite wrong to suggest that what I said was any closing of the door by Britain. . . . I made it plain that there is no refusal on the part of Britain.' I was dining with him alone that night, when a message came through that at a press conference in Rome, Eden had just announced the refusal of Britain to participate in the European Defence Community on any terms; and I can testify that he was on the brink of resignation.

The effect of this on the Council of Europe was traumatic. Spaak immediately resigned the Presidency of the Consultative Assembly; and, with the co-operation of Jean Monnet and the support of Schuman, Adenauer and de Gasperi, set about the creation of a Common Market of 'The Six'. On 3 December the Conservative members of the British delegation, of whom I was one, sent a letter to the Prime Minister (Churchill), signed by the lot, from which I give the following extracts:

We feel obliged to bring to your attention the great and increasing difficulty of our present position as Conservative delegates to the Consultative Assembly of the Council of Europe. A week ago events appeared to be moving in a manner favourable to British interests. The Conference between representatives of the Assembly and the Congress of the United States had been successfully concluded. The Congressmen, although disappointed that we could not see our way to join a European political federation, had by the end of the day been brought to a much better comprehension of our special position. At the same time, they had made it quite clear that, in their judgement, a good relationship between Great Britain and the United States would depend largely on the lead we gave in building a United Europe, whatever its precise form might be. . . .

It is no exaggeration to say that the unexplained and unqualified refusal of Great Britain to participate in a European Army, announced by the Foreign Secretary in Rome, came as a shattering blow to most members of the Assembly. Had the Home Secretary been anyone other than Sir David Maxwell-Fyfe, few could have been persuaded that he was unaware of the decision when he spoke. . . . In moving the Resolution for the immediate creation of a European Army last year, you said: 'Those who serve supreme causes must not consider what they can get but what they can give. . . . We should make a gesture of practical and constructive guidance by declaring ourselves in favour of the immediate creation of a European Army under a unified command, in which we should all bear a worthy and honourable part.' The Minister of Supply said that the Atlantic alliance was not an acceptable alternative, for the simple reason that nobody knew how long it would last. He concluded his speech by saying: 'We all have a positive duty to bring through to success this historic project which we ourselves initiated here. If it should fail through lack of support or lack of conciliation on the part of any of us, or of our countries, we shall bear a terrible responsibility before future generations.'

The Minister of Housing [Mr Macmillan] said: 'Last August we voted for a European Army and that was a tremendous decision . . . of course there are doubts and fears. . . . It is surely the purpose of this broad and generous conception of a European Army to reduce these apprehensions and inhibitions to the minimum. . . . Perhaps there is

a suspicion that Britain may be so blind as not to see the danger
through European eyes, and that she may, in a mood of despair, of
weariness, seek safety in isolation. Mr President, there is a single answer
to that. . . . Britain's frontier is not on the Channel; it is not even on
the Rhine; it is at least the Elbe. I believe that if our German comrades *join with us* in a European Army, they must be granted, from the
beginning, equally honourable military status. . . . There should go
out tonight a recommendation which should send to the peoples and
governments in every part of the world a ringing note of courage and
of faith.'

At the end of this week, we shall have to listen to speeches by the
Chairman of the Committee of Ministers, Dr Lange, M. Schuman,
Dr Adenauer, Signor de Gasperi and M. van Zeeland; with a British
statesman of the front rank conspicuous only by his absence. We must
admit that we do not find this a very agreeable prospect. . . . In conclusion, we venture to appeal to you to take some positive action
designed to restore British prestige in the Consultative Assembly, and
to show that His Majesty's Government meant to play their part in the
military defence and economic development of a united Europe.


To this letter there was no reply.

The whole idea of western European union was in fact blown
up by Churchill's Government of 1951. Eden did a hatchet job,
and made no bones about it. Did Churchill himself? I have
often wondered. Did he ever really believe in a United Europe?
I knew that he was playing a party political game at Strasbourg.
For example, when Layton asked me to tell him that he did not
feel able to stand against Whiteley, the Labour Chief Whip, for
election as a Vice-President, he said: 'Lock him in the lavatory.'
I think that at one moment he was genuinely attracted by the
idea. But when he was returned to power, he certainly lost interest in it. In his final year of office, when the mind was
beginning to fade, he became obsessed with the idea that he,
and he alone, could make peace with Stalin; and this came to
dominate all his thoughts and actions. Once, after he had
listened to one of my innumerable speeches on Europe in the
House of Commons, Oliver Lyttelton, who had been Colonial
Secretary in the Government of 1951–5, said to me: 'I cannot
remember a single occasion when the question of Europe was
brought before the Cabinet. If it had been, I should have been
sceptical, but interested.' David Maxwell-Fyfe, Harold Mac-

millan and Duncan Sandys, all of whom believed in European union, did nothing about it. We refused even to send a delegate to the conferences at Messina and Brussels, which drafted the Treaty of Rome and established the Common Market of The Six; so that ultimately we had to go on our knees to sign a treaty which we had played no part in framing. It was the final humiliation of a British foreign policy which had been almost as inept in the post-war years as in the pre-war years. For this Eden was primarily responsible. In the end, the combination of vanity with stupidity proved to be invincible.

A demoralized assembly at Strasbourg made one final effort to achieve something, in the shape of what became known as the 'Strasbourg Plan' for economic and monetary union, passed unanimously in 1952. As Vice-Chairman of the Economic Committee, I had a hand in drafting it. It was a good plan – certainly better than anything we have seen since. It was pole-axed overnight by the British Treasury.

Then in a rather forlorn attempt to secure some British participation in European affairs, Spaak, Monnet and Retinger tried to get me elected President of the Assembly. To my great surprise Churchill told me that the Government would put no obstacles in the way, and even Eden instructed his Minister of State, Anthony Nutting, to give me his support in Strasbourg. But by this time he knew he had won. The Council of Europe was dead. Sir Geoffrey Eastwood, the head of the Secretariat, told me afterwards that at lunchtime on the day of election, when the vote should have been taken, it was 'in the bag' for me. Then, suddenly, the French delegation moved an adjournment until the evening, and got to work. Among them Reynaud and Bidault were my only supporters. When the vote finally came to be taken, I was beaten. Reynaud said to me: 'Never mind, your turn will come.' But, for the first and last time in my political life, I was inconsolable. That night I walked, as I often did, alone through the streets of Strasbourg. I came across a garden, and sat down on a bench in the moonlight under a lime tree. The scent was overpowering. All of a sudden I was reminded of Sachs in the second act of *Die Meistersinger*; of his soliloquy *Wie duftet doch der Flieder*; and then of the Night Watchman when, after the uproar, he comes on alone with his lantern and walks slowly up the silent, empty moonlit street,

to one of the loveliest melodies ever written. That is what
Wagner did for Nuremberg. What had we done? Dropped
bombs on it for a whole long night, for no conceivable military
objective, and at colossal loss in Lancaster bombers and their
crews. I found myself in tears.

Next morning I could hardly bring myself to go to the
Assembly. But when I got there a charming, pretty girl who
was a member of the Secretariat, came up to me and said:
'Don't be sad. This place isn't going to realize the hopes we had
of it. If they had elected you President, you could have done
absolutely nothing.' I realized that she was telling me the
truth; and, in one minute, she turned me from a miserable into
a happy man. If I had dared, I would have kissed her. She is
now Mrs Enoch Powell.

Thereafter, the Consultative Assembly degenerated into
total impotence and irrelevance; and, as Herbert Luthy wrote:
'The Foreign Ministers of Western Europe, like actors on a
revolving stage which had got out of control, kept re-appearing
every few days against a different backcloth, always playing a
never-completed first act.' In 1957, after eight years, I left
Strasbourg in despair.

I have seen criticisms lately that the 'founding fathers' of the
European Movement, of whom Duncan Sandys and I were
certainly two, concentrated too much on the spire, and too
little on the foundations. This is not true. What we were looking for was architects; and these could only be politicians.
France found Schuman and Monnet; Germany found Adenauer, Carlo Schmid and Gerstenmaier; Italy found de Gasperi;
Belgium found Spaak; and Britain found no one. One thing
none of us envisaged was a European Parliament separate
from all the national parliaments, and therefore impotent; and
an expensive bureaucracy in Brussels, without political power.

The truth is that in the 1950s we missed the European tide,
and are unlikely to see it at the flood again in our lifetime. It
was a great opportunity in our history, which we did not take.
Louis XIV, Napoleon, Bismarck, and Hitler attempted to impose unity upon Europe by blood and iron. All failed. It remains possible that one day we shall achieve European unity
by democracy and consent. But this will now take a very long
time. Edward Heath tried to do something about it. He failed

because the political party which he led had already done it in.

In 1961 I went on a pretty comprehensive tour of central and eastern Europe with Sir Leslie (Dick) Plummer. Poland, Czechoslovakia, Hungary and Rumania. We were both overwhelmed by the beauty of Cracow, and the horror of the concentration camp at Auschwitz nearby – worse than Dachau.

On a Sunday morning we drove from Warsaw to Poznan. In every town and village the peasants were pouring into Mass from the countryside in the wooden carts which had served them for centuries, drawn by two beautiful animals in gleaming harness, and dressed in their best. The churches in Poland are still full, as indeed they are in Hungary. Our guide, who was by way of being a Communist, said: 'Their lives haven't changed much. They cultivate the soil, not very efficiently by modern standards, and often live to a great age. To them the doctor and the priest are the significant figures in town or village.' Then he added: 'Although we have been occupied and "partitioned" for centuries, you cannot say that we are not still a nation – and a nation of romantics at that. In the old days, when our noblemen had over fifty indoor servants in their castles, it was not so bad. They were comfortable and happy. Now, I suppose, we shall be "mechanized"; and our gypsies will be harried. But there is one thing that no Polish Government will dare to do for many years to come – take away their horses. We have far too many of them, and it is frightfully uneconomic. Each one eats three hectares of foddercrop a year. But, you see, you can love a horse in a way you cannot love a tractor. And they love them.' We stopped at a small house by the roadside, with a small crowd outside it. It was Chopin's birthplace. Inside was his piano, and a plaster cast of his hand. It was a national shrine.

In Prague they were eating dumplings, and trying to forget the day when the Russian tanks rolled into the city. We stood on the ramparts of the Hrâdcany Castle, and looked over the city. The last time I had stood there was alone with Beneš on the eve of Munich, when he said: 'We can't have that destroyed.' It wasn't. But for this the world had to pay a heavy price. In Budapest they were also trying to forget the day when the Russian tanks rolled back into the city. But the atmosphere was quite different. In Hungary the spirit of the Magyars is indestructible. The churches were packed, the restaurants were full, the food was good, the wine excellent, and the gypsies still sang. They talked about the revolution, about how they had pulled down the statue of Stalin and refused to restore it, and about our failure to come to their aid in 1956. I explained to them that, at that moment, we were trying to invade Egypt; but that, in any event, we should not have come to their aid, and never would. They accepted this quite cheerfully. They invited me to do a television programme, and when they asked me what my own programme at home was called, I said: 'One with which you will not be familiar. It is called *Free Speech.*' They put this out.

In Bucharest we expected to stay at the leading hotel. Instead we were taken to a comfortable villa with sentries outside it; and found ourselves alone. Next morning Dick said to me: 'We are under house arrest.' I said: 'I know. But as long as they give us delicious cured ham and brandy for breakfast, that suits me.' In each capital we were treated like royalty, and saw any minister we wanted to see. The only sign of the power that lay behind it all was when our Ambassador in Budapest asked us to lunch, and afterwards invited us to talk to him in the garden. I said: 'Is that because we are bugged here?' And he replied: 'Yes.'

As we talked about it all ourselves, Dick and I reached the conclusion that it was no good attempting to escape the results of Teheran, Yalta and Potsdam. Today the whole of central and eastern Europe is under the domination, not of Communism, but of Russia. They still fear the Germans; but for the Russians they have a deep hatred. East Germany, Czechoslovakia and Hungary are all occupied countries. In the first two the Russians are not afraid to display their armed forces. In Hungary their tanks are kept in the country, often under haystacks; and their troops are not allowed to wear uniform in the towns. So far as Rumania is concerned the Russian tanks are not actually inside the country, but within easy striking distance. No less than the others, it is in fact occupied. I believe that this, not the Middle East, is the greatest potential danger to world peace. Sooner or later, and in one form or another, there will be rebellion against Russian domination. The fires of national pride and patriotism still burn, unsteadily in

Czechoslovakia, but strongly in Poland, Hungary and Rumania. I don't think this necessarily means the nuclear destruction of the world. We should never forget that with the exception of Czechoslovakia (and then only for a brief period), none of these countries has known democracy as we in the West understand and interpret it; and that all of them have known foreign domination. As one Rumanian politician remarked to me when I asked him whether he did not resent the Russian domination: 'Don't forget that we were occupied by the Turks for five hundred years; and they took from us far more than the Russians have ever done.'

Before we left, Dick and I were asked to visit Mme Aslan's famous clinic in Bucharest, where many of the patients were over ninety, and some over a hundred. They asked us whether we would like a full medical check-up, which would involve examination by six doctors, and take two hours. Dick was a little doubtful, but I said that I would love it; so we had it. When it was all over, we went to the head doctor to hear the verdict. He said: 'Sir Boothby has recovered from his heart attack, and could live to a great age. Sir Plummer is suffering from severe hypertension. He must take a complete rest for a year. Otherwise he will die.'

I begged Dick to heed this advice. But he didn't. Instead he arranged to give a lecture tour in the United States, and died on arrival in New York.

# 15
# Into the Lords

I was introduced into the House of Lords by two old friends, Lord Brabazon of Tara and Lord Stanley of Alderley. Later I was to be asked by Lord Caradon (Sir Hugh Foot) to be one of his sponsors when he was introduced; and this made me feel very proud. Soon afterwards I was invited by a group of students to stand for election as Rector of the University of St Andrews. This was then one of the highest honours that Scotland could confer. If I got it, I would stand in a line which included Froude, J. S. Mill, Rosebery, A. J. Balfour, Carnegie, Marconi, Haig, Smuts, Nansen, Kipling, and Barrie. At the last moment the Conservative Party put up an official candidate against me. My student supporters told me that this would jeopardize my chances; and that my only hope now was to stand as an independent. I went to consult the Prime Minister, Harold Macmillan. He said: 'I had nothing to do with this. How much do you want to be Rector of St Andrews?' I said: 'More than anything else in the world.' 'In that case,' he replied, 'I would advise you to leave the Conservative Party, and sit on the cross-benches in the House of Lords where, in any case, I think you will be happier. I am glad that you will not be leaving us on a political issue.' A week before the vote was taken, A. J. P. Taylor wrote in the *New Statesman*: 'Next week a more important event will take place in St. Andrews than the dreary game [golf] which is played there, the election of a Rector.' He then gave the list of my opponents and added, characteristically, 'the reason for this escapes me'. When, years afterwards, I reminded him of this, I found, not to my surprise, that he had forgotten all about it. I won with a comfortable majority. Of all the messages of congratulation I received, the one I enjoyed most was a telegram from Isaiah Berlin: 'Congratulations on joining my profession from the top.' I asked Alan Taylor what I should make the subject of my Rectorial Address. 'Barrie did *Courage*,' he replied, 'and did it very well. Why not try *Cowardice*?' Eventually I chose *Tolerance*.

When I was installed I had to read the lesson at the Service in the university church. It was out of one of St Paul's epistles. Afterwards the Principal, Knox, said to me: 'Why did you leave out one sentence?' I said: 'Because I didn't agree with him.' In the course of my Rectorial Address I made an attack on the Reformation 'as it took place in this land, and from this town', which, I said, 'had plunged Scotland into a long dark night, from which she was ultimately rescued by Robert Burns'. This gave rise to a torrential correspondence in the *Scotsman*. The manses were ablaze; but I had my defenders, and much enjoyed an anonymous postcard from Argyllshire, written in red ink: 'With your love of the flesh-pots, and evident fear of death, you are easy meat for the Roman Catholic Church. I advise you to apply to Rome without delay. They will see you through – for a consideration.' At the Rectorial dinner, in proposing the toast of the university, Cyril Radcliffe, who had been given an LL.D. on my recommendation, made the best speech I have ever heard; and I have heard a lot.

As Rector, I was chairman of the governing body of the university, the University Court; and presided over many of its meetings because, during my tenure of office, we had to double the size of the university. I did not get on very well with the Principal. He was a puritan who shared the views of his famous or, as I would say, infamous namesake, John Knox. I was a cavalier. So we disapproved of each other. He was not very good with the students. I was. I loved their company. But one thing I will give him. When it came to the appointment of professors or lecturers he took infinite pains, he was quite unprejudiced, and he always chose the best.

I was later asked to stand for a second term of office, and my successor as Rector, C. P. Snow (now Lord Snow), pressed me strongly to do so. He told me that there would be no opposition. I said to him: 'Nothing will induce me to go back there for another three years.' He asked me why, and I said: 'Because I have read your books.'

From the very outset I enjoyed the House of Lords. On big subjects the standard of debate was higher than that of the House of Commons; and, as the years went by, became increasingly so. It was interesting to watch the rapid conversion of many Labour peers who came there with considerable prejudice against it. One of them, an extreme Left-winger, said to me: 'I never speak on a subject that I don't think I know a lot about. In this place I can always be sure that there are three or four people who know more about it than I do.' I have made many good friends in the Lords, and among them, rather to my surprise, was Field Marshal Lord Montgomery. In May 1953 he wrote warmly to me about an article I had written in the *News of the World*, adding that there were to be Questions in the House that week about a speech of his own, and that he relied on me to protect him! In 1956 he wrote me a letter from Versailles about a lecture I had given in Canada in which he said: 'I agree with all you say as I always have. The trouble in Western Defence has been that the nations thought they could make progress in economic and military affairs without first getting their political affairs clearly defined. We shall make no further progress until we can get out of the political morass in which we are floundering.' He added that he was going to give a lecture at the Royal United Service Institution in which he would have certain things to say about the lack of a central authority to direct the political and military affairs of the western world, adding that he would like me to attend, as my contribution to the discussion would be valuable. This gave rise to a continuous correspondence between us, which lasted until his final illness; and I have many letters from him in his own rather school-boyish writing, all of which brought me great encouragement. For example, I got a letter dated February 1961 beginning: 'My dear Bob, I have just been reading your article in the *Sunday Dispatch* of yesterday. It is absolutely first class and you have put the issue squarely before the world. I do congratulate you on a superb article.' I am re-printing two of his letters in full, both written towards the end of 1970, because I think they are of great historic interest and importance.

The first is dated 14 October 1970:

My dear Bob,

Thank you for sending me your review of *The Recovery of Europe*. I must get a copy of the book.

The trouble in the 1939/45 war was that the Americans didn't understand the political side of war. You go to war for political reasons, and when it is clear you are going to win (which was in 1943) it is essential to ensure you win with a political balance favourable to win the peace. We did not do so. Why? Because the Americans considered that all military action must be based on military factors, and politics come later. Once we had won the Battle of Normandy I said we must go all out to get possession of the great political centres of Central Europe – Berlin, Prague, Vienna. If we had fought the war properly we could have had the lot; we got none of them; Stalin got all three.

Stalin was a great leader; he had vision. The Russians might well have left the war in the winter 1940/41, but Stalin kept them in because he wanted to achieve his political object – which was to fasten his grip firmly and ever more firmly on eastern Europe, which he did. He made practically no mistakes. Yalta was his greatest victory. We British have a good deal to answer for; we could have had the leadership of western Europe after the war; we refused it. It is a fascinating subject and I would like to discuss it with you one day.

Winston should never have become Prime Minister in 1951; he was an old and tired man. I have never had any use for Anthony Eden; he was a good No. 2, but failed when he became No. 1.

If you are going to be a political leader, you must have vision and courage. Winston had both. Eisenhower did not understand the conduct of war.

I would like to lunch with you one day in the House of Lords and have a good talk.

> Yours ever,
> Montgomery of Alamein.

To this I answered on 18 October, 1970:

Dear Field Marshal,

Thanks for a fascinating letter, of absorbing interest.

During a long political life I have been a great one for espousing lost causes; and, on the whole, it has been a frustrating experience.

I was an opponent of our return to the Gold Standard in 1925 at the pre-war parity of exchange, which led to a General Strike, a long coal stoppage, and massive unemployment for fifteen years.

I was against Winston's disarmament in the 1920s, based upon his ridiculous 'ten-year rule'. I tried in vain to get re-armament going again in the 1930s against the growing menace of Hitler. I tried in vain to get a constituent of mine, Jock Burnett-Stuart, whom I think you knew well, made CIGS. He believed in armour. But Duff Cooper wouldn't look at it – on the ground that he was unpopular!

I was against Munich. I was the first MP publicly to advocate compulsory national service before the Second World War. I was against Yalta. I thought, and said, that we ought to get Berlin, Prague and Vienna. I wanted us to take the leadership of a united Western Europe in the 1950s when we could have had it on our own terms. I was against the Suez escapade. And I failed every time.

It is therefore a great consolation for me to know that, on practically all these tremendous issues, the views of a comparative nonentity like myself co-incided with yours.

I would love to lunch one day in the House of Lords and talk with you about it all.

> Yours ever,
> Bob Boothby.

His second letter was written on 13 November, 1970:

My dear Bob,

I listened to you last night on Radio 4 after the 10 p.m. news on great leaders, and lack of them today. I just want to say that I agreed with everything you said; it was exactly right.

Stalin was a great leader. If it had not been for him the Russians would have left the war in the winter of 1940/41 – as they did in 1917. I made friends with him at the Potsdam Conference in Berlin in 1945 and went to stay with him in Moscow in January 1947 when I was CIGS – with Attlee's approval. I can tell you a lot about him.

Mao tse-tung is a friend of mine, and I have the entrée to China whenever I like. I went to China as his personal guest in May 1960 and again in September 1961. In the days of the Emperors, the War Lords, and the landlords, the Chinese were the most miserable people in the world; I visited *that* China in 1934. Mao swept all that away. Today the Chinese people are happy and contented; they have a welfare state, with free education, hospitals, and food. Formerly if

they had floods, or famine because of bad harvests, the people died;
now the Government buys corn from Canada, Australia, the USA.
A leader is a man who can dominate the events which encompass him;
Mao did just that. I doubt whether Ted Heath will.

I would like to discuss these matters with you. I will be in the House
of Lords for the Censure debate on November 18. I will not be able
to get there before about 3 p.m. because I am due to lunch at No. 10
– at the invitation of Ted Heath. Could we have tea together?

I reckon I am the only person from the Western world who has sat
round the table and talked with the Russian Chiefs of Staff and also
with the Chinese Chiefs of Staff.

> Yours ever,
> Monty.

I had many talks with him. He said once: 'If I had known
you then, you would have been on my Staff during the war –
and much better off.' I said: 'Field-Marshal, if you think that
I would have run a mile before breakfast every morning you
would have had another thought coming.' He replied: 'To
begin with I would have made you, and you would have been
a much fitter man today.' On another occasion, when he was
complaining bitterly about our failure to take Berlin, Prague,
and Vienna before the Russians got there 'which we could
easily have done', I asked him who had actually stopped it.
Rather to my surprise, he said: 'Eisenhower.' I once asked him
why on earth he liked me. He said: 'No one can tell why they
like anyone, but there are two things I can tell you. I have
found, since the war, that we have always agreed about the
things that matter most. I like that. Then, I knew that they
tried to destroy you during the war, and I also knew the
strength of the force that you were up against. You fought
back, and won. I like that. I did it myself.' 'Against whom?'I
asked. 'Rommel,' came the instant reply. He never minded
anything you said to him. When I asked him what had made
him the great field commander which was his undisputed
claim to fame, he said: 'During the First World War I hardly
ever saw my Army Commander, and never my Commander-
in-Chief. I then made up my mind that, if ever I reached high
command, my troops should know me, and understand quite

clearly what I was trying to do.' If Lawrence was the only man John Buchan would have followed to the end of the earth, I can only say that, for reasons I don't know, Montgomery was the only man for whom I would have done the same. I once asked him what was Stalin's greatest victory, expecting him to say the Battle of Kursk. Instead he replied 'Yalta'.

The last time I saw him he said: 'I believe you are an Officer of the Legion of Honour.' I said I was. Then: 'Have you got unrestricted permission to wear it?' I said that I had – from Ernest Bevin. He said: 'That's rarely given. It is a good honour to have, and you are a good European. I am now going to give you an order. "Wear it." ' I was proud to wear it at his funeral; and have obeyed his order ever since.

In June 1967, the Six-Day War in Palestine broke out. Reports appeared in the English newspapers including one from the Beirut correspondent of *The Times*, of starvation, wholesale eviction, looting and the destruction of houses in the walled city of Jerusalem after it had been captured by the Jews; and on the West Bank of the Jordan. I thought I would go out and see for myself what was happening. I rang up El-Al, the Israeli airline, and asked them whether I could fly there. They said they had one plane going there that afternoon, but that it would be empty. I said that that suited me, and went. It was the day the Six-Day War came to an end with complete victory for Israel. I saw some of my friends in Tel Aviv, including Ben-Gurion who had come up from his desert retreat; Eliahu Elath; and Arthur Lourie. The Government very kindly put a military car at my disposal, and during the next three days I was taken all over the place – to Gaza, Bethlehem, the West Bank and Jerusalem. Many tanks were still smouldering, and in several places I lunched with a military commander who, only hours before, had been in battle. The pathetic little white flags, sometimes handkerchiefs, which the Palestinian Arabs had hung outside their houses were gradually being taken down. The general commanding in Gaza told me that he was replacing his troops with Arab police that day, and that next day he proposed to re-arm them. The only thing he could not bear to think of was the refugee camp; but that was a political, not a military problem. Everywhere I went I was allowed to move about freely, wherever I liked, and without a guard. Perhaps the most moving experience of all was walking, with Arthur Lourie, into the Old City of Jerusalem. He showed me where his parents were buried. There was no sign of looting or destruction, still less of starvation. On the contrary, the bazaars were well stocked with food, and busy; while Arab and Jewish children were playing happily together in the streets. The only note of gloom was struck when we went up the *Via Dolorosa*, and on to the Wailing Wall. But that was nothing new.

This was a moment of euphoria, as Golda Meir has well described it in her autobiography. If the Jews had seized the opportunity to make a generous political offer to the Arab Palestinians of the West Bank and Gaza, accompanied by whatever provisions they thought necessary for their own security, there might have been a chance of real and lasting peace.

When I got back to London I found that the House of Lords was having a debate on the refugee problem the following day. I rang up the Government Chief Whip and told him that I had just returned from Israel, and was certainly the only peer who had been there during the past week. He arranged for me to be called early in the debate, and I told them all I had seen and heard. I ended by saying: 'My Lords, they asked me to give a broadcast over the radio the night before I left Jerusalem, and I did. My last words were: "Be kind not cruel." That goes for all of us.' It was certainly the best speech I have ever made. It is not easy to move their Lordships, but this time I managed to do it.

I would not be honest if I did not confess that I have sometimes found the atmosphere of Israel rather oppressive. My religion is humour. As Maugham said in *The Summing Up*, it is man's only retort to the tragic absurdity of fate. This is not the strong suit of the Christian, Muslim, or Jewish religions – or indeed of any other, outside China. After a time the combination of prophets, commandments, sermons, wailing, kneeling, crucifixion, churches, mosques, synagogues, shrines, skull-caps, circumcision, Kosher food, chanting, candles, incense and souvenirs, all mixed up in a small space, gets me down. One day I fancied salt-herring and sour cream followed by chicken for lunch, and found I had to go to a different restaurant for each. I wondered why. And sometimes I found myself wondering how much cruelty, misery, suffering, torture and slaughter had been exported to the rest of the world from this tiny land.

I would like to end on a lighter note. When I went to Israel for the opening of the forest planted in memory of my old friend Baffy Dugdale, at which Vera Weizmann made a delightful speech brimming with humour, Violet Bonham-Carter was a member of the party; and we were taken to the Church of the Beatitudes above the Sea of Galilee, where Christ is supposed to have preached the Sermon on the Mount. As usual, we had had a strenuous morning; and Violet was hot, tired and rather cross. She marched out of the church and said: 'I don't believe the Sermon on the Mount was preached here.' 'Where was it preached?' I asked. She looked down at a field beneath the church, in which there was a little mound. She pointed to it There.' 'Well, Lady Violet,' said our Jewish guide from the Foreign Office, 'it's your religion. Have it where you like.'

Chaim Weizmann also had a great, if somewhat sardonic, sense of humour. Dick Crossman told me that once, when he was staying with him as President of Israel in Rehovoth, Meyer Weisgal rang him up on an open line from New York and said he was flying back that night, and was there anything he could bring him? The President thought for a moment, and then said: 'Yes, bring me a couple of peach-fed hams.' On another occasion, when he was attending a Zionist conference at Geneva, and thought that a rabbi was talking a lot of nonsense, he turned to a friend of his and mine and said: 'This is when all my latent anti-semitism rises to the surface.'

My final political campaign in the House of Lords has been about gold. In several speeches, all to be found in *Hansard*, I advocated an increase in the price of monetary gold as the only solution to our monetary problem. I found only one supporter – the late Lord Fraser of Lonsdale. The only other word of encouragement I got was from Thomas Balogh. When I quoted to him Keynes's dictum that the individualistic capitalism of today, precisely because it entrusts saving to the individual investor, and production to the individual employer, *presumes* a stable measure-rod of value, and cannot be efficient – perhaps cannot survive – without one, he said to me: 'If you believe, as you do and I do not, that gold alone can provide that measuring-rod, because everyone believes in it and no one believes in anything else, then of course the case for raising the price of bullion is unanswerable.' In what turned out to be his final speech as Leader of the House, Lord Jellicoe made the best case against gold that I have ever heard; but it did not convince me.

I have fought the Treasury all my life. In 1968 I said in Parliament: 'Those who have most consistently opposed the Treasury policies during the past forty-five years have been the most consistently right; and I'm nearly at the top of the list.' Upon this Nicholas Davenport commented: 'It was no idle boast.' During the dreadful decade of depression between 1925 and 1935, Sir Otto Niemeyer rendered Hitler just as great a service at the Treasury in London as Dr Schacht did at the Bank in Berlin. The Bank of England was even worse. On 25 April 1932, in a speech in the House of Commons, I said that the policy pursued, which had been consistently wrong and absolutely disastrous in its results, could be summed up in the single word 'deflation'. While we should have been reconstructing our own industries and developing the limitless resources of our Crown Colonies, we had been deliberately prevented from doing either of these two things. All we had done was to double the burden of our internal debt, while money which was denied to Britain, its industries and its Empire, was never stinted to European countries. I continued:

A statesman is judged by results. If his policy fails he goes. It may be unfair, but there is a kind of rough justice about it. Mr Montagu Norman, on the other hand, is never called upon to explain, justify or defend his policies. And it is his policies which have been carried out for the past ten years. Governments may come and governments may go, but the Governor of the Bank of England goes on for ever. It is a classic example of power without responsibility. . . . I do not ask for more, at the moment, than an assurance that the policy of deflation which has wrought such terrible damage and brought such misery to this country, is no longer to be continued.

'Economics,' said the late Lord Birkenhead, 'is a dismal and it is also a purely empirical science, if indeed it can be called a

science at all. Its professors grope more faithfully, but with less
certainty, towards the light (or towards the dark) than the
titular exponents of any other branch of human learning.' For
economists as such I have tremendous regard and affection.
They are good talkers, and good friends; and, unlike Churchill,
until they relapse into mathematics, I can understand what
they say. I have only one complaint to make against them.
They are always wrong. As they survey the present stricken
scene, they can hardly be proud of their handiwork.

The last time I saw Keynes, I said to him: 'You showed us
the way out of unemployment caused by deflation, falling
prices, low wages, and lack of purchasing power. What about
unemployment caused by inflation, rising prices, high wages,
and lack of production?' 'Ah,' he said, 'that is more dangerous.
I have seen it at close quarters. When the time comes, I will
show you the way out of that too.' The time came all too soon.
But when it did he was dead. The last time I saw Hawtrey I
asked him whether he thought we should ever have a viable
international monetary system. 'Not before the end of the
century,' he said. As by that time I shall be dead, I have now
given up.

I kept in touch with the Royal Air Force. Sholto Douglas,
by now Lord Douglas of Kirtleside, invited me to join a party
to go to Vienna, in order to celebrate the maiden flight of the
Trident, and his own retirement as Chairman of British
European Airways. On the way there he said to me: 'This is by
far the best short-distance aircraft that has yet been made; and
I chose it.' The choice has since been abundantly justified. We
had a marvellous time. We went to the Vienna woods, to the
Blue Danube which belies its name, and to the opera – still the
best in Europe; and one night we dined at a restaurant near
the Hungarian frontier. A few hundred yards away there was
a watch-tower. We walked over to look at it, while the armed
sentry looked at us from the top. On each side the watch-
towers continued as far as the eye could see. Here was the 'Iron
Curtain' which we had brought upon ourselves. We thought
of it stretching for hundreds of miles right across Europe. The
thought was eerie.

On the last night they gave a dinner for Sholto, and asked
me to propose his health. My speech was very short. I simply

mentioned the posts he had held – Commander-in-Chief
Fighter Command, Commander-in-Chief Coastal Command,
Chairman of BEA – and ended with three words, 'he never
failed'. Instead of replying, he got up abruptly and left the
room alone, with tears in his eyes. It was not my speech that
did it. It was, as he told me afterwards, the sudden realization
that this was the end. He was, as Lord Balfour of Inchrye said
in his admirable Address at the Memorial Service in Westminster Abbey, a born leader of men.

On another occasion I was asked to speak at the annual
dinner of the Air Gunners of Bomber Command. I found myself sitting next to Sir Arthur Harris. They called him 'Butch',
but with affectionate regard. I well knew that for four years as
Commander-in-Chief, and under terrific strain for all concerned, he had never ceased to command the loyalty of his
crews; and that for four years he had carried out his bombing
policy with the unswerving personal support of Churchill
himself. Terrible mistakes were made, but they were not all
his. The destruction of Dresden, a few weeks before the war
came to an end, was one. It soon gave rise to a wave of revul-
sion throughout what was left of the civilized world; and
Harris was blamed. I was later told that he had sent his Chief
of Staff, Air Vice-Marshal Saundby, to the Air Ministry to
protest against this raid. Saundby alone can answer this. Not
even Lindemann was responsible for the raid. At that moment
he was obsessed (he was always obsessed with something) with
the bombing of oil refineries. I think that this tragic raid was
an American decision. Anyway Harris was left to bear the
blame alone.

I hope I have never attached undue importance to peerages.
But when they are conferred upon commanders at the end of
a great war, they have a certain symbolic significance. The
casualties of Bomber Command were heavier than those of any
other. The Commander-in-Chief was the only one who was not
given a peerage; and this was greatly resented by all who
served in it. After I had spoken at the dinner, Harris made a
powerful speech in defence of his strategy and tactics, supported by figures which certainly convinced even the doubters,
like myself, that it had not all been a waste of time, of engineering skill and of valuable young lives. When it was over, I stood

aside to let him go out. He put his hand on my shoulder, and said: 'No. Peers first.' It was almost the only time in my life that I have felt ashamed.

In addition to the House of Lords I joined a number of organizations – The European-Atlantic Group, the Anglo-Israel Association (of which I became President), the British-Atlantic Group, and the British Association of Manipulative Medicine (as Chairman). Under the guidance of Ronald Barbor, one of our great orthopaedic surgeons, the last helped to give to the osteopaths the status they now enjoy. The others achieved nothing; but gave one the opportunity to go places, and meet interesting people. One conference sticks in my memory. It was in Munich. For old times sake I went to the Oktoberfest, drank six tankards of Löwenbrau beer, and then went round the Big Dipper (the highest in Europe) twice. I had a restless night. Next morning, when I was listening to a speech by Gladwyn, I felt an unmistakable pain in my chest. I took a taxi to my hotel, and asked the Manager whether there was a heart specialist in Munich. 'Only the best in Europe,' he replied. He made an appointment for me at two o'clock. The doctor was a charming man, who spoke perfect English. I told him my story, and he took a cardiogram. Then he said: 'My diagnosis is a slight tremor, but nothing like an infarct. My prescription is as follows: "Never drink more than two tankards of Löwenbrau at a time; never go on the Big Dipper again; never go to another international conference; and never listen to another speech by Lord Gladwyn." Now go back to your hotel, have a double whisky, and take the first plane back to London.' I telephoned home, and when I reached my flat found two doctors, Walter Somerville and John Henderson, awaiting me. After another cardiogram they told me that the diagnosis and prescription of the German doctor were both absolutely right; and we then sat up talking until midnight sinking a bottle of whisky between us. When I subsequently told Gladwyn about this, all he said was: 'I had no idea I was capable of moving you so much.'

I kept in close touch with General Paul Legentilhomme until the end of his long life. He became Military Governor of Paris, where he lived in state in the 'Invalides', and was given a KCB and the Médaille Militaire. But he never achieved his greatest ambition. This was to bring peace to the Far East. He wanted to withdraw all the French military forces from Indo-China immediately after the war; and to negotiate a peace treaty, and a trade and cultural agreement, with his friend Ho-Chi-Minh. I have seen a letter to him from Ho-Chi-Minh in his own handwriting and in perfect French, which left me in no doubt that if Vincent Auriol (the President of France) had had the guts to send Legentilhomme to Hanoi, he would have succeeded. If he had, there would have been no battle of Dien Bien Phu, and no Vietnam war. He said to me, at the time: 'It is no longer possible, even if it were desirable, for European countries to keep troops on the mainland of Asia; and this applies also to the United States. If we try to do it, they will be thrown out.' Later he convinced General de Gaulle. When, on the only occasion they met, President Kennedy asked de Gaulle whether he had any advice to give him, he replied: 'Only one piece of advice. Keep out of Indo-China.' He didn't take it. He plunged into Vietnam, and Lyndon Johnson plunged deeper. The result was the most humiliating defeat the Americans have ever suffered.

Paul Legentilhomme was one of the nicest and most intelligent Generals I have ever known; and I knew him pretty well, because he married my secretary. He had a profound admiration for Auchinleck, who, he said, had stopped Rommel at first Alamein 'with almost nothing', and whom he thought was very badly treated; and for General Platt, commanding our forces in East Africa, who has never been heard of since. It was he who gave me the chance to do some useful work during the last years of the war, which my Station Commander in the RAF urged me to take. It was he who so often smoothed the path for de Gaulle in London, when he was being more difficult than usual. He once told me about a particularly stormy meeting between de Gaulle and Churchill. At the end of it Churchill said: 'Am I to understand, General, that you are prepared to make no concessions at all?' De Gaulle replied: 'At the moment, Prime Minister, I am too weak to make any concessions.' Legentilhomme said that he then detected a glint of admiration in Churchill's eyes. Long after the war I said to Churchill: 'Roosevelt hated de Gaulle, and that was understandable. You did something worse. You underestimated him. He is in your class, and that is where the historians will put him.' He did not answer.

Now I have resigned from everything. After this book I intend to do nothing more than try to enjoy myself. But where? and how?

# 16
# The Media

After the war, when I had been re-elected to the House of Commons, I consulted Lord Woolton, a shrewd old bird, about what I ought to do. He said: 'You will never be happy in the corridors of political power. You are no good at intrigue; and you are incapable of keeping your mouth shut. My advice to you is to stay in Parliament for as long as you wish, and say what you think. They won't turn you out, because they know that they can't. But make your career on the media – journalism, the radio and television for which you have a vocation. And never underestimate their power.'

This, coming from the Chairman of the Conservative Party machine, was advice not to be disregarded; and I took it. I have never regretted it. I never really wanted to become involved in what Harold Macmillan has aptly described as 'the vast dullness of the administrative structure'.

I was also much strengthened in my determination to make such career as lay ahead of me on the media by two letters from Sir Arthur (subsequently Lord) Salter, one of our most distinguished Civil Servants, in the aftermath of his book *Slave of the Lamp*.

In one he wrote:

The differences between us are (1) you have your voice, both as a physical fact and in all that it has meant in speaking and in broadcasting, and (2) as a person with public fame, your power is not precariously based. As a 'slave of the Lamp' I have more than once brought a sudden change in the political scene, found myself in a moment from having had substantial power to having no more than that of a complete nonentity. 'Public fame' is not similarly precarious: it has as its foundation the memories of millions. It is usual too for 'screened' power to develop a kind of timidity that erodes character and personality. It is therefore with some touch of envy as much as admiration that I look at you. To be fiercely attacked and opposed – even for a time battered painfully – brings its own rewards, as the opposite experience does not.

(I sometimes thank God that I was never a member of 'The Establishment'; and that I have fought it all my life.)

In the other letter from Lord Salter, in the 1960s, he wrote:

My mind has recently gone back to the trivial technicality which, a quarter of a century ago, interrupted your political career – and I have been reflecting that since then no one in public life has, as one can see in retrospect, been so uniformly right on each of the great issues on which he has fought, or devoted such courage, ability, and persistent effort in contending against those who took the opposite (and disastrously wrong) side at the time.

Arthur Salter was a great public servant; and I would rather have had his praise than that of anyone else. In quoting what he wrote to me, I am of course boasting. Why not?

My journalistic career had been started, when I was at Oxford, by St Loe Strachey, then editor and proprietor of the *Spectator*. 'When you are writing an article,' he said, 'think you are writing me a letter.' After this, for several years, I wrote the *Parliamentary Sketch* under a *nom-de-plume*, first for the *Spectator* and then for the *New Statesman*. It was always delivered by hand, and no one except the Editor knew who had written it. Occasionally some of my parliamentary colleagues used to say to me 'Have you seen what the *Parliamentary Sketch* said this week? Do you know who wrote it?' I always replied that I had no idea, but agreed that it was absolutely monstrous. For a while I 'free-lanced' all over the place. But then, during and after the war, I was taken on first by the *News of the World* and then by the *Sunday Dispatch*. I loved every second of it. The truth is that I love Fleet Street, and all the people in it; and feel happier there than anywhere else – except perhaps the television studios. I suppose I am by nature an extrovert.

For several years an article of mine on the central page of the *News of the World* about the future of the Council of Europe, or of the United Nations, or of gold, appeared sandwiched between the crime and the sex. The combination must have worked, because the circulation of the paper reached vertiginous heights. Often on a Saturday night I would go down to Bouverie Street and watch the presses thundering out eight million copies. It was always exciting. It would be invidious to mention names; but I can say, with my hand on my heart, that I have never received anything but help and encouragement from all the editors I have ever worked for. And of how many other professions can that be said?

I started my career on radio and television in the *Brains Trust* during the war. Donald McCullogh pulled me in. As 'question master' he had what can only be described as genius. His handling of such diverse personalities as Cyril Joad, Julian Huxley and Commander Campbell was brilliant; and put the programme second only to ITMA in audience ratings. Joad, the star, told me that his favourite pastime was travelling on railway trains without a ticket. He regarded it as a game. I begged him to chuck it; but he enjoyed it too much. In the end it brought him down. He always began his answers by saying: 'It depends what you mean by . . .'. And that floored us all. Donald wanted to go on to television, but the strange thing was that, superb as he was on radio, he was no good at that. Never at ease with the cameras. However, he made a good career for himself in public relations; and everyone loved him.

Television was rather a different kettle of fish. After the war Edgar Lustgarten thought up a programme for the BBC to be called *In The News*. There was to be a regular team, which he chose. It consisted of A. J. P. Taylor, Michael Foot, W. J. Brown and myself. In those days television was very different from what it is today. The heat was terrific, and we had to sweat through a heavy greasepaint make-up. On the first night I couldn't find Alexandra Palace, but I got there in the nick of time, to be smothered in greasepaint and almost stifled. The programme was an immense success. It went on, weekly, from triumph to triumph. To our astonishment Michael Foot and I saw ourselves being built up, rapidly, into national figures by an unseen force outside Parliament. Understandably the politicians couldn't take this. The Conservative and Labour Central Offices, under the direction of Lord Woolton and Herbert Morrison, moved in. 'These fellows,' they said, 'say exactly what they think.' 'That,' replied the Director General of the BBC, Sir William Haley, 'is the whole point of the programme.' Grace Wyndham Goldie, in the best book that has yet been written about British television, *Facing the Nation*, has well described how they killed it. It took quite a long time. Sir George Barnes, then Head of BBC television, even went to the length of asking the Conservative Chief Whip for a list of speakers who would put the party point of view. Practically all those on the list, including David Eccles and John Boyd-Carpenter, refused. Barnes once said to me: 'I was glad to be knighted by the Queen on the field of battle' – meaning the television studios.

Norman Collins was made of sterner stuff. He revived the programme on ITV, with the name of *Free Speech*. It soon became, with the joint, part of the Sunday lunch. The British are a very funny people. They are all conservative, with a small *c*. If they like something, they like it regularly, and without change. On the rare occasions when we had a guest, we could all feel the resentment coming back at us through the camera – including the guest. I nearly always wore a bow tie. If I ever wore another one, I could count on at least a hundred letters of protest from all over the country. On the whole we were lucky that the two programmes lasted for nearly ten years. They were no small part of my life; and all the memories are happy ones. Bill Brown was a 'natural' on television. He understood the medium to perfection. He had only three faults. He never took a taxi, never stood anyone a drink, and for two years never changed his suit. One day Michael Foot, Edgar Lustgarten, John Irwin, Alan Taylor and myself decided to put up £10 each to buy him a new one. Next week he died, and left over £200 000. Alan Taylor rang me up and said: 'We've had a lucky escape. He'd have taken it.'

One Sunday Randolph Churchill came to the studio to do another programme. 'For God's sake don't bring him in here,' said Michael Foot. I went with Randolph to the room in which he was lunching. 'Spam!' I said, 'how nostalgic! It takes me back to the war.' He looked at me suspiciously, and said: 'What are you having?' 'Come and see,' I said. It was lobster and hock. As Michael had predicted, there was a fearful row. But in the end Randolph had to go back and lunch off Spam.

Gradually, but steadily, the political pressure against *Free Speech* built up. Rumours abounded. One was that Norman Collins had been offered a safe seat by the Conservative Central Office if he would take us off the air, and had refused it. In the end we went down; but we had a good run for our money. I am the first to take off my hat to the 'interviewers' who have succeeded us, and brought their profession to a fine art. But, as one senior official of the BBC, now retired,recently said to me: 'There will never be a programme quite like *In the News* and *Free Speech* again.'

When, in 1953, I was made a KBE, the team gave a dinner in my honour. Sir Dingle Foot (one of our chairmen and a member of a band of brothers the like of which we have never seen, and the only family in British history who have them-selves constituted a 'Brains Trust' on the BBC, under the chairmanship of their distinguished father Isaac, a Liberal, a Cornishman and a devout Cromwellian) brought with him a poem the second verse of which, with his gracious permission, I now print. I can never ask for a better epitaph.

Dinner to Robert Boothby, K.B.E.

by the original team of
IN THE NEWS

8th June 1953

R.B. – K.B.E.

But now a new phenomenon is seen
A television knight from Aberdeen,
Even the Tory whips dared not refuse
The man who keeps their party in the news.
The cry goes up from several million hearts
'With such a knight, who gives a damn for barts?'
Just listen while the Heralds' College gloats –
'A herring rampant on a field of oats'.
While listeners from the Danube to the Dee
Acclaim with shouts the latest K.B.E.

> And in the Elysian Fields, when shadows fall,
> An old, fat man – the greatest knight of all –
> Says to Doll Tearsheet as he quaffs his sack
> 'Thank God, my sort of knight is coming back.'

Another programme I was asked to do by ITV was *Dinner Party*, at which I acted as host. It came off all right, but the food and drink were both so good that by the end of the evening my guests were apt to be a bit too cheerful. The two that stand out in my memory are Hugh Gaitskell and Jo Grimond. It was a perfect setting for them; and they both talked with brilliance.

One night the distinguished editor of one of our most famous national papers, who had been ill and was very tired, arrived absolutely sloshed with gin. I believe the notes which I exchanged with the control room are still preserved in the ITV archives. My first was: 'Regret to say X is drunk.' I got back 'Perhaps he will sober up.' To this I replied: 'On the contrary, he is sobering down.' (By this time he had poured three glasses of port on to the tablecloth.) My last note was: 'X now hopeless and helpless. Do your best.' Next day Peter Black wrote an amusing review in the *Daily Mail*:

> Lord Boothby's dinner-parties continue to supply us with their eccentric joys. Last night it was the Invisible Man. I could have sworn I saw cigarette smoke which appeared to come from human lips, floating across the screen. And occasionally a voice, to which Lord Boothby paid not the faintest attention, could be heard saying, 'I say, chaps, what are we talking about?'

But such incidents were rare. One eminent art critic fell fast asleep with her head on my shoulder. The series, as a whole, was judged to be a success.

Then, one day, I was asked to do an interview with an old friend, John Freeman, called *Face to Face*. I was the third. I was a little surprised when they told me that they wanted me to sit for a portrait by Topolski. I was still more surprised when I reached the studio at Lime Grove, and received a message: 'Mr Freeman thinks you will understand that he does not wish to see you before the programme.' I was then taken to a studio draped in jet black, with God knows how many cameras and lights. Then, suddenly, John appeared, and sat opposite to me

with the cameras behind him. And it began. I was not frightened, because I am always happy in a studio. But it was rather
a daunting experience.

The programme was later repeated, and this is what John
said:

The programme that you are about to see is different in one
important way from all the others we have done in *Face to Face*. Baron
Boothby, of Buchan and Rattray Head – to give him his full title,
which he rather enjoys – is a personal friend of long standing. That
meant two things, First, that I already had very clear views about his
character and personality. Secondly, that I had to ask myself whether
I was tough enough to give a friend the full treatment, and not let
him off lightly.

As to the first, many of you have your own opinions about Bob
Boothby, but I will tell you how I see him. I think he is one of the most
gifted and idealistic and truthful men anywhere in public life. He is
also lazy and self-indulgent and over-generous. All these qualities
mixed up together have resulted in the comparative failure of his
public life, and the total success of his personal friendships. He has
usually backed the right political horses; but when, in the end, they
gallop home, Bob seldom shares the winnings. He is either in disgrace
for having blurted out something indiscreet, or he is off playing
baccarat at Deauville. Occasionally he amuses himself by trying,
with perfect good humour, to deny these charges. You will be able to
judge whether he does so in this programme – and whether I have
succeeded in making them stick.'

This portrait is far too flattering. But I know, in my bones,
that it is also the best that has been painted of me, or ever will
be. John Freeman and Malcolm MacDonald are the two men,
of a younger generation than mine, whom I have most admired.
The *Face to Face* programmes are certainly the best that have
ever been seen on television – with Jung perhaps the winner;
and they will last for years. Malcolm MacDonald did more than
any other single man to liquidate the British Empire without
bloodshed. Now they have both chosen to disappear, untitled
and unsung. Who am I to blame them? I am off myself. But I
sometimes think that I have lingered on too long, although I
must confess that I enjoy being Baron Boothby, of Buchan and
Rattray Head.

I was lucky to meet, and to know, some of the great American columnists who blossomed during and after the war. Walter Lippmann, the Alsop brothers, Reston, Edgar Mowrer, Walter Duranty, Knickerbocker, Louis Fischer. It is a tribute to his character, and to the esteem in which he was universally held, when I say that no one on either side of the Atlantic will disagree with me that Walter Lippmann was the greatest journalist of our time. I always went to see him when I was in Washington; and he never failed to bring his delightful wife to lunch with me when he came to London.

One of my most precious possessions is a letter he wrote to me from New York, dated 8 March 1954, in which he said: 'I don't know anyone speaking these days with whom I find myself agreeing so much or so often as with you.' When he left Washington for New York, I asked him why he did it. He replied: 'I couldn't take it any more. The corruption was too widespread. Kennedy was vastly over-rated, Lyndon Johnson is a disaster, and Nixon will be worse.'

Now we have developed our own breed of columnists; and they are bloody good. My only criticism of them is that, as Beecham said of Wagner, they are apt to go on too long. Walter Lippmann once said to me: 'I always write a two thousand word article, quite easily, in less than a couple of hours. Then it takes me six hours to cut it down to one.' I am sure that every editor in Fleet Street would approve of this. I must add a word about Ed Murrow. He put me on many of his programmes, including *One World* and I enjoyed working under his direction more than that of anyone else. One programme sticks in my memory. Senator Kennedy (as he then was) in Washington, Krishna Menon in New York, and myself in London. Ed sat by my side. He was a marvellous friend. Whenever I went to New York he took care to see that, on radio and television, I was always paid my expenses. One night I watched him destroy McCarthy in a single programme on television. It was an astonishing demonstration of the power of the medium in the hands of a master. The last time I saw him I said: 'Ed, you are killing yourself with cigarettes.' He replied: 'I know. But I like it that way.'

In conclusion I must refer to the radio programme *Any Questions?* It started on western radio for a week; and has lasted ever since. Freddie Grisewood, who taught me to sing at Oxford, saw to it that I was a regular member. I must have appeared on it about thirty times. Once, when Hugh Gaitskell took part in it, we travelled down together. He said: 'You don't care a damn what you say, but I have just been Chancellor of the Exchequer, and must be careful. Are we likely to be asked any embarrassing questions?' I said: 'Not at Bournemouth.' The first question was 'Were we right to throw out Seretse Khama?' I knew that he thought we were wrong, and his face paled. The next question was 'Should we now throw out South Africa from the British Commonwealth?' He became paler. The third question was, 'What would the team do if they woke up tomorrow morning and found that they had changed their sex?' There was dead silence. Then Freddie Grisewood said: 'What would you do, Bob?' I replied: 'Go for a walk and see what happened.' By this time Hugh's face was parchment.

Then, one day, I found that I was becoming bored with the programme; and I knew that this was not because of any defect in it but because I was stale. I wrote to Michael Bowen, the producer, and called it a day. In a charming letter he replied that he was saddened, but not surprised. He ended by saying: 'It is no coincidence that in most of the outstanding *Any Questions?* in my memory over nineteen years the name of Boothby is to be found in the team. Yours is a magnificent record, for which we are all immensely grateful. Yours, in admiration and affection.' It is always a good thing in life to know when to go.

One other memory of *Any Questions?* One Good Friday the team consisted of Lady Violet Bonham-Carter, Tom Driberg, Arthur Street and myself. It was to be at Minehead. In those days I had a car, and I offered to drive Lady Violet and Tom down there. They had never met. At eight o'clock in the morning Tom rang me up and said: 'I'm afraid I can't come.' I said: 'You can't chuck it at this stage. What's the matter?' He said in sepulchral tones: 'I have fallen in love.' I said: 'Don't be ridiculous. Come round at once, and I will put you right.' He came, and I gave him two aspirins and half a bottle of champagne. I said: 'You are not to mention this to Lady Violet.' No sooner had we got into the car than he gave a deep sigh, and said to me: 'Have you ever been in love?' I said: 'Shut up.' And he did. After lunch he said that, as it was Good Friday, he must do the stations of the Cross, and that he had looked up a High Anglican Church, which he showed to us on the map. It involved a 'detour' of twenty miles, but we went. When we got there he invited us to come in, but we said we would rather stay in the car. After about twenty minutes, he came out, with a face of wooden gravity, and said: 'I prayed for you both at each station.' We thanked him very much. But later, on the way to Minehead, Lady Violet said: 'I think, Mr Driberg, that you are more interested in the Army Orders of religion than in religion itself.' I was always interested in Tom's obsession with liturgy and High Anglicanism. I once told him that I had attended a service in a high Anglican church in Cornwall. We got the full works – candles, incense, vestments – the lot. Then, suddenly, a wooden pigeon whizzed over our heads on an electric wire stretching from the porch of the church to the altar. I said to my neighbour in the pew: 'What was that?' He replied: 'The Holy Ghost.' All Tom said was: 'How very moving.' On this at least we could agree.

# Epilogue

I am glad that I have lived so much of my life by, and about, the North Sea. I never read the concluding paragraph of Harold Nicolson's *Tennyson* – a beautiful piece of prose writing – without emotion. After telling us to forget the delicate Laureate, the shallow thought, the honeyed idyll, the complacent ode, the magnolia, the roses, the laurels and the rhododendrons, he ends: 'Let us recall only the low booming of the North Sea upon the dunes; the grey clouds lowering above the wold; the moan of the night wind on the fen; the far glimmer of marsh-pools through the reeds; the cold, the half: light and the gloom.'

All the major causes I have espoused – for a good monetary policy, against appeasement, for rearmament, and for a united Europe – were lost. But life has its compensations. Recently, when I was sitting alone in a pub, a distinguished old man with flowing white hair and a white beard, came over and sat opposite me. He said, in a singing Welsh voice: 'I know you. When you kick the bucket, we will drink your health not only in our fishing villages, but in our valleys.' I said: 'Why the valleys?' And he replied: 'Because we know that you were a great friend of Lloyd George and of Aneurin Bevan; and that, from within the Tory Party, you fought for the miners all your life.'

I think I have managed to do something practical to help the fishermen, the farmers, the cancer-sufferers, the Czech refugees, the buggers and the osteopaths. It is not precisely the programme I planned for myself when I first entered public life. But it is something.

When Oscar Hammerstein died they gave him a lovely memorial service in Southwark Cathedral, to which I went. After that the BBC asked me to do a programme about him, and gave me an hour. It was by far the most enjoyable programme I have ever done on radio or television. With the invaluable help of Anna Instone I recorded with comments song after song. Nearly all the music was by Jerome Kern and Richard Rodgers, for whom he wrote the lyrics. It was part, and a great part, of my life. Now, I suppose, it has all been supplanted by 'beat' music. More's the pity. One day, I hope, the BBC will give me a record of this programme. It will bring me more pleasure than anything else could do. I listened to it in a motor-car while a cousin and godson of mine was being married. He understood.

Then Julian Amery said to me one day, long after the war: 'I suppose you realize that you have now become a professional memorial service addresser.' I went straight back to my flat, and looked up my diary. It was too true. Lloyd George, Weizmann, Duff Cooper, Clement Davies, Sir Lewis Namier, Compton Mackenzie, Sir Jameson Adams, Sir Edward Beddington-Behrens, Mary Borden, Bill Allen – the list was endless. Immediately I wrote a codicil to my will. In no circumstances was there to be a memorial service to myself. All I wish is that my ashes should be thrown over Buchan and the North Sea from the light-house at Rattray Head, which was built by Robert Louis Stevenson's father. Perhaps the Royal Philharmonic Orchestra might give a concert in my memory. I would like them to begin with the overture to *Die Meistersinger*, go straight on to *The Siegfried Idyll*, then to Debussy's *La Mer* or *L'Apres-midi d'un faune*, and finally to Delius, *Brigg Fair*, *In a Summer Garden*, or the *Walk to the Paradise Garden* – it doesn't matter which. The audience will find no difficulty in discerning the thread which runs through all three composers. It is woven round one word – melody.

I would like it to be an emotional concert. No Beethoven, no Mozart, certainly no Bach. In the second half, a Brahms symphony, or perhaps Tchaikovsky 5 or 6. Or perhaps Yehudi Menuhin (a friend of mine) would come back to play Elgar's violin concerto which, when he was a boy, made his name and fame. Finally, a lollipop – preferably the *Sleigh Ride*.

In short, a typical Beecham concert of the music he loved most.

If they play the programme I have suggested, they will make money: and that is what I would like best.

# APPENDIX 1

# The Battle of Jutland

Of all the accounts I have read of the Battle of Jutland, and I have read many, the best seems to me to be that of Corelli Barnett in his book *The Swordbearers*.*

Jellicoe was keenly aware of the fact that, as Churchill subsequently pointed out, he was the only man on either side who could lose the war in an afternoon. And, unlike St Vincent, Nelson or Collingwood, he did not feel sure of his own ships. For this reason he avoided close action in his initial deployment, and subsequently turned away twice. He knew more about the respective merits of the Grand Fleet and the High Seas Fleet than anyone else, and was convinced that in *matériel* the High Seas Fleet was superior. In 1910, as Controller of the Navy, he had written a powerful memorandum in which he pointed out that the German ships were better designed, better constructed, better engineered, and better armoured with better steel than ours. Jellicoe was also dissatisfied with the quality of British shells. They could not pierce armour at an oblique angle. He asked for new shells capable of long-range plunging fire, with an explosive more stable than Lyddite. He did not get them.

All this was, and remains, a severe reflection on British naval constructors and armament manufacturers before the First World War. The truth is that Fisher's much vaunted fleet, from the *Dreadnought* onwards, was a poor one. Above all his battle-cruisers, in which armour was sacrificed for speed and

* Eyre and Spottiswoode, 1963; Penguin, 1966.

heavy guns which failed to sink, and often to hit, enemy ships, proved death-traps. Perhaps the greatest service rendered to the Royal Navy by Churchill as First Lord before the First World War was to scrap the battle-cruiser programme he found awaiting him, and substitute for it the construction of a fast division of well-armoured oil-driven battleships (the *Queen Elizabeths*), carrying eight fifteen-inch guns. These, at long last, turned out to be the answer. Churchill himself has paid high tribute to our naval constructors. But in July 1914, just before he assumed command at sea, Jellicoe sent him a memorandum in which he said that the inferiority of the protection of British ships of the 1909–11 classes against German guns and torpedoes was very striking; and that it was highly dangerous to consider that our ships as a whole were superior or even equal fighting machines. After Jutland I never met a captain in the Grand Fleet who did not agree that Jellicoe's forebodings had proved to be fully justified, except Richmond, who fiercely criticized his caution. But he himself was not there.

When Beatty reached Jellicoe after the run to the north he was, with all his courage, a beaten Admiral. And he had been beaten not by Scheer's battleships but by Hipper's battle-cruisers. He had lost a third of his force. And he was unable to fulfil his primary function, which was to tell the Commander-in-Chief the position, course and speed of the High Seas Fleet. When Jellicoe signalled to him, 'Where is the enemy's Battle Fleet?' he could not answer. In the circumstances Jellicoe's deployment must be regarded as the peak of his achievement. He put Scheer in a corral, and his own fleet between him and his bases. For forty minutes, ten of them at close range, he had the High Seas Fleet in sight under his guns, and subjected it to the heaviest bombardment ever fired at sea, while his own ships remained shrouded in mist, and presented no target to the enemy. He hit the German ships many times. But he did not sink them. At 6.36 Scheer, by means of a masterly manoeuvre unknown to the British – *Gefechtskehrtwendung nach steuerbord* – escaped from the trap. Some of our battleships saw the German ships turn, but they did not report to the Fleet Flagship. In fact they did nothing. Nor did any division of the Grand Fleet attempt to act independently for the rest of the battle.

In the voluminous and detailed Battle Orders drawn up by

Jellicoe in 1914 it was laid down that, after deployment, there would be need for an extensive decentralization of command. At Jutland this did not happen. It was partly due to Jellicoe's own obsession with detail and temperamental inability to delegate, which led ultimately to his replacement as First Sea Lord by Wemyss; but mainly to the hierarchical tradition of strict obedience to orders from above, which had been built up in the Royal Navy over many years.

After the war Admiral Sir Reginald ('Blinker') Hall, who had been Director of Naval Intelligence and subsequently took charge of the Conservative Central Office, talked to me at some length about Jutland. He blamed the divisional commanders of the Battle Fleet, particularly Jerram and Leveson (Second Battle Squadron in the van), for their lack of initiative. He said that, when they had the High Seas Fleet in sight and range, they should themselves have altered course to close the enemy, in which case the remainder of the fleet must have conformed in support. Instead they kept rigidly to the course which had been ordered by the Fleet Flagship astern, from which Jellicoe could not see what was happening.

Corelli Barnett disputes this view. He writes:

In view of the performance of Beatty's and his own cruiser squadrons – except for Goodenough – limp, bewildered and ineffective – and of Evan-Thomas's and Beatty's misunderstandings over simple and obvious manoeuvres, it is difficult to believe that Jellicoe was wrong to centralize his battle fleet and its tactics. The truth was that the Grand Fleet was only capable of rigid text-book manoeuvres; and Jellicoe was cool-headed enough to realize it.

The fact is that communications within the Grand Fleet were very bad. With the brilliant exception of Goodenough, the Commander-in-Chief was ill-served by his cruiser squadrons. Even his own battleships seldom reported what they saw. In consequence, Jellicoe fought the Battle of Jutland blind. Despite this, he twice engaged the High Seas Fleet under visibility conditions extremely favourable to himself. It is clear evidence of his skill as a tactician.

One great mystery remains. Why did the Grand Fleet steam steadily south during the night of 31 May–1 June, against all the odds, while Scheer broke through to his bases astern of it, inflicting heavy losses on the British light forces as he did so? Did Jellicoe really want to fight a fleet action on 1 June, with a whole day before him? He said afterwards that he did, and bitterly reproached the Admiralty for not passing on Scheer's signals ordering course for the Horn Reef, all of which they received and deciphered, to him. Admittedly the conduct of the Admiralty, then under the direction of Balfour and Sir Henry Jackson, was throughout the battle supine. Tyrwhitt lay at Harwich with thirty-five destroyers, of which Jellicoe was short. He left harbour to join in the action, and was immediately ordered back to base. As for the failure to transmit Scheer's signals, with one exception, to Jellicoe, the comment made to me years afterwards in the House of Commons by Admiral Sir William James suffices: 'It would be incredible if it were not true.' Nevertheless the sound and flashes of heavy gunfire and the beams of searchlights astern of him must have indicated to the British Commander-in-Chief that Scheer was making for the Horn Reef. *Malaya*, of the Fifth Battle Squadron in the rear of his own battle line, actually saw a German battleship. But not a single ship reported to Jellicoe. Until long after midnight he had time to turn and intercept the High Seas Fleet. When at last, he did turn northwards, the sea was empty, and Scheer was home.

In the light of subsequent knowledge derived from exhaustive enquiries into the structure of our ships and the quality of our shells, particularly the report of the Projectile Committee, the question must be asked – what would have happened if Jellicoe had fought a fleet action in daylight on 1 June? It is at least possible that Scheer would still have broken through to his bases, after inflicting heavy losses on the British Battle Fleet which, as it was, emerged unscathed.

The day after the Battle Fleet reached Scapa, a funeral service for those who had been killed was held in Orkney. Jellicoe stood alone in front of his Admirals. Later *Bartimeus* was to write: 'In the courage, judgement and sober self-confidence of that solitary figure had rested the destiny of an Empire through one of the greatest crises in her history.' And this verdict will almost certainly stand. But the final word lies with Beatty. Sitting in the chart-room of his badly damaged flagship *Lion* as she limped back to Rosyth, he suddenly looked up and said wearily to his staff: 'There is something wrong with our ships; and with our system.' He was right on both counts.

The Battle of Jutland brought the unchallenged sea power of Britain, which had lasted since Trafalgar, to an end. It was fought on 31 May 1916. The Battle of the Somme began on 1 July. Our casualties at Jutland were six thousand. Our casualties on the Somme were six hundred thousand.

[In the 1920s, when I was Parliamentary Private Secretary to Churchill, statues to Jellicoe and Beatty were unveiled in Trafalgar Square. Churchill went; and when he got back we had a drink together in the House of Commons. I asked him how the ceremony had gone, and he said: 'For me it was a moving experience, because I appointed them both to their commands.']

# APPENDIX 2

# The European Movement

In 1950 I wrote and circulated the following memorandum for the European Movement:

*Confidential*

## MEMORANDUM ON POLICY
### by
### ROBERT BOOTHBY, M.P.

1. I cannot see the use of continuing a propaganda movement unless there is substantial agreement between its members regarding the policy which it is desired to propagate.

2. At the Congress of the Hague we were all agreed in principle that the first step towards European union must be the creation of a Council of Europe, with a Committee of Ministers and a Consultative Assembly. This objective was achieved in a miraculously short space of time.

3. Again at Brussels, in February 1949, a Committee over which I had the honour to preside issued a Statement – Principles of European Policy – which commanded unanimous assent. The salient features of this Statement were that a synthesis between a free and a collective economy should be created which would combine the merits of the two systems for constructive purposes; that no State should be admitted into the European Union which did not accept the fundamental principles of a Charter of Human Rights, and bind itself to ensure their application; that Western Germany should be invited to become an integral part of the new community; that the Union must take

account of the special ties which unite certain nations with countries overseas; that economic policy should be directed towards the harmonious and rational exploitation of Europe's resources; that there must be an overall plan of production accompanied by the progressive removal of existing national barriers against the free movement of persons, goods and capital; and that integration of the heavy industries was urgently required as 'the necessary foundation of the economy of the Union as a whole'.

4. The Brussels Statement of Principles thus embodied and exemplified what may be described as the 'functional' method of approach towards European Union; and, in so far as it contributed to the drafting of a Charter of Human Rights, to the invitation to Western Germany to join the Consultative Assembly, to the recognition by the Assembly of the special relationship between certain member States and countries overseas, and – last but not least – to the Schuman Plan, it may be said to have been successful.

5. Since then the European Movement has been in a state of continuous and progressive disintegration; and, as a result, has ceased to give any effective leadership in the cause which we all have at heart.

6. The cause of this is, in my opinion, the internecine disputes arising from the repeated attempts of our federalist friends to substitute a 'constitutional' for a 'functional' approach, as a result of which the Movement has literally been tearing itself to pieces. It is an issue of principle which must now be faced and decided.

7. Unless and until this dispute is settled, it is useless to discuss questions of organisation, such as the Statutes of the Movement, and finance. I hope, therefore, that the question of policy will come first on the agenda of the Committee which is to meet in Brussels at Whitsuntide; and, in this hope, I propose briefly to trace the lines of a possible solution.

8. It is to be found, I think, in the French statement on the proposed unification of the European coal and steel industry. This statement makes the federation of Europe a declared aim, but adopts – without equivocation – the functional as against the constitutional approach. 'Europe', it says, 'will not be made all at once, or according to a single general plan. It will be built through concrete achievements which create a *de facto* solidarity.'

In other words, national sovereignty, in the present phase of human development, can only be broken down by practical action within defined fields of activity. It is this principle which has, in my opinion, to be accepted by our Movement, in spirit as well as in the letter, if we are to serve any useful purpose in the future.

9. If it is accepted, the difficulties confronting us will still be enormous, and should not be underestimated. It is easy to draft paper constitutions which no responsible Government has any intention of accepting, and which no serious attempt will, therefore, be made to realise in action. It is easy to talk glibly – as many of us, including the Federalists, are inclined to do – about Customs Unions and free currency convertibility. The real problems confronting us are much more complicated and difficult than that.

10. Assuming that we accept the principle of the functional approach, let us consider for a moment some of the vital problems which demand immediate attention, and towards the solution of which the European Movement might reasonably be expected to make a useful contribution.

11. In the political field, there is the relationship between the Consultative Assembly and the Committee of Ministers; the relationship between the Council of Europe, as a whole, and the national Governments and Parliaments; the relationship between the Council of Europe and the associated countries overseas; the question of migration, not only within Europe, but from Europe to less developed territories; the coordination of the social services; the status and position of Germany within the new community.

Last, but not least, there is the question of the relationship between Western Europe and the proposed Atlantic Union – or, as I prefer to call it, Western Union. Are certain European countries to be encouraged, individually, to join the Union? Or is a united Europe, including Germany, to be made one of the piers upon which a wider Western Pact should rest? No easy solution, I venture to suggest, is to be found for any one of these problems.

The 'synthesis between a free and a collective economy', advocated in the Brussels Statement of Policy, must be achieved; but it will cut right across many existing political beliefs – and prejudices. The whole conception of planned national socialism, upon which the structure of the British economy has been built up over the past five years, will have to be subordinated to the wider aim of international economic integration. At the same time cut-throat international competition, upon which the Communists so confidently rely to bring about the collapse of the Western economy, will have to be eliminated. A union of competitive industrial producers, all in deficit to an even more competitive industrial producer, could only give rise to massive unemployment and increasing economic disequilibrium.

Let us make no mistake about it, the Schuman Plan spells the doom of the free market economy so far as the basic industries are concerned;

and some means other than competition will have to be found to produce the requisite efficiency in production.

Then there is the question of the Sterling Area, on the basis of which half the world's trade is still conducted. The political separation of the agrarian countries in Eastern Europe from the industrial countries of the West means that the national economies of the countries composing the Sterling Area must be closely associated with those of Europe, in order to ensure an adequate supply of raw materials for the latter, and achieve a balanced economy for the whole. This involves the creation of a Central Bank, the coordination of monetary and fiscal policies, reciprocal trade and payment agreements on a limited multilateral basis, and preferential arrangements.

It need not be assumed that the adoption of the principle of planned international investment, production and trade, and the final abandonment of the principle of non-discrimination will be easily acceptable to the United States. Nevertheless, they are both essential, if any effective economic integration is to be achieved.

13. To sum up. The task confronting us is to break down national sovereignty by concrete practical action in the political and economic spheres; and to use modern technical progress to build up an international political Western Union, and a coordinated and complementary post-capitalist Western Economy. It is a revolutionary project, at least comparable to the nationalistic industrial revolution of the nineteenth century. But the alternative is the gradual absorption of the Western world into the suffocating totalitarian unity of the Communist Empire.

14. Seen in this light, the task confronting us is, in all conscience, formidable. Must we make it even more difficult by superimposing hypothetical paper constitutions, for which the Western world is certainly not ready? I, therefore, appeal to our Federalist friends to abandon theories which are, at the moment, unacceptable, and to join us wholeheartedly in a supreme effort to save our Western democratic civilization, by methods which are severely practical, while there is still time to do it.

# Index

QM LIBRARY (MILE END)

WITHDRAWN
FROM STOCK
QMUL LIBRARY

WITHDRAWN
FROM STOCK
QMUL LIBRARY